D1084468

AMERICA'S ROYALTY

AMERICA'S ROYALTY

ALL THE PRESIDENTS' CHILDREN

Sandra L. Quinn and Sanford Kanter

GREENWOOD PRESS
Westport, Connecticut • London, England

R973.009
Quinn

Library of Congress Cataloging in Publication Data

Quinn, Sandra L.
  America's royalty.

  Bibliography: p.
  Includes index.
  1. Presidents—United States—Children—Biography.
2. Presidents—United States—Children. I. Kanter,
Sanford. II. Title.
E176.45.Q56   1983   973'.009'92 [B]   82-12006
ISBN 0-313-23645-3 (lib. bdg.)

Library of Congress Catalog Card Number: 82-12006
ISBN: 0-313-23645-3

First published in 1983

Greenwood Press
A division of Congressional Information Service, Inc.
88 Post Road West
Westport, Connecticut 06881

Printed in the United States of America

10 9 8 7 6 5 4 3 2 1

Copyright Acknowledgments

  The authors and publishers are grateful for permission to reprint from Joseph J. Perling,
Presidents' Sons: The Prestige of Name in a Democracy (Freeport, New York: Books for
Libraries Press, 1947). Reprinted by permission of Esther Ruth Perling.

  Every reasonable effort has been made to trace the owners of copyright materials in this
book, but in some instances this has proven impossible. The publishers will be glad to receive
information leading to more complete acknowledgments in subsequent printings of the book,
and in the meantime extend their apologies for any omissions.

chum

To
John and Charlene

CONTENTS

PREFACE

As professors of government and history, each day faced with the need to stimulate and intrigue students to study, we found that with the addition of the personal, human touch, even the dullest of students was not only able to relate to the past, but also ofttimes developed an interest in the subjects previously considered only as boring. The stories collected in this book are entertaining. They can be instructive in themselves, and as we use them they aid in the understanding of the times.

One day, between classes, in the midst of idle chatter, a fellow instructor asked, "Do you know the story of Lincoln's son, Bob?" "No, what is it?" was the reply, little suspecting the response would lead on a path to this book. The tale of Robert Lincoln, his father, and his generation is central to American history and made a good story. How much better a way to convince students that history was made of "real" people—living, dying, absurd, boring, and all of the other adjectives applied to people each of us knows.

We expected to find material *ad nauseum* on the subject of children of the presidents. After all, were they not close to the chief magistrate of the land? Were they not at the center or at the development of political power? It seemed reasonable, especially in the twentieth century when the presidency has been described as the "imperial presidency," to indicate the vast powers that war and the threat of war have given to the chief executive, that there would be excesses of revelations of all those surrounding the president. Moreover, revelations of even the most distant of relatives of European royalty have constantly enticed writers and fascinated a sector of the public throughout the world. What would be more natural, then, than a book on all the presidents' children. It was found that no book included all of the children, and, so, simple as the task appeared to be, we jumped to it.

Rapidly a strange bag of collected characters was accumulated, including some incredible stories generally unknown to the public. The stories, many of which are fun, including those about people whose lives were uneventful, are intriguing because of their association with great people and times of this country. Though the tales began as anecdotal, the impact of the stories grew. Questions were raised as to the meanings of the success or lack of success of many of the children. From this we withdrew. Psychohistory is for others, though the basis for many interpretations may well begin with these collected stories about children of all of the presidents.

On the way to the compilation of the materials, including endless biographies of totally unassociated persons, only happening to live in the time of the studied child, help was received from all manner of individuals. Stories were told by distant relatives of some of these people who claimed to have firsthand and hitherto unknown information or even sources of information. Most were followed up, especially when desperate for material. We enjoyed the hunt, and hope you, the reader, enjoy the creatures "bagged."

Many individuals contributed both effort and inspiration in the accumulation of the material within this collection of stories of presidents' children. Assuredly, a special note of gratitude is extended to Esther Ruth Perling, widow of the late Joseph J. Perling, author of *Presidents' Sons*, for her gracious permission to make use of the extensive research done by her husband. Others that certainly are owed a major thank-you are Parker Williams and Thomas Spencer, administrators of San Jacinto College, and the entire library staff of the same college, especially Elizabeth Evans and Colleen McKenna.

We sincerely hope you enjoy the reading as much as we have enjoyed the telling of these stories.

INTRODUCTION

Who were the presidents' children? What are their vital statistics? What were their relationships with their families? Was it, or is it, an advantage to be born to a man who becomes the president of the United States? Do presidents' children share common characteristics throughout the history of the presidency? Are they more political than the average citizen? Do they form an elite group, in any sense, other than through their birth? If so, in what way? Who do the children of presidents marry, for who could be their social equal? Is there evidence to suggest that men who have become presidents transmit special abilities to their offspring? What kinds of parents do presidents make? Is there similarity between the man as president and the man as father? Are the children of presidents markedly different from their contemporaries? Do they favor one occupation? How much of a "boost" in life does the child who happens to be born to a president of the United States receive?

There is an assumption that being the child of a president assures a place in life somewhat bigger than the ordinary. This commonly held view may be exemplified by the story, attributed to John Adams, that when John Quincy Adams was elected president and during his first appearance before a joint session of Congress, his father, and second president of the United States, sat and listened with some of his closest friends. After the speech John Adams's friend leaned over and said, "You know, Mr. Adams, your son made a finer speech than you did at your inauguration." The old gentleman responded, "Yes, he did. And, he'll probably be a greater president than I was. And all of his speeches will be better. But, remember, he started where I could not . . . from my shoulders." But, if true in John Adams's case, with this single son (and there are those who argue that John Quincy would have made it to the top regardless of his father's position) do the facts really support the theory that having a royal family heritage is an advantage? The answers to this and many other questions are the contents of this book. For the first time readers have an opportunity to test their own theories.

The children of the presidents of the United States are a highly select group, for no other reason than their fathers happened to be chosen to become the nation's chief executive officer. But not all children were considered equal. The simple fact is that prior to the twentieth century males and females were expected to lead very different lives. In America, the land of opportunity, any profession was open to men, and especially to the sons of presidents. Daughters, even the daughters of presidents, were limited by social, economic, and intellectual convention. Wife and mother was the profession for which most women were prepared. Increasingly in the twentieth century women would prepare for other professions, and thus the opportunity for daughters to impact as personalities on American life did not occur until society changed and allowed women to select their own professions.

Some people claim that the role of president is modeled on that of a king. The American president combines both the attributes of the ceremonial chief of state and the head of government. From this duality stems the aura that so far exceeds that of the common man, that many see a quasi-royalty attached to the president and the family of the president. While the mystique of this artificial prestige may be abhorrent to many, nevertheless, one cannot deny that it exists now and has existed since the founding of our nation. All the desire for social distinction, so apparent in America's social climbers, and which is forbidden to Americans in the Constitution with its prohibition against the establishment of nobility, has been lavished upon the man and the office of the American president.

The book may be read as a whole from beginning to end, or it can be read as support material for various presidents and times, or it may be read only for the human interest of the lives of the individuals that happened to be the sons and daughters of presidents. Above all, the human interest of these children will amuse, stimulate, or even arouse pity. Some of the children are surprisingly average, and yet others touch the heart.

All historians develop likes and dislikes about the people they study. We too have favorite stories, including the stories of George Washington Adams, John Scott Harrison, Robert Todd Lincoln, Ruth Cleveland, Margaret Wilson, Theodore Roosevelt, Jr., Margaret Truman, and Amy Carter. The reader also will surely find personal favorites.

AMERICA'S ROYALTY

1 CHILDLESS PRESIDENTS

Of the forty presidents of the United States through Ronald Reagan, six had no children. Of the six, only one, James Buchanan, was a bachelor. The other five, Washington, Madison, Jackson, Polk, and Harding, were married only once, and each marriage lasted for many years. One of the five, Washington, acquired a family when he married a widow, and another, Jackson, adopted a child. Though these presidents produced no children, certainly an explanation of each, and the progeny they inherited, adopted, or did not have, is due.

GEORGE WASHINGTON

George Washington, the first president of the United States, married widow Martha Dandridge Custis, the mother of four children, two of whom had died as small children. At the time of the marriage Washington was close to twenty-seven years old and she was almost twenty-eight years old. Martha had become a widow when her husband, who was twenty years her senior, died from tuberculosis. Coming into the marriage with a daughter, who died unexpectedly when the child was only thirteen years old, and a son, John Custis, Martha immediately provided Washington with a family.

The son, John Parke Custis, served as Washington's aide-de-camp in the Revolutionary War and was with Washington in all of the war's battles through the final British surrender at Yorktown. Shortly after the war young Custis died from a fever. The young man had married and left four small children to be provided for and raised. The two youngest, a three-year-old girl, who died while still young, and little George Washington Parke Custis, only months old, were taken into the care of George and Martha Washington. Years later some biographers refer to this child as Washington's adopted son, but Washington did not adopt the boy and in letters he referred to him as his ward.

Washington raised the boy, sending him to both St. Johns College and Princeton, though Custis showed no special abilities. Leaving school when he was just seventeen years old, he went into the military, receiving a commission as an officer of dragoons. Washington wanted to see that the boy was secure and requested he receive a higher rank so that he might be a leader in battle should the need arise. Custis never did lead troops. Instead, Washington died in 1799, leaving the boy land, including property on the Potomac River.

When George Washington Parke Custis was twenty-three years old he married, built a home on the west side of the Potomac River, named his home Arlington, and lived the life of a "country gentleman," receiving visits periodically from the Washington, D.C., elite, including President Andrew Jackson. The couple had a daughter who married Robert E. Lee, and it is this child that in later writings referred to her father as "the adopted son of George Washington," giving credence to the adopted-son hypothesis of Washington's biographers.[1] Maintaining his pride in his heritage by association, Custis's final request was that, as the last descendant of George Washington, his only child, a daughter, rename her son with the Washington name, to continue the name, if not the line.

JAMES MADISON

The fourth president of the United States, James Madison, had no children. He married Dorothea "Dolley" Dandridge Payne Todd when he was forty-three and she twenty-six, and the marriage lasted for almost forty-two years. Dolley was the mother of two children, one of whom had died the year prior to her marriage to Madison. The other, John Payne Todd, was brought into her marriage. The boy evoked no interest in contemporary biographers or later chroniclers and thus the child disappeared from history's pages.

ANDREW JACKSON

Andrew Jackson married Rachel Donelson Robards, supposing her to be divorced from Lewis Robards. Later he found the marriage to be invalid, necessitating a remarriage of the Jacksons.

At the time of their first, invalid, marriage, both were twenty-four years old and their marriage lasted thirty-seven years, until her death. When no children were born to the couple after several years of marriage, they adopted a son. The boy, one of a pair of twins born to Rachel's brother's wife, was named Andrew Jackson, Jr. Though Jackson's career kept him from the boy during the early years, his wife wrote progress reports on their son and Jackson responded, frequently giving advice on how to raise the adopted Andrew, Jr.

Just as Andrew Jackson was elected to the presidency in 1828, his beloved Rachel died. Andy, Jr., spent his time between the family home, The Hermitage, supervising the plantation's overseers; in Washington, D.C., with his father; and in Philadelphia, with his twin brother who had been raised by his natural mother and had accepted a government appointment. The young man also became engaged twice before settling upon Sarah Yorke for his wife, whom he married in 1831. The president approved of his son's wife, and was so fond of her that he turned over his deceased wife's jewelry to the girl, stipulating that it would be his granddaughter's (should the couple produce a daughter) and that they should name the daughter Rachel. Jackson set his son to the task of learning to manage the Jackson's large land holdings. In time Jackson bought a plantation for Andy and Sarah very near The Hermitage. But his son was incapable of management—so much so that he soon acquired major debts, necessitating Jackson's paying off his adopted son's debts repeatedly. During one period when Jackson thought his life to be near an end, he wrote to his son:

My dear Andrew, I have been quite unwell. . . . My son, as my life is uncertain, and we know not at what moment we may be called hence, I now address you with the fondness of a father's heart. I wish to bring to your view the situation you now, and will hereafter, occupy, that it may be a stimulant to your proper conduct in all time hereafter. It is well known that I have adopted you as my own son and you are to represent me when I am called hence. Your conduct standing as my representative, the son of a President, draw upon you the eyes of the world, and the least deviation from the rules of strict decorum and propriety are observed and commented on by all our enemies.[2]

Jackson did not die at this time, and neither did his son observe any "propriety." Instead he continued to accumulate large debts, which his father continued to make good. Before Jackson died in 1845, he was advised to make his will in the name of Andy's wife, Sarah, but the senior Jackson felt the act would not show good faith. He left to Andy's guardianship massive holdings. The young man repeatedly risked the family's finances. Each time his venture failed, exhausting funds further, until finally Andy, Jr., sold the family home, The Hermitage, and its surrounding lands to the state of Tennessee, though Andy maintained the right to live in The Hermitage during his lifetime.

The adopted son survived his father by twenty years, dying in 1865 at the close of the Civil War. Though Andy had maintained his neutrality during the war between the states, he did have two sons that fought for the South.

While climbing a fence during a hunting expedition, Andy's gun accidentally discharged. He received minor injuries to his hand, but within a week he was dead from lockjaw.

JAMES KNOX POLK

The marriage of James Polk, the eleventh president, and Sarah Childress took place when he was twenty-eight and she was twenty years old. No children resulted from the twenty-five-year marriage. Sarah Polk, noted for her piousness, devoted her entire time and energy to her husband before and during his presidency.

WARREN GAMALIEL HARDING

The fifth and final married president to have no children was the twentieth-century president, Warren G. Harding, and his wife Florence Kling DeWolfe, who had been married and divorced some nine years prior to their marriage in 1891. Florence Harding, five years older than her husband, had a son, Marshall DeWolfe, but he died of tuberculosis. The Harding marriage lasted for more than thirty-two years, though there was a great deal of gossip as to the quality of the marriage. The couple, both of whom died during his term in office, bore no children of record.

There have been periodic claims, however, that a Harding child was born of an illicit union. Some of the rumors have a ring of truth, but there is no proof for any of the stories.

JAMES BUCHANAN

The fifteenth president of the United States, James Buchanan, is the only president never to have married. Buchanan remained a bachelor for all of his seventy-seven years, though he had been engaged to marry at the age of twenty-eight. His fiancée died from an overdose of a sedative in 1819, and never again was there discussion of an engagement or even the possibility of a Buchanan marriage.

Such are the stories of the presidents to whom no children were born. All other presidents produced heirs, some surviving long years, living full and influential lives. Some children developed as eccentrics, while others lived lives not unlike those of children born to ordinary people of the United States.

2 JOHN ADAMS'S CHILDREN

ABIGAIL AMELIA ADAMS SMITH

First child of John Adams and Abigail Smith

Born: July 14, 1765   *Birthplace:* Braintree County, Massachusetts
Died: August 15, 1813   *Age at Death:* 48 years, 1 month
Cause of Death: Breast Cancer
Education: Tutored at Home   *Profession:* Housewife, Mother
Spouse: William Stephens Smith
Number of Children: 4

AN INNOCENT VICTIM OF FORTUNE'S TREACHEROUS GAME

Abigail Amelia Adams, known familiarly as Amelia, Nabby, or Emmy, was a quiet and withdrawn person. She had blue eyes, reddish hair, a round face, and a fair complexion. Educated at home, in the manner common to women of the time, Amelia was strongly influenced by her dominating parents, particularly her dictatorial father. Whether by natural inclination or through conditioning by her parents, Amelia was to be dominated by everyone with whom she had any affiliation.

At the age of seventeen she fell in love with a young lawyer, Royall Tyler, who practiced law in Boston but moved to Amelia's home county, Braintree. Royall, classically tall, dark, and handsome, fancied himself a poet. Quite a lady's man, with the Braintree County belles vying for his attention, he eventually courted Amelia. The courtship did not go smoothly. Indeed, the Adams family found Tyler lacking in essential qualities for connection with the family. Nevertheless, Amelia and Tyler became engaged.

Engagement or not, father John Adams was not the type to allow Amelia to choose her own way against his wishes. Hoping to break the engagement, Adams sent his daughter to Boston. But the maneuver did not work. Amelia returned to Braintree County and resumed her engagement. Next, the resourceful father ordered Amelia and her mother to join him in Paris, where he was representing the United States. Amelia agreed to go to Paris on the condition that after one year, if she and Tyler maintained their affection for each other, then Royall would travel to the continent to marry her.

As was to be expected, a heavy correspondence quickly developed between the separated lovers. But it was not long until the correspondence became one-sided, from Amelia to Royall. Weeks passed with only silence from Royall. Amelia grew dejected. She became even more introspective than was her normal character.

In May of 1785, John Adams was appointed America's first minister to England. Abigail, Amelia, and John Adams moved to London. From London Amelia continued her regular correspondence with her brother, John Quincy, as well as her unanswered correspondence with Royall. During a presentation at the Court of St. James, Amelia was introduced to her father's aide, the secretary of the American legation, William Stephen Smith. Smith, a New Yorker and former aide to General Washington, as well as a seven-year veteran of the Revolutionary War, personified the kind of man that was acceptable to the Adamses as a son-in-law. The introduction was the beginning of a relationship that would signal the end of her relationship with Royall. Soon after meeting Smith, Amelia finally gave up hope of hearing from Royall and broke their engagement. "Sir," she wrote, "Herewith you receive your letters and miniature with my desire that you return mine to Uncle Cranch, and my hope that you will be well satisfied with the affair as is."[3] The response from Royall was completely unexpected. He had written to her, he claimed, during travels to expand his business, and he pleaded that he had never received her letters except the last one. But he was too late. Amelia was in London and Smith was in London. Royall was in the United States.

Amelia and Smith became constant companions. Smith gave letters and testimonials to his character to Mrs. Adams with his purpose "to gain the confidence of her daughter to lay a proper foundation for a future connection."[4]

Amelia's letters to her brother now often spoke of *le colonel*. On the recommendation of John Adams, Smith was made consul general to Great Britain. Amelia became Smith's bride on June 26, 1786. The Smiths made their home near the Adamses' home in London. Smith continued to serve under John Adams. Amelia continued life more as the daughter of John Adams than as the wife of Smith.

Meanwhile, back in the United States, Royall was crushed by news of Amelia's marriage. He left his law practice and moved back to Boston. Although badly hurt, he was able to express his poetic nature. He wrote two plays, which became hits.

It was upon the return of the Adams and Smith families to the United States in 1788 that the true character of Smith began to emerge. He would disappear for months on end, and when home paid very little attention to

Amelia. He became involved in an insurrection in Venezuela and land speculations in the West, none of which came to fruition.

Amelia developed cancer of the breast and died at the age of forty-eight "in the wilds of Western New York," as John Quincy was later to observe—"an innocent victim of fortune's treacherous game."[5]

Ironically, Royall, the man whom the Adams family had so opposed as unsuitable for Amelia, achieved success in the law and became the chief justice of the Supreme Court of Vermont, "universally loved and respected."[6]

JOHN QUINCY ADAMS

Second child, first son of John Adams and Abigail Smith

Born: July 11, 1767   *Birthplace:* Braintree County, Massachusetts
Died: February 23, 1848   *Age at Death:* 80 years, 7 months
Cause of Death: Cerebral hemorrhage
Education: Tutors, continental schools, Harvard University
Profession: Presidential aide, Professor, Politician
Spouse: Louisa Catherine Johnson
Number of Children: 4

THE ONLY SON OF A PRESIDENT TO BECOME PRESIDENT

John Quincy Adams, the eldest of John Adams's sons, graduated from Harvard in 1788. He had already crossed the Atlantic four times, including three trips during the Revolutionary War, and had served as secretary and interpreter on the U.S. mission to the Russian court of Empress Catherine while yet in his teens. John Quincy's linguistic abilities had been acquired when he studied in both Paris and Leyden during his father's diplomatic service. At Harvard he specialized in literary and classical studies but later turned to law.

Excelling in all that he tried, John Quincy was the most brilliant of any student the school had ever had, according to one professor. But perhaps academic excellence was attained at the cost of personality development. The drive to achieve had been hammered into the young boy by his father, who constantly harangued him to surpass all others in scholarship, thus little or no time was left for development of social and emotional awareness. Instead of acquiring his own unique personality, John Quincy adopted his father's maxims as the rules upon which to run his life. It was the puritanic code of the seventeenth century that the elder Adams imposed upon his son. Thus, his father admonished him, "Morals, my boy, morals should be, as they are eternal in their nature, the everlasting object of your pursuits."[7] It was this kind of advice that shaped the brilliant but haughty and stern character of John Quincy Adams.

Completing his studies at Harvard, John began a brief term as a lawyer in Boston, but shortly thereafter, in 1794, he was appointed by President George Washington as minister to the Netherlands. From the Netherlands he was sent to Sweden to negotiate commercial treaties in 1798.

During a brief interlude in London, John Quincy met and married Louisa Catherine Johnson, the daughter of the American minister to England. A driving, fiery character in her own right, though chronically suffering from numerous unspecified illnesses, it can be said that in the twenty-five years of their marriage Louisa never really understood her husband.

By 1802 John Quincy, his wife, and child returned to the United States. Immediately he entered the political scene, and was successively elected to the Massachusetts Senate and then to the U.S. Senate. While serving as the U.S. senator from Massachusetts, John Quincy also fulfilled the duties of professor of rhetoric and oratory at Harvard College. But it was not for his teaching or public speaking abilities, rather, it was his expertise and personal experience in foreign affairs that recommended him to successive presidents.

He was appointed as minister to Russia, leaving that nation only when he was appointed to the commission that negotiated the Treaty of Ghent, ending the War of 1812 with England. Back in the United States, John Quincy became secretary of state under President James Monroe. Many historians have claimed that he, alone, should be credited with the origination of the Monroe Doctrine, enunciated in 1823, which announced to the world that the United States would oppose the growth of European colonies, or the reconquest of former colonies in the Western Hemisphere.

In 1825 John Quincy Adams became the only son of a president to also become president of the United States, though neither in the Massachusetts Senate, the U.S. Senate, nor in the presidency was John Quincy popular with the people. Even his election to the presidency came after a dispute in which the House of Representatives came to determine the issue of who would be president. He had, in fact, lost the general election to his nemesis, the extremely popular General Andrew Jackson. The electoral vote was ninety-nine to eighty-four against John Quincy, yet the House of Representatives decided that it would be the politically experienced John Quincy, not the popular hero, Andrew Jackson, who would be president.

Adams's attempt at reelection became the first real "gut-level," name-calling election in American presidential politics. Jackson called John Quincy extravagant, corrupt and an aristocrat. Adams responded in his moralistic tone that Andy was an ignoramus, a vulgarian, a murderer, and an adulterer. The public must have believed Jackson, for they overwhelmingly denied John Quincy's second presidential term. He returned to his Massachusetts home, anticipating retirement from public life. Instead, he later returned to Washington as a member of the House of Representatives and remained there until 1848. During his years in the House, his reputation was of a moral fanatic. Said one observer about a discussion over slavery, an institution Adams violently opposed, "I remember the appearance of Mr. Adams as he sat day after day watching his opportunity to present his mammoth petition on the subject of slavery. Mr. Adams was excessively bald, and as he sat in the middle of the House, with his immense petition rolled around a kind of windlass to sustain it, his excitement was manifest in the flaming redness of his bald head, which acted as a chronometer to his audience."[8] It may well have been a petition such as the one he presented from several Massachusetts citizens, defiantly requesting the dissolution of the United States over the issue of slavery.

A solitary person before, during, and after his marriage, much of Adams is yet a mystery. To the public he had the appearance of a dour, bitter, and cranky old man. But to the statesmen of the age, John Quincy Adams was known for his brilliance, tempered by a difficult and obstinate nature.

SUSANNA ADAMS

Third child, second daughter of John Adams and Abigail Smith

Born: December 28, 1768   *Birthplace:* Boston, Massachusetts
Died: February 4, 1770   *Age at Death:* 1 year, 1 month
Cause of Death: Unknown

A CHILDHOOD DEATH

Susanna Adams was the only John Adams child not to survive infancy. Life was very harsh for a newborn in the colonies, and Susanna only lived slightly more than a year. Her short life was spent in Boston, at the family home on Brattle Square, in a house called The White House long before the same name would be given to the home of the chief executive in Washington, D.C.

Susanna is the first child of a future chief executive to die, as George Washington never had children. All that we know is that Mrs. Adams long suffered the pain of her second daughter's early death.

CHARLES ADAMS

Fourth child, second son of John Adams and Abigail Smith

Born: May 29, 1770   *Birthplace:* Boston, Massachusetts
Died: November 30, 1800   *Age at Death:* 30 years, 6 months
Cause of Death: Cirrhosis of the liver
Education: Tutors, private schools, Harvard University
Profession: Lawyer   *Spouse:* Sarah Smith
Number of Children: 2

FOREVER LOST

In September 1779, Charles accompanied his older brother, John Quincy, to London, where their father was to negotiate on behalf of the United States. In less than two years the young boy became so homesick that his father determined that the boy must return home to preserve his health. Departing London in August 1781, the eleven-year-old boy was stranded in Spain when the ship was forced to seek shelter for repairs. The family lost contact with Charles and believed him lost at sea. After four months, Charles arrived home but was ever after to appear a "lost" soul.

Charles attended Harvard with his younger brother, Thomas, studied law, and passed the bar, though his Harvard days were marred by involvement in campus unrest. However, despite his studies he never practiced law. Following Harvard, Charles moved back to Boston to stay with his mother's family. It was there that he fell in love with his cousin, Sarah, and despite family objections that he was too young, they married in August 1795.

We do not know how Charles came to be impoverished, but by 1797 he was already unsuccessful at supporting his wife and two children, and was floundering in depression and alcoholism.

In October 1800 Abigail Adams set out to New York City to check on her son and his family. Instead of finding a happy home she found Charles "laid upon a bed of sickness, destitute of a home. The kindness of a friend afforded him an asylum,"[9] his wife no longer living with him. On November 30, 1800, Charles died of cirrhosis of the liver.

Charles was mourned by his mother and father, who commented upon "the melancholy death of a once loved son,"[10] indisputably reflecting the Adamses' inheritance of intellect, potential, and tragedy.

3 THOMAS JEFFERSON'S CHILDREN

MARTHA WASHINGTON JEFFERSON RANDOLPH

First child of Thomas Jefferson and Martha Wayles Skelton

Born: September 27, 1772
Birthplace: Monticello, Albemarle, Virginia
Died: October 10, 1836   *Age at Death:* 64 years, 1 month
Cause of Death: Apoplexy
Education: Tutors, private school in France
Profession: Housewife, Mother, White House hostess
Spouse: Thomas Mann Randolph, Jr.
Number of Children: 12

HER FATHER'S CLOSE COMPANION

Martha Washington Jefferson was only ten when her mother died. "Patsy," as she was called by her father, became the feminine head of her father's household, a position she never relinquished.

Described as bright and studious, bearing a strong resemblance to her tall, red-haired father, she attended small private schools, studied the classics, and managed to master the French language. Her cheerful and obedient character made submission to her father's prescribed regime easy. Jefferson desired that his children be paragons of learning and accomplishment. To attain his goal for his children, Jefferson established a strict regimen for Martha to include:

Practice music: 8–10 A.M.

Dance one day and draw another: 10 A.M.–1 P.M.

Draw on the day you dance, and write a letter the next day: 1–2 P.M.

Read French: 3–4 P.M.

Exercise yourself in music: 4–5 P.M.

Read English and write: 5–until bedtime

As a dutiful daughter, Patsy obeyed her father, studied her lessons, and attained a quality of education equaled by few, if any, women of her time.

The bond between father and daughter was close, and became even closer as the child matured into a woman. Martha accompanied her father to Philadelphia where he attended the Continental Congress. In 1784 she went with him to France, where they were to stay for some years.

Martha married a man she had known all her life, Thomas Mann Randolph, Jr., on February 23, 1790, at the age of eighteen. The Randolphs made their home at Edgehill, a plantation near Monticello, and the couple became the parents of twelve children between 1791 and 1818. Monticello, the Jefferson family home, had come to Jefferson through inheritance by way of his wife, as the inheritance of a married woman became the property of her husband. Given the proximity of the Randolph home, Edgehill, to Monticello, and the close attachment of father and daughter, it is not surprising that Monticello became a second home to Martha and her growing family.

Randolph was elected to Congress, serving with a remarkable lack of distinction. Notwithstanding his record in Congress, he was later elected governor of Virginia for the years 1819–1822. But all was not smooth in the marriage. Randolph suffered a series of mental breakdowns and bankruptcies, as well as eventually developing a hatred and envy of his famous father-in-law. The Randolph family finances went from bad to worse. Through all the trials, the single stable element in Martha's life was her love for her children and her father. The death of her sister, Polly, brought father and daughter even closer together. But the death of Jefferson, in 1826, removed her mainstay of emotional and financial strength.

Martha inherited her father's debts, and she considered selling Monticello or turning it into a school. Randolph had become remote from the family and died in 1828, leaving her with official responsibility for the family and Monticello. But both the family and Monticello were saved by the state legislatures of South Carolina and Louisiana, that, upon hearing of her economic plight, appropriated $10,000 each for her maintenance.

In 1836 Martha died of apoplexy at age sixty-four. But Martha was not buried at the home she had shared with her husband, Edgehill, but at her father's beloved home, Monticello.

JANE RANDOLPH JEFFERSON

Second child, second daughter of Thomas Jefferson and Martha Wayles Skelton

Born: April 3, 1774   *Birthplace:* Monticello, Albemarle, Virginia
Died: September 1775   *Age at Death:* 1 year, 6 months
Cause of Death: Unknown

ANOTHER NONSURVIVOR

Jane Randolph, the second of the Jeffersons' six children, was born when the nation was heading for its dramatic separation from the mother country, England. Not much is known about this child who lived only eighteen months, but it is clear that her birth was not difficult, unlike all of the following pregnancies of Martha Jefferson. Also, Thomas was at home during her death, and the little girl had lived long enough to be "greatly loved, and her death must have compounded Jefferson's reluctance to leave his wife."[13] Thus, when Thomas Jefferson was involved in the serious business of giving birth to a new nation, he was torn between his two loves, his wife and his country. Martha, never a healthy woman, became progressively ill following Jane's birth and childhood death.

"SON" JEFFERSON

Third child, only son of Thomas Jefferson and Martha Wayles Skelton

Born: May 28, 1777   *Birthplace:* Monticello, Albemarle, Virginia
Died: June 14, 1777   *Age at Death:* 17 days
Cause of Death: Unknown

AN UNNAMED SON

He was the only son of Thomas Jefferson and Martha Skelton, but he seems not to have had a name. There is no record of his receiving a name but, perhaps, it has simply been lost to history, as he only survived seventeen days. The lack of a recorded name implies that his health was unstable from the moment of his birth. For, by the laws of primogeniture, property was inherited through the son, and as this was Jefferson's only son, and therefore, only heir, more care would most likely have been taken in naming the child and filing all proper documentation had there been some surety of the baby's health. The same care would not have been so important a few years later, when primogeniture laws were eliminated in Virginia through the efforts of Thomas Jefferson.

MARY JEFFERSON EPPES

Fourth child, third daughter of Thomas Jefferson and Martha Wayles Skelton

Born: August 1, 1778   *Birthplace:* Monticello, Albemarle, Virginia
Died: April 17, 1804   *Age at Death:* 25 years, 8 months
Cause of Death: Childbirth complications
Education: Tutors, private school in France
Profession: Housewife, Mother
Spouse: John Wayles Eppes
Number of Children: Unknown

SECOND TO NONE

Mary Jefferson, called Polly or Marie by her family, lived her life in the shadow of her older sister, Martha. In an attempt to reassure Polly and quiet her constant fear that she was always in competition with Martha, the stern, but fair father wrote to her from the White House, shortly before the end of her life and during a time when she was suffering some characteristics of depression, that, "No, never imagine that there could possibly be a difference to me between yourself and sister. You have both such dispositions as to engross my whole love and each so entirely that there can be no greater degree of it that each possess."[14]

Polly was educated in France by her father's tutelage and also attended a Catholic convent near Paris. Having traveled to Paris following the death from whooping cough, of her sister Lucy II, and from which she herself just barely survived, nine-year-old Polly made the trip accompanied by a Jefferson household slave, fourteen-year-old Sally Hemings. Separated from her father and sister for almost six years following the death of her mother, it had taken two years after the death of her sister Lucy II, for Polly to get to Europe once Jefferson had determined that she was not safe in the United States. When she arrived in Paris she just barely remembered her father and held no memory of her older sister, Martha.

Unlike Martha, Polly bore a strong resemblance to her mother and was considered very lovely. She married her cousin John Wayles Eppes, whom she had known and loved all her life. The marriage further strengthened the ties of the Jefferson family with the Wayles family—her mother's family. Polly's husband became a member of the House of Representatives, and the economic and social strength of these united families represented major sources of power in Virginia and in all of the United States.

During the years of her marriage, Polly, like her mother, gave birth to several children, and the final birth ended her life at age twenty-five, during Jefferson's second term as president. Her father, emotionally distraught, turned even more strongly to his only surviving child, Martha, for emotional support during the rest of his life.

LUCY ELIZABETH JEFFERSON I

Fifth child, fourth daughter of Thomas Jefferson and Martha Wayles Skelton

Born: November 3, 1780   *Birthplace:* Richmond, Virginia
Died: April 15, 1781   *Age at Death:* 5 months
Cause of Death: Unknown

THE FIRST OF TWO LUCYS

Lucy Elizabeth, the first of two Jefferson daughters to be so named, was named after Jefferson's two sisters, eleven-year-old Lucy and twenty-one-year-old, mentally retarded Elizabeth. Her birth weight of ten-and-one-half pounds was high, especially for those days.

Jefferson was away at the Virginia state capital, Richmond, when Lucy Elizabeth I died. He did not learn of her death until he returned to Monticello. The profound grief he felt at the death of this child was further deepened by the effects of that death on his wife, Martha. Martha fell into a deep state of melancholy resulting from the deaths of three of her five children, and she continued in this condition for the next seventeen months, when another birth destroyed her health and she died.

LUCY ELIZABETH JEFFERSON II

Sixth child, fifth daughter of Thomas Jefferson and Martha Wayles Skelton

Born: May 8, 1782   *Birthplace:* Monticello, Albemarle, Virginia
Died: November 17, 1785   *Age at Death:* 3 years, 6 months
Cause of Death: Whooping cough

THE FINAL PREGNANCY

Lucy Elizabeth Jefferson, the second Jefferson daughter named after his two sisters, was born a bit more than a year after the death of her sister, the first Lucy. Lucy II was the last of the Jefferson children, for her birth resulted in Martha's death. Martha Jefferson, who had had a succession of pregnancies regularly resulting in miscarriages, died shortly after the difficult birth of the second Lucy.

Jefferson, who loved his wife passionately, was distraught. Monticello now represented memories that he was unable to bear. To escape the scene of his wife's death, Jefferson took the position of U.S. minister to France. He took with him only his daughter Martha, and left the two younger girls, Polly and Lucy II, with his sister-in-law, Mrs. Eppes. The thoughtful father left the little girls in Virginia to avoid exposing them to the dangers of the journey, as well as to the potential health problems of the unfamiliar surroundings in Paris.

However, his caution went for naught. Three years later, while Jefferson was still in Paris, his baby daughter, Lucy II, died of whooping cough. The Jefferson children's poor survival rate was, indeed, unusually high, even for the times.

TOM, HARRIET I, BEVERLY, HARRIET II, ESTON, AND MADISON HEMINGS

Supposed illegitimate children of Thomas Jefferson and Sally Hemings

Born: Tom: 1790

Harriet I: October 5, 1795

Beverly: 1798

Harriet II: May 1801

Madison: January 1805

Eston: May 21, 1808

Birthplaces: Tom: France

All others: Monticello, Albemarle, Virginia

Causes of Death: Unknown

Spouses: Several married, as specified below, but times and names of mates are unknown.

FANCY AND FACT OF THOMAS JEFFERSON AND "BLACK SALLY"

Thomas Jefferson had only been in the office of president of the United States for a short time when the Washington rumor mill began saying that several of the Jefferson slaves bore a strong resemblance to the president.

Sally Hemings, born to Betty Hemings, a household slave of Thomas Jefferson's father-in-law from a supposed union between Betty Hemings and her master, became a Jefferson slave upon the death of his father-in-law. Nine-year-old Sally, described as "very pretty" and "mighty near white" moved with her mother to the Jefferson home. Both she and her mother were given the duties of caring for Jefferson's dying wife, Martha Wayles Skelton Jefferson. Sally became a runner for the sickroom, while her mother cared for the rapidly failing Martha. Running to the sound of a "tinkling silver bell," Sally carried messages throughout the household. (The bell, handed down through four generations of Hemings, was presented to Howard University in the 1960s.)

A physically mature fourteen-year-old Sally accompanied Jefferson's youngest daughter, Polly, journeying to join her father and sister in France. Two years later Sally returned to the United States with an infant son.[15] Shortly thereafter Jefferson returned.

The Jefferson "Farm Book" records the births of four children as follows: "Beverly 1798; Harriet 1801; Madison 1805; and Eston 1808." There is some question whether a fifth child recorded "Harriet," ambiguously, belongs to Sally Hemings. The case for parentage of these children by Jefferson rests on the following points:

1 . The "Farm Book" does not mention the father, as was common practice.
2 . Harriet I was born October 5, 1795, during a period of two years (1794–1796) that Jefferson spent at Monticello.
3 . Harriet II was born in May 1801, and Eston was born in May 1808, each of which is exactly nine months after Jefferson's regular August vacation at Monticello.
4 . Madison was born in 1805, just nine months after Jefferson attended the Monticello funeral of his daughter, Polly.

Madison and Eston were made apprentices to Sally's brother, John, Jefferson's chief carpenter, to learn carpentry. Harriet II became a favorite household slave. When Jefferson died in 1826 he freed Madison, Eston, and Sally's brother, John Hemings. Sally, fifty-three at the time of Jefferson's 1826 death, disappears completely from all records.[16]

After being freed, Madison, supposed son of Jefferson, claimed that his mother came home from France and gave birth to a son by Thomas Jefferson. Also, "She gave birth to four others and Jefferson was the father of all of them. Their names were Beverly, Harriet, Madison (myself), and Eston. We all became freed because of a treaty entered into by our parents before we were born."[17]

Madison married the daughter of a slave and worked in Ohio, becoming a respected member of the community. Sister and brother Harriet and Beverly moved to Washington, D.C., married whites, and lived as members of the white community. Brother Eston married a black woman, produced three children, and died shortly after moving to Wisconsin, according to Madison.[18]

Such is the story of Jefferson's children by Sally Hemings. Whether it is true or not, or whether any part of it is true, cannot definitely be said.

FOR FURTHER READING

Brodie, Fawn M. *Thomas Jefferson: An Intimate History*. New York, New York: W. W. Norton & Company, Inc., 1974.

Burnham, Sophy. *The Landed Gentry: Passions and Personalities Inside America's Propertied Class*. New York, New York: G. P. Putnam's Sons, 1978.

Dabney, Virginius. *Jefferson Scandals: Rebuttal*. New York, New York: Dodd, Mead, 1971.

Malone, Dumas. *Sage of Monticello: Jefferson and His Time*. Vol. 6. Boston, Massachusetts: Little, Brown, 1981.

Miller, Hope Ridings. *Scandals in the Highest Office*. New York, New York: Random House, 1973.

McDonald, Forrest. *Presidency of Thomas Jefferson*. Lawrence, Kansas: University Press of Kansas, 1976.

Randolph, Saval Nicholas. *Domestic Life of Thomas Jefferson*. Charlottesville, Virginia: University Press of Virginia, 1978.

Schachner, Nathan. *Thomas Jefferson: A Biography*. New York, New York: Appleton-Century Crofts, Inc., 1951.

Smith, Page. *Jefferson: A Revealing Biography*. New York, New York: American Heritage Publishing, 1976.

4 JAMES MONROE'S CHILDREN

ELIZA KORTRIGHT MONROE HAY

First child of James Monroe and Elizabeth Kortright

Born: December 1786   *Birthplace:* Virginia
Died: 1835   *Age at Death:* 49 years
Cause of Death: Unknown
Education: Madame Campan's School for Girls, Paris, France
Profession: Housewife, Mother, White House Hostess
Spouse: George Hay
Number of Children: 1, at least

A LIFELONG FRIENDSHIP WITH ROYALTY

Eliza Monroe, a tall, glossy-haired, black-eyed beauty, received her education in Europe. At the age of seven, when her father was minister to France, she entered Madame Campan's renowned school for girls on the outskirts of Paris. It was there that she established a lifelong friendship with Hortense Beauharnais, the daughter of Josephine Bonaparte, the future Queen of Holland, and mother of Napoleon III of France. So intense was this long-lasting friendship that Eliza named her daughter Hortense, in honor of her royal friend.

In 1817, when James Monroe entered the White House, Eliza was a married woman. She had married George Hay, a prominent attorney noted for his role as prosecutor in the infamous treason trial of Aaron Burr. Her role as wife was interrupted frequently by the necessity of substituting for her mother as hostess at the White House because her mother could not tolerate the ordeal of being the White House mistress. At the White House, Eliza is primarily remembered for her domineering style and insistence that every iota of protocol be followed, making many enemies for herself. While Eliza served as hostess, her husband George became secretary to the president of the United States.

Following Monroe's presidency, Eliza and her family moved to a new Virginia home. The home, whose rough plans had been drawn by her father and Thomas Jefferson, was the site of family gatherings. Life was not difficult for the Hayses. The family's income was assured when John Quincy Adams, successor to Monroe as president, repaid debts to the Monroe family by appointing Eliza's husband as judge for Virginia's eastern district court.

Upon the death of James Monroe, Eliza returned to France to visit her friend Hortense. The two traveled to Rome, where Eliza was converted to Catholicism by no less than Pope Gregory XVI.

Eliza died in Paris, where she is buried. In the case of Eliza Monroe Hay, it is more fitting that she rests forever in a nation with an exalted royal past, than in the soil of a nation devoted to a rough equality among all.

J. S. MONROE

Second child, only son of James Monroe and Elizabeth Kortright

Born: May 1799   *Birthplace:* Unknown
Died: September 28, 1801   *Age at Death:* 2 years, 4 months
Cause of Death: Unknown

"J. S. M."

In the Monroe family burial plot there is a gravestone bearing only the initials "J. S. M."[19] which are believed to be those of James Monroe's only son. It is assumed that the initials represent James, after his father, and Spence, after Monroe's father and brother, though it is only speculation, for almost nothing is known about the Monroe boy.

The child suffered from "a series of childhood diseases"[20] as Monroe informed Thomas Jefferson by letter. Apparently Mrs. Monroe traveled far from the family's Virginia home in search of a healthy place to revitalize her sickly son, but to no avail. "J. S." Monroe died shortly after his second birthday.

MARIA HESTER MONROE GOUVENEUR

Third child, second daughter of James Monroe and Elizabeth Kortright

Born: 1803   *Birthplace:* Paris, France
Died: 1850   *Age at Death:* 47 years
Cause of Death: Unknown
Education: Private schools in Washington, D.C.
Profession: Housewife, Mother
Spouse: Samuel Lawrence Gouveneur
Number of Children: 3

THE FIRST TO WED IN THE WHITE HOUSE

Born in Paris, France, the daughter of the future president of the United States, Maria did not see her parents' homeland until she was four-and-one-half years old. Her arrival in America sparked a new fashion fad, for little Maria wore "pants." The pants, more properly known as "pantalettes," represented haute couture on the Continent.

Attending schools in Washington, D.C., where her father was very active in the politics of the city, young Maria became known as a fashion pace-setter and was very popular with the younger set of the city's elite.

When Maria was fourteen years old, her father was elected to the presidency. Shortly after her father's term had begun, he employed Samuel Lawrence Gouveneur to work for him as a junior secretary in the White House. For Maria, it was love at first sight. She immediately set her cap for him. Her goal was attained when, in 1820, she married her father's secretary in the first White House wedding.

With the end of Monroe's presidential term in 1825, Maria and her husband moved to New York City, from which he had originally come. Samuel was appointed as postmaster of New York City by Monroe's successor to the presidency, John Quincy Adams. In this way Adams repaid political debts owed to James Monroe, and, thus, Maria, Samuel, and their three children were able to live comfortably.

By the late 1820s Maria's father was in financial difficulties and had to turn to Maria and Samuel for help. He sold his Virginia home, in part designed by Thomas Jefferson, and moved to New York City to live his final years with his daughter.

FOR FURTHER READING

Cresson, William Penn. *James Monroe*. New York, New York: Archon Books, 1971.

Kane, Joseph Nathan. *Facts about the Presidents*. New York, New York: H. W. Wilson, 4th ed. 1981.

Klapthor, Margaret Brown. *First Ladies*. Washington, D.C.: White House Historical Association, 1979.

Richardson, James D. *A Compilation of the Messages and Papers of the Presidents, 1789–1897*. Vol. 4. Washington, D.C.: n.p., 1897.

Whitney, David C. *American Presidents*. New York, New York: Doubleday, 1978.

5 JOHN QUINCY ADAMS'S CHILDREN

GEORGE WASHINGTON ADAMS

First child of John Quincy Adams and Louisa Catherine Johnson

Born: April 13, 1801   *Birthplace:* Berlin, Germany
Died: April 30, 1829   *Age at Death:* 28 years
Cause of Death: Drowning
Education: Tutors, preparatory schools, Harvard University
Profession: Lawyer   *Spouse:* None
Number of Children: 1

A FLAWED BRILLIANCE

George Washington Adams, born in Berlin, Germany, where his father was serving as America's minister to Prussia, was named after George Washington, whose death had occurred only a little more than a year previously. The birth followed numerous miscarriages and was extremely difficult for his mother. The difficult birth was prophetic in that the burden of a great name would prove to be more than the young man could handle. George Washington Adams was never to reach even the minimal expectations of his stern, demanding, and, perhaps, even cruel father, John Quincy Adams.

In early childhood George showed signs of brilliance, but, as his grandfather, John Adams, second president of the United States, warned, "George is a treasure of diamonds. He has genius equal to anything; but like all other genius requires the most delicate management to keep it from running into eccentricities."[21] A sensitive soul, with a strong preference for art and music, he was never to experience that "delicate management" prescribed by his grandfather. On the contrary, his entire life was spent with his father's scoldings, commandments, and periodic tirades raining down upon him.

Acknowledged by his family as a nervous, overgrown boy of unsteady health, George was privately tutored in preparation for his admission to Harvard. Once at Harvard, George received directions by mail from his father on how to conduct every aspect of his private life. His father told him when to work, at which times of the day to play, and reminded the young man that he was an Adams who must recognize that, "My sons have not only their honor but that of two preceding generations to sustain."[22]

John Quincy thought George's aspirations inappropriate to the Adams family, for George wanted to practice the poetic arts. As if to confirm his father's opinion, George became involved in a student riot at Harvard, and, as was later to be discovered, led a double life. Nonetheless, he managed to graduate from Harvard and was admitted to the Massachusetts bar in 1824. He practiced law in Boston and in 1825 reached the zenith of his achievements when he was elected to the Massachusetts state legislature. During this short period of success, George seemed to be on the road to fulfilling his father's ambitions for him. As much of the Adamses' property was located in Boston, George took over the management of the family finances, thus earning a short-lived acceptance from the family.

George traveled frequently to Washington, D.C., when his father occupied the White House. It was during these trips that he fell in love with his cousin, Mary Catherine, who, along with several other orphaned children of his mother's sister, stayed at the White House during the John Quincy Adams administration. As John Quincy was Mary Catherine's guardian, George approached his father about marriage to her. Both father and son agreed that it would be better if George developed his law practice for four or five years, and, then, possibly the marriage could be considered. So, George returned to Boston to work.

In his absence, the fickle Mary Catherine became deeply attached to George's younger brother, John II, who also lived at the White House. Eventually Mary Catherine broke the engagement in order to marry John II. Thereafter, George's apparent devotion to his family and career began to dissipate. He began to neglect his law practice, acquire numerous debts, and stay out late drinking.

In the summer of 1827 his mother visited Boston during one of his periodic illnesses to nurse him back to health. She wrote to John Quincy, describing George as "the same old exaggerated conceited timid enthusiastic negligent cold and eccentric being that he had been since he was born."[23] John Quincy asked that George send him his diary for evaluation. Later that year, the president traveled to Boston to visit his eldest son, whom he described as "dutiful and affectionate, and wants nothing but a firm purpose to be all that I could wish."[24]

When the spring of 1829 came, George went to Washington to visit his family, and those that saw him recognized that something was seriously wrong. His appearance and actions showed physical and mental degeneration. Returning home by way of New York City, George left Washington on April 29, 1829 complaining of a very bad headache.

Returning from Washington he began telling fellow passengers on a ship that he heard voices of people who were spying on him. At 3 A.M., April 30, he went to the ship's captain and demanded that he stop the ship so George could be let off, even though the ship was at sea. Following his orders to the captain, George disappeared. Later, his hat was seen in the water off the stern of the ship. Within two weeks, George's body was discovered near City Island in New York. It was determined in the investigation only that he fell or jumped overboard. His body was returned to the family's Braintree County home for burial.

Soon after his death it was discovered that George had been leading a double life. Papers were found in which George acknowledged his parentage of a child by a maid of the family's Boston doctor. The affair was known in the Boston area, but was a surprise to the Adams family. It was then that a blackmailer entered the scene. To keep the sordid secret quiet, the blackmailer demanded payment. On behalf of the family, Charles Francis Adams, George's younger brother, refused to pay for suppression of the scandal. In anger the blackmailer published and circulated a forty-four-page pamphlet intended to embarrass the Adams family. George's mother always maintained that her son was a sacrifice to the political ambitions of the Adams family. Charles Francis later observed of his brother, "Poor fellow, he had wound himself nearly up in his own web."[25]

JOHN ADAMS II

Second child, second son of John Quincy Adams and Louisa Catherine Johnson

Born: July 4, 1803   *Birthplace:* Boston, Massachusetts
Died: October 23, 1834   *Age at Death:* 31 years, 3 months
Cause of Death: Alcoholism
Education: Preparatory schools, Harvard University
Profession: Secretary, Presidential aide, Grist Mill Manager
Spouse: Mary Catherine Hellen
Number of Children: 2

ANOTHER SACRIFICE TO POLITICAL AMBITION?

It was his mother who frequently observed, following the early death of John Adams II, that he was another sacrificial lamb on the doorstep of the Adams family ambition for political power.

As a young man, John and his brother George accompanied their father to England, where Adams, Sr., served his third major diplomatic post. At this stage of his life, John Adams II was outgoing and eager. In 1817 the family returned to the United States. In the accepted manner of prominent families of the time, John was educated in preparatory schools, and was admitted to Harvard in 1819. He excelled in sports, but was only a fair scholar.

Finding that John II stood only forty-fifth in a class of eighty-five at Harvard, his father would not allow John to return home for Christmas vacation, stating in a characteristically harsh letter that, "I could feel nothing but sorrow and shame in your presence."[26] Spurred on by his father's anger, John managed to move his standing up to twenty-fourth in his class. It was not good enough for John Quincy. He would not attend the graduation ceremonies of his son unless he stood fifth or better. Further, despite his father's warnings of dire consequences, John became involved in a student rebellion as a member of the notoriously rowdy Harvard class of 1823. Just before commencement John and forty-two other students were expelled.

Leaving Harvard, John became secretary to his father, president of the United States. In a White House wedding, John married his cousin Mary Catherine, who had previously been engaged to his older brother, George. Describing the wedding in a letter to brother Charles Francis, his mother wrote that John looked as if "the cares of the world lay on his shoulders and my heart tells me there is much to fear."[27] It was a prophetic observation. Trouble did not surface, however, during the first years of their marriage when John and Mary lived at the White House, where their first child was born. It was a time of family entertainment, such as playing musical instruments and taking part in family theatricals, as well as presidential politics and government. But the tranquility was short-lived.

During the 1828 New Year's Eve celebration at the White House, the president insulted a guest, Russell Jarvis, in front of other guests, as well as in the presence of John II. As the president was not liable to challenge because he was president, Jarvis challenged John II to a duel. Jarvis sent a letter to John II demanding a duel, but received no response. Not to respond to such a challenge was thought cowardly by many Americans. To further humiliate the president through his son, Jarvis felt it necessary to provoke an incident. Jarvis intercepted John II in the rotunda of the capitol as he carried a message from his father's office to Congress. Jarvis yanked John's nose and slapped his face, all standard and approved provocations for a duel. But, again, John did not respond. Adams, Sr., disapproved of dueling, and responded for his son by sending a message to Congress that "his secretary" had been waylaid and assaulted by "a person," requesting that Congress should provide funds to secure the way between the president's office and Congress so that future incidents could be prevented. The press had a great time with the "nose-pulling" episode, and Congress went so far as to investigate by having both John II and Russell Jarvis appear before it for examination. John's mother always maintained that the humiliation of the nose-pulling incident ruined her son's career.

John moved from the White House to take over management of a family-owned business, a gristmill. The business had never been successful, and under John's management it began to go broke. John began to drink heavily. By the late 1820s John Quincy observed that "my dear son has been in declining and drooping state of health."[28]

With the loss of his bid for a second term, John Quincy returned to the family home near Quincy, Massachusetts. John II remained at the gristmill near Washington, D.C., his health steadily deteriorating. In late October 1834, John Quincy received notice that his thirty-one-year-old son was gravely ill and rushed to the bedside, arriving only four hours before John II died.

John's death was a cause for heightened tensions within the family. Louisa accused John Quincy of sacrificing another son to political ambition. Whether or not mother Louisa's accusation was justified, it is certain that John Quincy's treatment of his son lacked parental warmth and affection. It was not easy to be a member of the Adams family, and more particularly the son of John Quincy Adams.

CHARLES FRANCIS ADAMS

Third child, third son of John Quincy Adams and Louisa Catherine Johnson

Born: August 18, 1807   *Birthplace:* Boston, Massachusetts
Died: November 21, 1886   *Age at Death:* 79 years, 3 months
Cause of Death: Stroke
Education: Tutors, private schools, Harvard University
Profession: Writer, Politician   *Spouse:* Abigail Brown Brooks
Number of Children: 6

A THIRD ADAMS PRESIDENT?

Educated through travel with his family on trips to Russia and England during John Quincy Adams's service in the diplomatic corps, Charles spoke French, German, and Russian fluently at a very young age. Following attendance at several European schools, as well as the Boston Latin School, Charles graduated from Harvard College in 1825.

From Harvard, Charles went to apprentice in law under the tutelage of the famous Daniel Webster. Yet, with this excellent beginning, he was never to practice law.

At the age of twenty-two, Charles married Abigail Brown Brooks, "the daughter of Peter Brooks, at the time the wealthiest citizen of Boston."[29] Following his marriage, Charles turned from law to writing, editing, and publishing family documents, as well as writing on subjects such as economics and foreign policy, often taking controversial stands on the social and political issues of the time. Charles championed the radical position of the abolition of slavery, and even went so far as to assist in the black cause by initiating Boston laws to prevent discrimination on public conveyances.

With the death of his wife's father, Charles inherited a huge estate, enabling him to pursue politics without monetary difficulties. In 1841, Charles became his father's and grandfather's successor apparent when he entered the Massachusetts state legislature. By 1848 he had become a leading spokesman for the abolitionist movement, a delegate and then chairman for the state convention seeking to destroy slavery. The convention was part of the separatist movement that split from the Democratic party and took the name of "Free-Soil party." Former president Martin Van Buren was selected to head the new party's national ticket, and Charles Francis Adams was chosen as the vice-presidential candidate. But the time was not yet ripe, for Van Buren, an abolitionist, and Adams were soundly defeated by the Whigs' southern candidate, Zachary Taylor.

Elected to the House of Representatives in 1858, Charles was strangely silent on his abolitionist stand, causing the nickname "Silent Charles" to be hurled at him by his detractors. Following in the tradition of his grandfather and father, Charles was appointed as minister to Great Britain, where he served with a high level of popularity. "This scion of the Adams clan was 'to the manner born' so that his family prestige and the wealth of his wife paved the way into the inner circles of British society."[30] It was said that, "though he had his father's name, he lacked personal magnetism."[31]

In 1872 and again in 1876 Charles's name was placed in nomination at the Republican convention for candidate for president of the United States. But Charles was an advocate for civil service reform and control of big business—much in advance of his peers—and neither convention nominated him.

Charles retired to Boston, concluding his public life. He was free to devote time to his continuing scholarly work on the Adams family, a massive undertaking which extended to ten volumes. Charles died on November 21, 1886. According to newspaper accounts, "he had not been well for some time, and suffered more or less for the past five years from some brain trouble, the result of overwork."[32]

But for his championing of the right causes at the wrong time, there is reason to believe that Charles might well have been the third in a dynasty of American presidents.

LOUISA CATHERINE ADAMS

Fourth child, only daughter of John Quincy Adams and Louisa Catherine Johnson

Born: 1811   *Birthplace:* St. Petersburg, Russia
Died: 1812   *Age at Death:* 1 year
Cause of Death: Unknown

AN AMERICAN IN ST. PETERSBURG

Louisa Catherine, conceived and born in St. Petersburg, Russia, (renamed Leningrad) lived only a short time. While John Quincy Adams was serving as United States minister to Russia, his last child was born. When John Quincy was ordered to Paris to negotiate the Treaty of Ghent in 1814, ending the War of 1812, his wife's major concern was "that the baby would be left behind in Russia's inhospitable clime."[33]

What killed Louisa Catherine? Nobody knows. She may have been the victim of the high infant mortality rate characteristic of the time, or the especial rigors of the Russian winter may have been responsible for her early death. Even her exact birth and death dates are unknown.

Somewhere in the city of Leningrad, in the Union of Soviet Socialist Republics, lie the remains of a child of the eighth president of the United States.

FOR FURTHER READING

See list following the chapter about John Adams's family.

6 MARTIN VAN BUREN'S CHILDREN

ABRAHAM VAN BUREN

First child of Martin Van Buren and Hannah Hoes

Born: November 27, 1807   *Birthplace:* Kinderhook, New York
Died: March 15, 1873   *Age at Death:* 65 years, 3 months
Cause of Death: Unknown
Education: West Point   *Profession:* Soldier, Presidential Secretary
Spouse: Angelica Singleton
Number of Children: 3

THE HUSBAND OF ANGELICA

Spectacularly unspectacular may be the best description for the eldest son of Martin Van Buren. Constantly in attendance on his father's needs and desires, Abraham Van Buren seemed to have no life of his very own. It was a pattern that he did not break throughout his life. Known only as his father's son when a child, in manhood he was known primarily as the husband of his wife, Angelica.

Entering West Point at age sixteen, Abraham graduated in 1827 with the rank of second lieutenant in the U.S. Army. He was posted to an infantry regiment and served not quite two years on the frontier. Five years passed before he was promoted to the rank of first lieutenant, and it took nine years in all before Abraham was made a captain, a slow promotion rate considering his father's exalted position. In 1837 his father became president of the United States, and Abraham resigned his army commission to become his father's secretary.

It was Dolley Madison who introduced Abraham to her cousin, the beautiful and accomplished Angelica Singleton. Abraham married her in 1838. Angelica, heir to a wealthy South Carolina family, spurned convention and earned a lively reputation for herself. During Van Buren's presidential term,

Angelica acted as White House hostess, creating a stir in Washington society with her assumed airs.

With the outbreak of the Mexican war in 1846, Abraham was commissioned as a major and was actively involved in the campaign from Vera Cruz to Mexico City. Finally, in recognition of his service he was promoted to the rank of lieutenant colonel. Promoted at the same time was Robert E. Lee, who would command southern forces in the Civil War. Abraham served in the army for a total of eighteen years, until he retired in 1854.

Following his retirement, he and Angelica earned a reputation for elegant and gracious hospitality. While the Van Burens thus appeared consumed with the social graces, Abraham was, in fact, busy editing and publishing Martin Van Buren's works.

It was said of Abraham that "he [is] very different from 'Prince' John, his younger brother, who resembles his father in using his fellow man as a ladder upon which to mount and when he is up he kicks it down and without scrupples of conscience denies he has had any aid."[34] Abraham did not only not kick the ladder down but, instead, acted during his entire lifetime as the "steadier" for his father and brother.

JOHN VAN BUREN

Second child, second son of Martin Van Buren and Hannah Hoes

Born: February 18, 1810   *Birthplace:* Hudson, New York
Died: October 13, 1866   *Age at Death:* 56 years, 8 months
Cause of Death: Kidney failure
Education: Private studies, Yale University
Profession: Lawyer, Politician
Spouse: Elizabeth VanderPoel
Number of Children: 1

"PRINCE JOHN"

John Van Buren was one of the most colorful of all presidential children. His life was marked by escapades as well as accomplishments, with equal numbers of followers and detractors. Perhaps, had he had less of an aversion to hard work and more ambition for public office, John Van Buren may very well have equaled his father's achievement.

Tall, well built, maintaining a personable attitude and an unpretentious demeanor, this son of a president was nevertheless described by contemporaries as extravagant, bold, notorious, and brilliant. He chose to live life fully, thus his pleasures took precedence over developing his potential.

Reaching manhood in the 1830s, when young gentlemen were expected to have prowess in drinking, gambling, and lovemaking, John certainly achieved notoriety and caused concern in the first two areas. Graduating from Yale in his late teens, John studied law in Albany, New York, and was admitted to the New York bar when barely twenty years old. He did not proceed directly to the practice of law because his father was selected as minister to England, and John accompanied his father as secretary to the American legation. John delighted in the elegant life of European nobility and was accepted into high society. It was during this first European sojourn that John developed the close associations with influential Europeans which would be further cultivated in later years.

After two years in Europe John returned to Albany, where he opened a law practice. Initially his law practice was highly successful and lucrative. However, the habits acquired during college days, habits associated with drinking and gambling, soon showed themselves. News of John's growing notoriety reached the ears of his father, who by 1837 was president of the United States. The president wrote to his son expressing his concern: "What you may regard as an innocent and harmless indulgence will take you years to overcome in the public estimation," further relating that "I was informed that you had been twice carried drunk from the race course."[35] What John needed to reform were new habits and associations with good people, thought his father, so he suggested a vacation in the London John had so much enjoyed.

To direct John on the right track in London, Martin Van Buren asked former President Jackson for letters of introduction to the Duke of Wellington, the British hero of Waterloo. Jackson complied with the request. Thus, John was reintroduced to the most elite European society through the auspices of the conquerer of Napoleon. It was to be this very elitism that would cause him difficulties in equality-loving America. John's name appeared on the guest list of a social event, with his name listed between royal titles as "John Van Buren, Son of the President of the United States."[36] An uproar appeared in the American press. A member of the U.S. House of Representatives stood "to denounce this flagrant departure from the ideals of equality for which the Founding Fathers fought against England."[37] Henceforth, in ridicule John Van Buren became known to American people as "Prince John."

Notwithstanding the negative press, John engaged in some solid politicking among his constituents and was elected to Congress for the term beginning May 1841. Among his fellow representatives were the former president, John Quincy Adams, and the soon-to-be president, Millard Fillmore, as well as James Roosevelt, grandfather to one and granduncle to another president. Either despite his reputation for indulging in the bottle, or because of his prowess at imbibing, John was repeatedly reelected to the House of Representatives. Observations such as "John Van Buren is a rowdy, the associate of rowdies"[38] did him no harm in political contests. On the burning issue of the day, slavery, John supported his northern colleagues, affirming, "I look with detestation upon the practice of buying and selling live bodies."[39] However he did not support slavery's abolition by proclamation, believing the method unconstitutional. Further, despite his abhorrence of slavery, John Van Buren did not support Abraham Lincoln's presidential bid, but ironically supported the state's rights candidate John Breckenridge, the nominee of the southern faction of the Democratic party.

In his legal practice, John's most famous case was *Forrest* v. *Forrest* (1851–1852), a scandalous divorce action. The sordid details of infidelity by both parties made lurid headlines and advanced John's legal practice.

For the last few years of his life John was an invalid. For his health, as well as to see again places of pleasant memories, John went abroad in 1866. On the return journey, accompanied by his only child, John set sail aboard the *Scotia*. But he was never to see America again, for he suffered complete kidney failure and died at sea.

John Van Buren, an American president's son, was actually called "royal" during his lifetime. Possessing the physical and mental characteristics and the proper associations, John had all the credentials for high achievement, possibly even the presidency itself, yet there was something lacking in his ambition and self-discipline. He chose to taste the world rather than to shape it.

MARTIN VAN BUREN, JR.

Third child, third son of Martin Van Buren and Hannah Hoes

Born: December 20, 1812   *Birthplace:* New York, New York
Died: March 19, 1855   *Age at Death:* 42 years, 3 months
Cause of Death: Unknown   *Education:* Unknown
Profession: Presidential Secretary
Spouse: None   *Number of Children:* None

FIRST PRESIDENTIAL SON TO DIE UNDER A FOREIGN FLAG

Martin Van Buren, Jr., called Mat by family and friends, spent his entire life as a very sedate, controlled individual. Working as secretary to his father during Van Buren's presidency, he certainly was not the man to inspire either love or hate from those who knew him.

Described as very literary and not at all physical or robust in appearance, Mat developed his father's notes for the senior Van Buren's planned biography. By the fall of 1849, however, Mat's lack of physical well-being had finally taken its toll and left him a very sick man. Though ill, he maintained a wide correspondence with his father's friends.

His seventy-year-old father was extremely worried about his son's health. He finally prevailed upon the failing Mat to seek help from European doctors in Switzerland and England, as well as searching out the restorative powers offered by waters in France and Germany—to no avail. "It had been the boast of Martin Van Buren that he had been the first President of the United States born under the American flag. It was the destiny of Martin Van Buren, Jr., to be the first presidential son to die under a foreign flag."[40] Mat Van Buren died in Paris while seeking relief from the illnesses that had plagued him all of his life.

SMITH THOMPSON VAN BUREN

Fourth child, fourth son of Martin Van Buren and Hannah Hoes

Born: January 16, 1817   *Birthplace:* New York, New York
Died: 1876   *Age at Death:* 59 years
Cause of Death: Unknown   *Education:* Unknown
Profession: Presidential Aide, Editor
Spouses: Ellen James, Henrietta Irving
Number of Children: Van Buren/James: 4
                                      Van Buren/Irving: 3

A TIGHT-FISTED DEFENDER OF HIS FAMILY

Named after Van Buren's close friend and chief justice of the New York State Supreme Court, Smith Thompson Van Buren was raised in an atmosphere of political intrigue, compounded by controversy over the capabilities of his father, President Van Buren. Unlike his namesake, Smith avoided the judicial arena and instead spent most of his life defending his father and elder brother, John, who became known to the nation for his escapades in Europe. Occasionally, however, Smith Thompson, too, became the recipient of political attacks, particularly in reference to his reputation as being extremely tight-fisted.

Never a candidate for public office himself, he did, however, attend numerous political gatherings, where his intensity on behalf of his father's political actions was well known. Considered knowledgeable about important people and issues of the day, the youngest Van Buren son worked avidly for his father during his presidency. Smith rendered real aid to his father by writing and preparing speeches and documents.

Little of Smith's private life is known. Though he married twice and sired seven children, his impact in history stems from his writings on the presidency of his father. Living fourteen years beyond his father, Smith completed and edited his father's treatise on the development of political parties.[41] Because of his invaluable contributions to our understanding of the Van Buren presidency, he may be credited with some responsibility for what there is of the senior Van Buren's mark on American history.

FOR FURTHER READING

Kane, Joseph Nathan. *Facts about the Presidents*. New York, New York: The H. W. Wilson Company, 1981.

Whitney, David C. *American Presidents*. New York, New York: Doubleday, 1978.

7 WILLIAM HENRY HARRISON'S CHILDREN

AN INTRODUCTORY NOTE

The ninth president of the United States, William Henry Harrison, was the nation's chief executive for only one month. The sixty-eight-year-old military hero of the War of 1812 came into the presidency following a hard-fought, vigorous campaign to win the office. On the day Harrison was inaugurated (March 4, 1841), the winds blew and there was a strong chill in the air. Harrison took an hour and one-half to read his inauguration speech. His speech, combined with the other official speakers of the ceremonies, added up to a long exposure to the chilled Washington, D.C., temperature. The elderly man was felled by pneumonia shortly after his entry into the office, and he died thirty-two days later. Immediately succeeded by his vice-president, John Tyler, it was almost as if William Henry Harrison had never served as president of the United States. The first president to die in office, the shortness of his term is almost the only thing that is remembered of his service, though his actions as a military figure are well recorded.

Perhaps because of this short service in the nation's highest office, little has been recorded of his children. Though three of the sons achieved some renown on their own, including one that would be the father of the twenty-third president of the United States, Benjamin Harrison, the other children have received only the most perfunctory note in history.

The lives of most of the ten children were short, ending while in their thirties. Most of the children preceded their father to death before he achieved his brief moment in the nation's highest office.

ELIZABETH BASSETT HARRISON SHORT

First child of William Henry Harrison and Anna Tuthill Symmes

Born: September 29, 1796
Birthplace: Fort Washington, Ohio Territory
Died: September 26, 1846   *Age at Death:* 50 years
Cause of Death: Unknown   *Education:* Unknown
Profession: Housewife   *Spouse:* John Cleves Short
Number of Children: Unknown

A LOG CABIN BIRTH

Born at Fort Washington, Ohio, only shortly after her father was given the command of that fort, Elizabeth would survive five years beyond her father's death. Her death was but one in the string of deaths that would befall all of the Harrisons' daughters.

Elizabeth, who had married at eighteen years of age, survived only a year beyond her youngest sister, Anna.

JOHN CLEVES SYMMES HARRISON

Second child, first son of William Henry Harrison and Anna Tuthill Symmes

Born: October 28, 1798   *Birthplace:* Vincennes, Indiana Territory
Died: October 30, 1832   *Age at Death:* 34 years
Cause of Death: Unknown   *Education:* Unknown
Profession: Government Employee
Spouse: Clarissa Pike
Number of Children: 6

A SIMPLE EMBEZZLER

Born in the new capital of the Indiana Territory, Vincennes, John Cleves Symmes, always referred to as Symmes, spent almost all of his short life in Indiana.

Marrying the daughter of the famous General Zebulon Montgomery Pike, discoverer of Pikes Peak, Symmes fathered six children. To support his family he received an appointment, arranged by his father, to a position with the finance division of the government land office at Vincennes. It was a position of responsibility. Large sums of money regularly passed through his hands, as at the time the bureau in which he worked gave an expression to American slang of "doing a land office business." For ten years Symmes's honesty and integrity were unquestioned. Then his world dissolved beneath him. Symmes was accused of embezzlement.

Nearly $13,000 was missing from the government land office. The government took Symmes to court, with the result that judgment was passed in favor of the government. Symmes was condemned for embezzlement and commanded to make restitution of the missing money.

As his father had posted surety for his son, he, as well as Symmes, was made responsible for repayment. Father and son did not come to share equally the financial burden of the judgment, for Symmes died at the young age of thirty-four years.

Harrison's presidency was ten years distant when he was forced to pay for his son's embezzlement, while also grieving for his death.

LUCY SINGLETON HARRISON ESTE

Third child, second daughter of William Henry Harrison and Anna Tuthill Symmes

Born: September 1800   *Birthplace:* Richmond, Virginia
Died: April 7, 1826   *Age at Death:* 26 years
Cause of Death: Unknown   *Education:* Unknown
Profession: Housewife, Mother   *Spouse:* David Este
Number of Children: 4

THE JUDGE'S WIFE

Married to David Este, a judge of the Superior Court of Ohio, Lucy Harrison gave birth to four children before her death at the age of twenty-six. When Lucy died her father was a senator from the state of Ohio, with fifteen years to pass before he would be president.

WILLIAM HENRY HARRISON, JR.

Fourth child, second son of William Henry Harrison and Anna Tuthill Symmes

Born: September 3, 1802   *Birthplace:* Vincennes, Indiana Territory
Died: February 6, 1838   *Age at Death:* 35 years, 5 months
Cause of Death: Alcoholism
Education: Transylvania College
Profession: Lawyer, Politician, Farmer
Spouse: Jane Findlay
Number of Children: Unknown

MASTERED BY DEMON RUM

William, his father's namesake, showed little inclination toward the law career his father planned for him. The senior William had definite ideas about more than his son's career; he wanted his son to be his namesake in deed as well as in name.

At seventeen, young William was sent to Transylvania College in Lexington, Kentucky, despite perpetual family financial difficulties. But the young man soon became homesick and discontented, complaining that he should be transferred to a college in Cincinnati so that he might be closer to the family, who had moved to a North Bend, Ohio, home in 1814. The Harrison family refused to listen to the boy's pleas. Completing his studies at Transylvania College, though his grades were not particularly impressive, William did succeed in earning a law degree. He began a short-lived Cincinnati practice.

Within two years of William's graduation from law school, his father was appointed as minister to Mexico and secured the appointment of his son as aide. During this period of international public service William handled himself with the grace and skill of a political veteran, in contrast to his deportment in later years.

Following this brief career in the diplomatic arena, William returned to Cincinnati and the practice of law, marrying Jane Findlay, daughter of his father's close friend, James Findlay. Things did not go well for young William. By 1832 he had become addicted to "demon rum." He was forced to abandon his law practice because he could no longer cope with the demands of his profession. At his father's behest, William then turned to farming, unsuccessfully. Failure again was caused by his addiction to alcohol.

William never mastered his alcoholism. His father was eventually forced to take over the support of his son's family. In the end, alcohol brought William's death. With the burial of his namesake the future president's dreams were shattered. All the hopes and plans Harrison had envisioned for his dead son were then transferred to his remaining children.

JOHN SCOTT HARRISON

Fifth child, third son of William Henry Harrison and Anna Tuthill Symmes

Born: October 4, 1804   *Birthplace:* Vincennes, Indiana Territory
Died: May 25, 1878   *Age at Death:* 73 years, 7 months
Cause of Death: Unknown
Education: Old Farmer's College   *Profession:* Farmer, Politician

Spouses: Lucretia Knapp Johnson, Elizabeth Ramsey Irwin
Number of Children: Harrison/Johnson: 3
                    Harrison/Irwin: 6

A STOLEN BODY

Son of a president and father of a president, John Scott Harrison himself served in the U.S. House of Representatives, but never aspired to a higher office. He was a farmer at heart for the most part of his seventy-three years and he preferred his 400 fertile acres of land in North Bend, Ohio, to political intrigue. Nevertheless, the drama of political events followed him into his grave—and beyond.

John Scott, born in Vincennes, Indiana Territory, during his father's governorship of the territory, was educated at Old Farmer's College, where he studied law. Returning to the family lands, for his father was occupied with national politics and needed his son to run the farm, John Scott never practiced law. However, he was soon called upon by friends and neighbors to run for Congress. Successful, rather more for his popularity than any political ability, he served two terms in the Congress, but was defeated in his third bid for the legislative seat.

After his political career, John Scott returned again to Hamilton County, Ohio, and to the farm where he was to live for the rest of his life. He tended his crops and watched the developing careers of his many children, among whom was Benjamin Harrison, who would be the twenty-third president of the United States.

On May 25, 1878 John Scott died of an unknown ailment. His death was to be followed by a bizarre succession of events which to this day have not been satisfactorily explained. Several days before his death, a young nephew, Devin, died and was buried in the Harrison family plot, but the corpse was stolen from the grave and disappeared. Taking no chances that such would occur to their father's body, John's children directed that their father's grave be dug deep and a cement cover be used to protect the body from would-be violators. Such was, supposedly, done.

A few days after John Scott's funeral, his son and several neighbors went to Cincinnati to search the medical school dissecting rooms for the body of Devin, supposing that it had been sold to the school to be used in research.[42] The group searched all day, but did not find the remains of Devin. However, as they made ready to leave the morgue, a body was discovered hanging in a shaft with its face covered by a burlap bag. To the horror of John Scott's son, it was his father, John Scott Harrison, hanging in the shaft.

Of course, the newspapers had a field day with all the grotesque details of the case. It was through the body-snatching that John Scott Harrison, a simple man known only in Ohio, became a national topic of conversation.

When they buried John Scott Harrison again, in the family plot, his son and the future president, Benjamin Harrison, was standing by the grave. Some explained John Scott's disappearance as simply one of body theft for profit. Others found more devious reasons for the episode. It was suggested that Benjamin Harrison had made bitter and unforgiving enemies, who, not being able to triumph over Benjamin's Indiana political successes, had taken their vengeance out upon the unresisting corpse of his father.

Fame is a strange commodity. John Scott Harrison was a son of a president and father of a president and served his country in Congress. Yet he became known to his fellow Americans only in what must surely have been one of the strangest incidents ever to befall America's royalty.

BENJAMIN HARRISON

Sixth child, fourth son of William Henry Harrison and Anna Tuthill Symmes

Born: 1806   *Birthplace:* Vincennes, Indiana Territory
Died: June 9, 1840   *Age at Death:* 34 years
Cause of Death: Unknown
Education: Medical studies   *Profession:* Medical Doctor
Spouses: Louisa Bonner, Mary Raney
Number of Children: Harrison/Bonner: 3
                           Harrison/Raney: 2

A SHORT, FULL LIFE

This is the first of the nation's Benjamin Harrisons. However, he died while his nephew who would be the twenty-third president of the United States was but a small child.

William Henry's son, Benjamin, accomplished much in his short lifespan. Twice married, he fathered five children, three by his first wife and two by the second, and completed medical studies, entering into a medical career—all before he was in his mid-thirties. As his father had studied medicine, the only president to do so, it is not surprising that his son should follow his father's example.

Benjamin died only months before his father would gain the presidency. Yet, this son of a president would have his name perpetuated when an older brother named his son in memory of his loved, admired, and accomplished brother.

MARY SYMMES HARRISON THORNTON

Seventh child, third daughter of William Henry Harrison and Anna Tuthill Symmes

Born: January 22, 1809 *Birthplace:* Vincennes, Indiana Territory
Died: November 16, 1842 *Age at Death:* 33 years, 10 months
Cause of Death: Unknown *Education:* Unknown
Profession: Housewife, Mother
Spouse: John Henry Fitzhugh Thornton
Number of Children: 6

MOTHER OF SIX

Carrying her mother's maiden name and representing a prominent family of the day, Mary Symmes Harrison married a physician when she was twenty years of age, and soon had a large family of six children.

But this daughter as well as her sisters died at a relatively youthful age. She left only her six children and almost no record of her personal life.

CARTER BASSETT HARRISON

Eighth child, fifth son of William Henry Harrison and Anna Tuthill Symmes

Born: October 26, 1811 *Birthplace:* Vincennes, Indiana Territory
Died: August 12, 1839 *Age at Death:* 27 years, 10 months
Cause of Death: Unknown *Education:* Unknown
Profession: Lawyer *Spouse:* Mary Anne Sutherland
Number of Children: 1

A COLOMBIAN ADVENTURE

Only seventeen years old when his father was appointed by President John Quincy Adams to be minister to Colombia, Carter Bassett, named after his grandmother's family, accompanied his father on the trip to the South American continent. William Henry took no note of the small concern that his son was completely unprepared for both the journey and the work. His father preferred to dwell instead on the importance of proper attire for his staff, including the attire of his son: "a plain coat with the diplomatic buttons, which could only be got in Philadelphia, is all the uniform we require. . . . The button has an eagle with an olive branch in one talon, with a thunderbolt in the other."[43]

Almost immediately upon the arrival of the Americans in Colombia, a revolution broke out. President John Quincy Adams recalled Harrison and his entire staff. Returning to the United States until the revolution ended, William Henry Harrison was not reappointed to the ministry, for the post fell to another office seeker.

By the age of twenty-five Carter Bassett completed his education. He became an attorney, opened a small practice, married, fathered a child, and died. He, too, died slightly more than a year before his father was elected as the nation's chief executive.

ANNA TUTHILL HARRISON TAYLOR

Ninth child, fourth daughter of William Henry Harrison and Anna Tuthill Symmes

Born: October 28, 1813   *Birthplace:* Cincinnati, Ohio
Died: July 5, 1845   *Age at Death:* 31 years, 9 months
Cause of Death: Unknown   *Education:* Unknown
Profession: Housewife   *Spouse:* William Henry Harrison Taylor
Number of Children: None

MARRIED TO HER COUSIN

Anna Tuthill Harrison was born only four weeks after her father had recaptured Detroit in the War of 1812, a battle that elevated William Henry Harrison to the status of one of the nation's great generals. Anna's birth took place in Cincinnati because her family was a victim of the war. They were forced to evacuate their Vincennes, Indiana, home to escape the campaigns in which her father played such a prominent role.

Anna married her cousin. Her life was short. She died before her thirty-second birthday, less than two years after her father's unexpected death while in office.

JAMES FINDLAY HARRISON

Tenth child, sixth son of William Henry Harrison and Anna Tuthill Symmes

Born: 1814   *Birthplace:* North Bend, Ohio
Died: 1817   *Age at Death:* 3 years
Cause of Death: Unknown

THE FIRST OF MANY MOURNINGS

The tenth and last child to be born to the William Henry Harrison family, James Findlay, was born at the family home in North Bend, Ohio, only shortly after his father had resigned from the army. Named for his father's Ohio friend, James Findlay, he was the first of many Harrison children to die at a young age. He was also the first of two children that would be associated with the Findlay family, as his brother, William Henry Harrison, Jr., would marry a Findlay daughter in later years.

The family mourned the death of this child, little knowing it was but the first of many of their children's deaths to follow.

FOR FURTHER READING

Beard, Charles. *Presidents in American History*. New York, New York: Julian A. Messner, 1981.

Donaldson, Norman, and Betty Donaldson. *How Did They Die?* New York, New York: St. Martins Press, 1980.

Kane, Nathan Joseph. *Facts about the Presidents*. New York, New York: The H. W. Wilson Company, 1981.

Whitney, David C. *American Presidents*. New York, New York: Doubleday, 1978.

8 JOHN TYLER'S CHILDREN

MARY TYLER JONES

First child of John Tyler and Letitia Christian

Born: April 15, 1815   *Birthplace:* Charles City County, Virginia
Died: June 17, 1848   *Age at Death:* 33 years, 2 months
Cause of Death: Unknown   *Education:* Unknown
Profession: Housewife, Mother
Spouse: Henry Lightfoot Jones
Number of Children: 2

A LITTLE SYLPH

Mary was the first of eight children by Tyler and his first wife. Her upbringing was strict but filled with love within the family. Her father was intent that she grow up to be a proper lady. Commenting to her, when viewing their first waltz, she received his warning that the waltz was a dance "which I do not desire to see you dance. It is rather vulgar, I think."[44] Mary blossomed from a little sylph to a woman with a fascinating way about her, who "beguiled people of their senses."[45]

She married Henry Lightfoot Jones in December 1835, in an elaborate and expensive wedding that could little be afforded by the financially strapped father, a U.S. senator. Young Jones was a tidewater planter of comfortable means who had inherited lands in North Carolina.

Following her father's request, Mary moved with her son, Henry, Jr., to stay with her parents until her mother's death. Thus, Mary's second son, Robert, who would be promoted for gallantry in the Confederate Army for his service at Gettysburg, was born in the White House during this stay.

ROBERT TYLER

Second child, first son of John Tyler and Letitia Christian

Born: September 9, 1816
Birthplace: Charles City County, Virginia   *Died:* December 3, 1877
Age at Death: 61 years, 3 months   *Cause of Death:* Unknown
Education: Private
Profession: Lawyer, Politician, Newspaper Editor, Presidential Secretary
Spouse: Elizabeth Priscilla Cooper
Number of Children: 7

A SOUTHERNER ON THE RUN

Robert Tyler, eldest son of Tyler's many children, was an extremely shy young man. His father, concerned for the young man's future, advised his son to "learn to make yourself popular by accommodating yourself to the feelings, nay whims, of others; we are put into the world and it is our duty to use, while we abstain from abusing it."[46] Young Tyler learned the lesson, and by the time he was an adult he had trained himself not only to overcome his shyness, but also to charm and sway people.

Educated as a lawyer, though never working at anything before his father became president when Robert was just twenty-five, he worked for the first time as his father's White House private secretary. During this period of his life, his great romance and marriage took place. Seeing the daughter of one of the nation's leading tragedians, Thomas Cooper, playing Desdemona, the young, tall, distinguished son of John and Letitia Tyler was immediately smitten, and he soon married her. Young Robert, conveniently, had married in time for his elegant wife to take over the role of White House hostess, for his mother was seriously ill and unable to perform the duties of White House hostess.

At the end of his father's term as president, Robert moved to Philadelphia to successfully practice law. But with the outbreak of the Mexican War in 1846, Robert heard the call of duty and raised a Pennsylvania volunteer regiment. So quickly victorious was the American army that Robert's troops were unneeded, and the U.S. Army declined to use his volunteers.

Robert's activities in forming the voluntary military contingent, in combination with the fact that he was the son of a president, brought him much attention and an important role in Pennsylvania politics. Young Tyler became a champion of the poor, particularly of Irish immigrants, and regularly championed their cause. His work in the state's Democratic party brought him acclaim and also the chairmanship of the Democratic party's central committee, a position of great power, given the weight of Pennsylvania in the day's national politics. In recognition of his assistance in electing Democrat James Buchanan to the presidency in 1856, Buchanan offered Robert a clerkship in the U.S. District Court. Robert refused, saying, "I am distinctly my own master and no office seeker,"[47] indeed an unusual statement for any politician.

With the outbreak of the Civil War sectional animosity turned bitter. Pennsylvania was no place for a public figure with a well-known Southern heritage. Forced to flee for his life and losing all he and his family owned and treasured, Robert returned to Virginia in 1861. His abilities did not go unrecognized by the new Confederate government, as he was immediately appointed registrar of the Confederate treasury, a position of great trust in the new nation.

Following the war, Robert did not return to the North, but began a practice of law in Montgomery, Alabama. "There, in a single upstairs room, unknown and without a single client, he resumed the practice of law. He cooked his own meals, washed his own clothes, scrubbed and cleaned his miserable habitation. James Buchanan, retired from the presidency, heard that Robert Tyler was in financial straits and sent him a $1,000 check, but he [Robert] declined to take it."[48]

Within ten years Robert had become Alabama Democratic state chairman, and editor of the leading Montgomery, Alabama newspaper, the *Advisor*.

Upon his death, obituaries throughout his readopted southern state observed that "no man was ever more unselfish. He devoted his time and talents to the cause of his people without reward or expectation of reward."[49] Truer words could only have been spoken if the obituary had added that this president's son not only did not expect reward, he completely refused it in order that he could remain his own man.

JOHN TYLER, JR.

Third child, second son of John Tyler and Letitia Christian

Born: April 27, 1819   *Birthplace:* Charles City County, Virginia
Died: January 26, 1896   *Age at Death:* 76 years, 9 months
Cause of Death: Unknown
Education: College, law studies   *Profession:* Lawyer, Politician
Spouse: Martha Rochelle
Number of Children: 3

IN THE SHADOW OF FATHER AND BROTHER

John Tyler, Jr., spent his entire life attempting to equal or surpass the accomplishments of his brother and his father, president of the United States. Though blessed with a gift for writing, John never developed his ability, and thus in the field in which he might well have achieved fame, his inherent ability was only superficially exploited.

Educated in law, he served as his brother's assistant in dealing with the press on behalf of their father. It was in this capacity that his extraordinary skill emerged. His flair for writing political tracts won him the admiration of many, including his father who published some of them. But, this talent also earned for him the enmity of those he attacked. One one occasion an editor of a Richmond, Virginia, newspaper defamed the president father and his writer son in such a manner that John felt himself compelled to challenge the editor to a duel. The upcoming duel became the subject of much talk and newspaper accounts, with newspapers unfriendly to the Tylers predicting that young John would play the coward and fail to appear at the appointed hour. To the surprise and chagrin of the Tyler detractors it was not John, but the editor who failed to show at the dueling ground. John came through this test of courage with his family's honor intact. His days of polemical writing and the publicized duel were the high points of John's life.

John spent the rest of his life attempting to equal his respected brother, Robert, but to no avail. For example, there is the instance of the Buchanan presidential election in which Robert played a role acknowledged in full by a grateful Buchanan. John, seeing his brother's success, attempted to imitate his role as confidant by sending unsolicited advice to Buchanan. Buchanan's response was to ignore the younger brother, though offering a position of trust to the elder.

By 1857 the aging former president was alarmed at his younger son's lack of career progress. His son had moved back to Washington, D.C., where he had experienced some small measure of fame, and took a minor position in the attorney general's office. His employment was short, but John remained in Washington, D.C.

In the last years of his life, John lived in difficult financial circumstances while he talked to all that would listen of the exaggerated tales of his influential role in his father's administration.

LETITIA TYLER SEMPLE

Fourth child, second daughter of John Tyler and Letitia Christian

Born: May 11, 1821   *Birthplace:* Charles City County, Virginia
Died: December 28, 1907   *Age at Death:* 86 years, 7 months
Cause of Death: Unknown   *Education:* Unknown
Profession: Housewife, Mother, Businesswoman, Educator
Spouse: James A. Semple
Number of Children: None

AN UNHAPPY MARRIAGE

The beautiful, high-spirited Letitia Tyler was already married to James A. Semple, the nephew and heir of a prominent Williamsburg judge, when her mother died. Periodically, while her husband worked as a purser on U.S. Navy ships, Letitia served as White House hostess, until her father married a much younger woman, Julia Gardiner. Thus, early in her life the two dominant themes were established: a husband that would increasingly become alienated from his wife and reality and a mutual hatred between stepmother and Letitia that would end with the death of one.

With the election of Abraham Lincoln as president of the United States in 1860, Letitia's husband resigned his commission from the navy to support the southern cause, as did all of the Tyler family and kin. During the war, Letitia's husband served the Confederacy as a member of the South's navy. At war's end, unable to comprehend the South's disastrous defeat, James Semple became clearly deranged. He disguised himself so as to engage in espionage against the Union though the war had ended. While the forces of the Confederacy disbanded, returned to their homes, and attempted to reorganize their lives, James continued to play at cloak and dagger in the year following the war. The entire family was forced to acknowledge James's mental disturbance. Letitia, forced into independence for most of their marriage, now permanently separated from James. Moving to Baltimore, she opened a private school, The Eclectic Institute. Meanwhile, James continued his private war against the North until 1867, when he announced that he had been overcome.

In a strange relationship, Julia Tyler, widowed in 1862, became the confidant and benefactor of the deluded James. Letitia, for her part, became enraged, feeling that humiliation was being heaped upon her by her hated stepmother; that Julia's only motive for the involvement with Semple was to bring further scorn and derision upon Letitia. Semple fell in love with his wife's stepmother, and publicly acknowledged the relationship. Julia denied all rumors and refused his romantic attentions, but the public was never sure of the actual relationship. Semple then turned from his mother-in-law, as he had from his wife, to launch himself into a life of wine, women and cards.

Seeking to strike back at her stepmother, Letitia instituted a suit against Julia over the possession of family portraits. In 1907, at the age of eighty-six, Letitia died, a married woman without a husband, still locked in eternal hatred for her father's second wife, who had died many years earlier.

ELIZABETH TYLER WALLER

Fifth child, third daughter of John Tyler and Letitia Christian

Born: July 11, 1823   *Birthplace:* Charles City County, Virginia
Died: June 1, 1850   *Age at Death:* 26 years, 11 months
Cause of Death: Childbirth complications
Education: Unknown   *Profession:* Housewife, Mother
Spouse: William Nevison Waller
Number of Children: 5

DEATH IN CHILDBIRTH

Elizabeth, known as "Lizzie," was eighteen when she was introduced to the White House social scene. Because of her mother's illness, she assisted her older sister, Letitia, in supervising the domestic affairs of the mansion, and acting as White House co-hostess. In 1842 Lizzie married William Waller in a White House wedding. A surprise to all at the wedding was the appearance of her mother, who emerged this single time from her sickroom to be present at the union of her much loved daughter, Lizzie, to a man considered unsophisticated, but very generous and honorable. It was the last time that Letitia Tyler would be seen in public, for only months later she died.

Lizzie, as was the case with her sister Letitia, would not at first acknowledge her father's marriage to a new, younger wife, Julia Gardiner. But, unlike Tyler's other children, Letitia and John, Lizzie came, in time, to be friendly with and even to admire her father's second wife.

In 1850 Lizzie died from complications arising from childbirth. Not yet twenty-seven years old, she died leaving five young children, including two sons who later fought for the South in the war between the states.

ANNE CONTESSE TYLER

Sixth child, fourth daughter of John Tyler and Letitia Christian

Born: April 1825   *Birthplace:* Charles City County, Virginia
Died: July 1825   *Age at Death:* 3 months
Cause of Death: Unknown

"CHILD OF MY LOVE"

Anne Contesse lived but a few short months and died. Tyler, the epitomy of American fatherhood, wrote a lament for his dead child:

> O child of my love, thou wert born for a day;
> And like morning's vision have vanished away.
> Thine eye scarce had ope'd on the world's beaming light
> Ere 'twas sealed up in death and enveloped in night.
>
> O child of my love as a beautiful flower;
> Thy blossom expanded a short fleeting hour.
> The winter of death hath blighted thy bloom
> And thou lyest alone in the cold dreary tomb.[50]

ALICE TYLER DENISON

Seventh child, fifth daughter of John Tyler and Letitia Christian

Born: March 23, 1827   *Birthplace:* Charles City County, Virginia
Died: June 8, 1854   *Age at Death:* 27 years, 3 months
Cause of Death: Bilious colic
Education: Private school   *Profession:* Housewife, Mother
Spouse: Henry Mandeville Denison
Number of Children: 2

"FAT" ALICE

Alice, described, perhaps a bit ungenerously, as "tall and fat" was fourteen when her father entered the White House. Under the wing of her sister-in-law, Priscilla, who acted as White House hostess for a short period, Alice received more attention than might have been expected from men, given her physical description. Considering her teenage ungainliness it may be assumed that "her popularity was enhanced in some measure by her father's political position."[51]

Tyler's remarriage, shortly after the death of Alice's mother, replaced sister-in-law with stepmother, Julia, who was only six years older than Alice. Julia decided that Alice must attend a boarding school for a proper education, and so Alice was packed off, despite her objections. Not lacking in the political acumen that had made her father president, Alice wrote such sweet and charming letters to her stepmother that Julia relented. She brought Alice back to Washington for the social season.

Plunging into the social world, Alice received her share of attention and marriage proposals, but she rejected all suitors. When her father left office, Alice was still single, though she had matured into a "tall and attractive young woman."[52]

In 1849, as friends and relatives of the twenty-one-year-old woman had just about given her up for an "old maid" she met the tall, rugged, lady's man, Reverend Henry Mandeville Denison, a twenty-eight-year-old Episcopalian rector of the Williamsburg parish. Alice immediately set her cap for him, and by July of the next year she was his bride. It was a romantic union, for her husband had neither economic nor social status commensurate with Alice's previous suitors.

Alice gave birth to two children, only one of whom lived to adulthood. She died in 1854 of bilious colic leaving a grieving husband and a distraught father, who had seen the death of three daughters in the space of seven years.

TAZEWELL TYLER

Eighth child, third son of John Tyler and Letitia Christian

Born: December 6, 1830   *Birthplace:* Charles City County, Virginia
Died: January 8, 1874   *Age at Death:* 43 years, 1 month
Cause of Death: Alcoholism
Education: Philadelphia Medical College
Profession: Medical Doctor
Spouse: Nannie Bridges
Number of Children: 2

"A GENIAL GENTLEMEN"

The youngest of the eight children born to John and Letitia Christian Tyler, the first wife of John Tyler, was named by the older children after the Tyler family's close friend, Littleton W. Tazewell. Taz, as he came to be called, was fourteen when his father married for the second time. Father Tyler, an exceptional man to his many children, declared, "My children are my principal treasures,"[53] which may have made up for the frequent financial problems of the family. Tyler's second wife lavished attention upon the young man as if he were her own child, frequently teasing him about his many lady friends, whom he pursued with all the vigor of his twenty years.

At the gentle age of twenty, during the height of the California gold rush, Taz sought his family's acquiescence to his journey to that state so that he might begin a life of financial ease. But his father stopped him and for four years the hard-pressed family spent $700 a year on an expensive medical education, finally ending when the talented young man studied under his uncle, Dr. Henry Curtis.

Little is known of his immediate beginnings in medical practice, but the Civil War found him in the Confederate Army serving in the medical corps.

After the war between the states, Taz practiced medicine in Virginia, then Baltimore, Maryland, and finally reached his long-sought goal, California, when he moved to San Francisco.

Though Taz earned a measure of success in his field, by 1873 his wife, Nannie Bridges, whom he had married in 1857, divorced him, citing "dissipation" as the cause.[54] The father of two children, neither of which reached maturity, died at the age of forty-three, the year after the divorce, leaving only the characterization in his obituary: "he was a genial gentleman."[55]

DAVID GARDINER TYLER

Ninth child of John Tyler; first child of John Tyler and Julia Gardiner

Born: July 12, 1846   *Birthplace:* Charles City County, Virginia
Died: September 5, 1927   *Age at Death:* 81 years, 2 months
Cause of Death: Unknown
Education: Private schools, Washington College
Profession: Lawyer, Judge, Politician
Spouse: Mary Morris Jones
Number of Children: 5

A CHILD OF HIS FATHER'S PRIME

"Pooh," said President John Tyler, "I am just full in my prime,"[56] when privately and publicly criticized for his second marriage to a woman half his age. He went on to prove his statement by fathering seven more children. The first of these children was David Gardiner Tyler, born one year after the 1845 summer marriage.

David, or "Gardie" as he was always called, was a sixteen-year-old student at Washington College at the outbreak of the Civil War. Ever a loyal southerner, as were all the Tylers, Gardie left college and joined the Confederate Army, serving first in the infantry and then in the artillery. At war's end, his father having died in 1862, his mother Julia sent him and his brother to Germany to study. But Gardie, both having difficulty with the German language and feeling an intense concern about the shape of the South that would emerge from defeat, returned to study at Washington College. He also read law and was admitted to the Virginia bar in 1870.

At the end of 1870 Gardie jumped enthusiastically into state politics, winning election to the position of attorney for Charles City County. Gardie opposed many of the changes being imposed on the South, but also was strongly opposed to the white supremacy policies instituted by southern reactionaries. His successful election was due to the combination of both white and black votes. Surprisingly, his realistic position was not a barrier to further elected office or success in business. Gardie went on to the state senate, to the circuit court judgeship, and finally into the U.S. Congress.

Marrying quite late in life, Gardie died having fathered five children. To the end of his days he was proud that, in his own way, and in his own definition, he was an unreconstructed southerner.

JOHN ALEXANDER TYLER

Tenth child of John Tyler; second child, second son of John Tyler and Julia Gardiner

Born: April 7, 1848   *Birthplace:* Charles City County, Virginia
Died: September 1, 1883   *Age at Death:* 35 years, 5 months
Cause of Death: Dysentery
Education: Private schools, Washington College
Profession: Surveyor   *Spouse:* Sarah Gardiner
Number of Children: 2

A QUESTIONABLE DEATH

Born in the family home of Sherwood Forest, Virginia, Alex was the second child of John and Julia Tyler. Growing up as a "straight and strong and devilish child,"[57] Alex became known for his vivid imagination. Tyler hoped that his son's "imagination would be governed by discretion,"[58] but it was not to be.

At the age of fourteen, his father having just died, Alex begged his mother to be allowed to go south from their home to "massacre Yankees." His mother refused, so Alex ran away to enlist in the Confederate Army at Baltimore. At that stage in the war the Confederacy seemed to be holding its own or better, so he was rejected as too young, and he was returned to his mother, where she and her children lived on Staten Island, New York. Later in the war Alex would, most assuredly, not have been rejected for such a reason.

But Alex would not give up in his attempt to fight for the South, and eventually Julia consented to his wishes, provided he join the Confederate Navy, not the army, as the army suffered from an extremely high casualty rate in comparison with the navy. Alex agreed, and joined the Confederate Navy, only to be assigned to a ship that was quarantined because of yellow fever. Upon release from quarantine in the summer of 1864, Alex left the navy; joined his brother at Camp Lee, where he became a member of a prison guard unit; and, once again, was returned to his mother—this time through the personal auspices of Jefferson Davis, president of the Confederacy.

Constantly besieged by the Tyler family to leave the hated North, Julia moved South to join many of the Tyler family. She placed her son in Washington College, in Lexington, Kentucky. One of only twenty-two students in the school, he remained only three months and finally returned to the Confederate Army, just in time to witness the South's surrender at Appomattox Courthouse.

With the war ended, Alex returned to the family home in Sherwood Forest to restore the estate to its original grandeur, but as the plantation had been thoroughly plundered, the task was beyond the young man's abilities. In the fall of 1865 his mother sent both Alex and his older brother, Gardie, to Germany to study. The costs entailed in this foreign education stretched Julia's finances to the limit, and each boy was allowed only twenty cents per week for necessities. Despite the frugality of his life, Alex was a good student. He mastered the German language rapidly, and finding that he had a flair for math and science, he set as his goal to become a mining engineer.

Given his experiences in the war between the states, Alex was not to be denied a war, and the Germans thoughtfully provided one. At the outbreak of the Franco-Prussian War in 1870, Alex enlisted in the German Army and served in France during its occupation for several months in 1871. For his services to the newly proclaimed German empire, the Kaiser awarded Alex a ribbon for faithful service. Alex had enjoyed the war thoroughly, so much so that he incurred large debts, which he and his family were unable to repay. In 1873 Alex returned to the United States.

Alex quickly found work in mining near Salt Lake City, but soon was out of work via that same year's depression. For almost a year Alex could not find a job. When he did find work it was for the railroad, at a salary that did not begin to equal his expenditures. Constantly on the run from creditors and accused of laughing his way through life by his younger brother, Lachlin, Alex finally appeared to settle down when he married his third cousin, Sarah Gardiner. Both families approved of the match, as Sarah came from a monied family, though she lacked physical attributes that would inspire other suitors. Her family welcomed Alex's devotion to their daughter. Shortly after their marriage Alex was again unemployed, a state in which he remained for two years, though he did father two children. Both the Tyler and the Gardiner family attempted to find the young man and new father a suitable position.

The job that Alex finally took was that of surveyor of Indian lands in the Dakota territory, working as an experienced surveyor. Anticipating a profit of at least $5,000, Alex bought into a surveyor partnership with funds provided by his mother. The venture was not a financial success. After 1879 Alex's wife rarely saw him. Appointed as an inspector and surveyor for the Department of Interior, Alex suddenly appeared at the Governor's Palace in Santa Fe, New Mexico, in 1883 after having been stranded on the desert without water. Half-crazed by the sun, Alex drank the desert's foul alkaline water, contracted dysentery, and died at the Governor's Palace, or so goes the story.

But Alex's widow, Sarah, lived on for many years periodically hearing from travelers a different version of her husband's end—that he had been murdered.

JULIA TYLER SPENCER

Eleventh child of John Tyler; third child, first daughter of John Tyler and Julia Gardiner

Born: December 25, 1849
Birthplace: Charles City County, Virginia
Died: May 8, 1871   *Age at Death:* 21 years, 5 months
Cause of Death: Childbirth complications
Education: Tutors, convent school, Halifax, Nova Scotia, Canada
Profession: Housewife, Mother   *Spouse:* William Spencer
Number of Children: 1

"HOT-BLOODED JULIA"

Julia Gardiner Tyler, named Julia in honor of her mother, Tyler's second wife, was born on Christmas Day, 1849. While her mother immediately predicted a beautiful future for her firstborn daughter, her father expressed some concern about the baby's prominent nose, observing, "I hope that organ will rest awhile in its maturity, for its prominence is quite amusing."[59]

Julie, as she was called, began her education at a boarding school, but as finances deteriorated after her father's death, she was withdrawn from private school until more prosperous times. Tutored at home, with her schooling paid for by the sale of pelts captured on the family estate by the older boys, Julie remained at home until the end of the Civil War in 1865. The end of the war coincided with the bursting forth of Julie's womanhood, and she appeared to her mother as wild and flirtatious.

Concerned about the future of her daughter, Julie's mother sent her away to a convent school in Halifax, Nova Scotia. The school had been chosen because it was far removed from the social world, restrictive, and inexpensive, as well as excellent in academics. But hot-blooded Julie was not long for the convent life. When the Protestant Tylers received a letter from Julie telling them that the Catholic life in her school was leading her to consider becoming a nun, the Halifax education was terminated.

In 1869 Julie married William Spencer. Though her family was elated that she was at last to settle down to a proper life, Spencer was deeply in debt and had no economic prospects for the future. The newlyweds settled down in Spencer's heavily mortgaged farm in upstate New York, where mother, daughter, and son-in-law spent much time together.

In the spring of 1871, giving birth to her daughter (also named Julia) Julie died. The grandmother's anguish was distracted by the requirements of caring for her granddaughter. William borrowed money from his mother-in-law with which to settle his long overdue debts, and then he disappeared. He would surface briefly in Colorado's silver mines and the California citrus groves, but then he disappeared from the family's sight forever. It was grandmother Julia who raised Julie's daughter, hoping to build for her the beautiful future she had so eagerly anticipated for her daughter.

LACHLIN TYLER

Twelfth child of John Tyler; fourth child, third son of John Tyler and Julia Gardiner

Born: December 2, 1851   *Birthplace:* Charles City County, Virginia
Died: January 25, 1902   *Age at Death:* 50 years, 1 month
Cause of Death: Unknown

Education: Private schools, medical school
Profession: Medical Doctor   *Spouse:* Georgia Powell
Number of Children: None

NAVY SURGEON

Yet a small boy when the Civil War erupted, Lachlin Tyler missed partici-
pating in the horrors of the nation's most costly war. Educated as a physician, he practiced medicine in the north, despite the Tyler family's southern
connection.

In 1877 Lachlin's analysis of his situation was that he had a practice with
few patients, yielding fewer dollars, and the expenses of a new wife. Therefore, he appealed to his mother to exert her influence, as former first lady,
to obtain for him a position as a police surgeon in Jersey City, New Jersey.
But Julia was unable to help her son acquire the position. Lachlin next decided that Washington, D.C., offered opportunities for success. So poor had
the couple become that Lachlin even considered letting his young, beautiful
wife, Georgia Powell, go to work in the Department of Agriculture, something simply not done by respectable women of the time.

Lachlin eventually found work in the medical division of the Department
of the Navy, where he performed well, but grew dissatisfied with the lack of
interesting and responsible work. To advance to the position of surgeon,
Lachlin would have to pass a battery of examinations, including tests in
grammar, geography, and history, disciplines in which Lachlin acknowledged his own lack of proficiency. Writing to his mother he expressed the
hope that he would be allowed to pass the examinations because "perhaps
they modified things for those applicants who came forward highly recommended, or were undoubtedly gentlemen."[60] But he failed to receive the appointment, the notification simply stating "general debility," which according to Lachlin "means in the medical vocabulary everything or nothing."[61]
He then embarked on a body-building program. In 1879 he tried again. This
time he passed both physical and academic examinations, the "general
debility" having in the meantime apparently disappeared. Certified a surgeon in the U.S. Navy, Lachlin also began a private medical practice.

In time Lachlin's private practice became very lucrative, and he gave up
his navy surgeonship to concentrate entirely on his private practice. At the
age of fifty, childless, Lachlin died, having, however, achieved some
measure of the success he so earnestly sought.

LYON GARDINER TYLER

Thirteenth child of John Tyler; fifth child, fourth son of John Tyler and Julia Gardiner

Born: August 1853   *Birthplace:* Charles City County, Virginia
Died: February 12, 1935   *Age at Death:* 81 years, 6 months
Cause of Death: Unknown
Education: University of Virginia
Profession: Teacher, Administrator, Lawyer, Politician, Author
Spouses: Anne Baker Tucker, Sue Ruffin
Number of Children: Tyler/Tucker: 3
                                      Tyler/Ruffin: 2

ACADEMICIAN

Following the Civil War, Lyon Gardiner Tyler studied at the University of Virginia, receiving from that school both a bachelor of arts and a master of arts degree, before taking up the study of law. But, because he found that the practice of law could not satisfy his quest for more information as well as the sheer joy of teaching, Lyon became a professor at the financially troubled William and Mary College in 1877. Then, for a short time, he went on to teach in a Memphis, Tennessee, high school.

Returning to Virginia, Lyon initiated his first and only substantial practice at law, though he taught night school at a school he founded, the Richmond Mechanics Night School. Indeed, so interested was Lyon in teaching that when this school suffered financial reverses Lyon managed to get state subsidies to continue the school. His law success continued and Lyon was elected to the state legislature. These experiences were the foundation for the balance of Lyon's life.

As the college of William and Mary had been forced to close in 1880, the directors of the college saw the state legislator, Professor Lyon Tyler, as a strategically placed man who could be interested in securing state funds to reopen the school's doors. Their assumptions were correct. Lyon was both willing and able to come to the aid of education.

In grateful response the directors of William and Mary College elected Tyler president of the college, a position he was to hold for thirty-one years. Lyon's administration of William and Mary was based upon the twin principles of academic excellence and financial security.

In 1919, retiring from this presidential position, with the title professor emeritus, he devoted himself to historical research, specializing in genealogy and early Virginia history. Publishing frequently, Tyler made a new name for himself in historical circles for his published works. He received honorary Ph.D.'s from Brown University, University of Pittsburgh, and Trinity College of Hartford, Connecticut.

In Lyon's later days he became a noted public speaker. As a historian of the South he spoke for a definite point of view when the subject of the Civil War or anything about it arose. At one time, speaking before the Sons of Confederate Veterans, he referred to Abraham Lincoln as the "boss slacker" and insisted "that histories by northern writers should be barred from Virginia schools."[62] Lyon believed that southerners were political slaves of the North, and "if through some cataclysm, the South should get control the North would secede tomorrow."[63]

At the age of eighty-one, the distinguished historian, twice-married father of five died.

ROBERT FITZWALTER TYLER

Fourteenth child of John Tyler; sixth child, fifth son of John Tyler and Julia Gardiner

Born: March 12, 1856   *Birthplace:* Charles City County, Virginia
Died: December 30, 1927   *Age at Death:* 71 years, 9 months
Cause of Death: Unknown
Education: Georgetown Academy, Georgetown University
Profession: Farmer   *Spouse:* Fannie Gluin
Number of Children: 3

THE BARON WAS A FARMER

Named Robert Fitzwalter in honor of Julia Tyler's ancestor, a baron of thirteenth-century England, he was the fourteenth Tyler child, and the sixth by the second wife to be born to the sixty-eight-year-old former president of the United States. His birth proved beyond all doubt that Tyler was correct when he said upon his marriage to the young second wife that he was "just full in his prime." As his mother converted to Catholicism after her husband's death, her son, Fitz, entered a Catholic school near Washington, D.C., at the age of fifteen. He continued his education at Georgetown College, now known as Georgetown University, near the nation's capital. But the family financial instability forced him to withdraw from college, and he never returned.

Instead of a professional career, Fitz would turn to the land and become a Virginia farmer, initially on leased land near the Tyler family home, Sherwood Forest. Fitz was successful and remained a farmer for the rest of his life. He fathered three children by his one and only wife, but his achievements, though highly desired by his mother, never matched the grandeur of his ancestral name, which had been carefully chosen to reflect the social aspirations of his ambitious mother.

PEARL TYLER ELLIS

Fifteenth child of John Tyler; seventh child, second daughter of John Tyler and Julia Gardiner

Born: June 20, 1860   *Birthplace:* Virginia
Died: June 30, 1947   *Age at Death:* 87 years
Cause of Death: Unknown
Education: Georgetown Academy, Sacred Heart Convent
Profession: Housewife, Mother
Spouse: William Mumford Ellis
Number of Children: 8

A HAPPY PEARL

Pearl Tyler Ellis, the last of the many Tyler children, was originally to be named Margaret, but was christened Pearl instead. She never knew her father, who was seventy-two years old at the time of her birth. With her mother's conversion to Catholicism when she was about eleven, Pearlie was sent with her brother Fitz to Georgetown Academy, a school run by the Catholic clergy. So intense were her convert mother's religious feeling and concern for her daughter's afterlife, that, when Pearlie fell ill, her mother demanded a bewildered priest to "rebaptize" her daughter, in order to insure that the rite had "taken."

Later educated at the convent of the Sacred Heart in Washington, D.C., Pearlie married Major William Mumford Ellis in St. Peter's Cathedral. The couple moved to Montgomery County, Virginia, where for more than fifty years they lived in the upper end of Happy Valley near Roanoke. The mother of eight was frequently visited by her own mother, Julia, and Julia's adopted daughter, Julia III.

Of all the Tyler children, the youngest, Pearlie, lived a life totally unaffected by the power of her father's office or her mother's ambitions.

FOR FURTHER READING

Gerlinger, Irene. *Mistresses of the White House*. Freeport, New York: Books for Libraries Press, 1950.

Klapthor, Margaret Brown. *First Ladies*. Washington, D.C.: White House Historical Association, 1979.

Seager, Robert II. *And Tyler Too: A Biography of John and Julia Gardiner Tyler*. New York, New York: McGraw-Hill Book Company, Inc., 1963.

9 ZACHARY TAYLOR'S CHILDREN

ANNE MARGARET MACKALL TAYLOR WOOD

First child of Zachary Taylor and Margaret Mackall Smith

Born: April 9, 1811   *Birthplace:* Jefferson County, Kentucky
Died: December 2, 1875   *Age at Death:* 64 years, 8 months
Cause of Death: Unknown   *Education:* Unknown
Profession: Housewife, Mother   *Spouse:* Robert Crooke Wood
Number of Children: 4

DIVIDED LOYALTIES

The first of the Taylor children, Anne Taylor, grew up on military posts as her father was transferred from one to another during his military career. As her sister would, Anne met her future husband, an army surgeon, at Fort Crawford, Prairie du Chien, Wisconsin. Unlike her sister's husband, Anne's choice was accepted by the family, and he remained with the military. The couple had four children, and Anne lived a life of a soldier's wife.

The Civil War split Anne's family. Robert, her husband, remained with the Union and served as surgeon general of the 14th Union Army. However, the couple's only sons, John and Bob, saw their duty in service to the Confederate States of America. Thus, father was pitted against sons. As the nation split, so too did the Anne Taylor family. At war's end, Anne was a widow.

Alone, Anne turned to her daughter for the emotional support and comfort so lacking in her life now that her husband had died. Anne moved to Germany, where her daughter lived, for her daughter had married Baron Guido von Grabow, of the German embassy staff, while he was in Washington, D.C. Anne remained in Germany, and in 1875 she died there.

SARAH KNOX TAYLOR DAVIS

Second child, second daughter of Zachary Taylor and Margaret Mackall Smith

Born: March 6, 1814   *Birthplace:* Fort Knox, Missouri Territory
Died: September 15, 1835   *Age at Death:* 21 years, 6 months
Cause of Death: Malaria   *Education:* Unknown
Profession: Housewife   *Spouse:* Jefferson Davis
Number of Children: None

THE CONFEDERATE PRESIDENT'S WIFE

Sarah Knox Taylor was called "Knox" throughout her life, after Fort Knox, where her father was stationed at the time of her birth. She is described as very feminine, a typical southern girl of the day, with long blonde hair falling in ringlets to her shoulders and a sweetness that could, and did, appeal to all that saw her.

When Sarah was a teenager, her father was transferred to Fort Crawford, which became Prairie du Chien, Wisconsin. In 1832, Knox met her future husband, Jefferson Davis. The man who would be the president of the Confederate States of America was a new West Point graduate, and the soldier's daughter and Davis were immediately attracted to each other. But her father, Zachary Taylor, disapproved entirely of young Davis, the two men having confronted each other over military matters with Indians. Davis, never known for his tact, had strongly expressed his opposition to the superior officer Taylor's judgment. Thus, there was enmity between the two men before love blossomed between Jefferson and Knox. In rejecting Davis as his daughter's suitor, Taylor used the argument to her that as the wife of a military man she would have to suffer many hardships. At this stage of the couple's relationship Davis was transferred to another post, far removed at St. Louis, Missouri, and the father breathed a sigh of relief, having separated the young lovers. But the couple's love for each other grew with distance, as long and passionate letters crossed between them for over two years.

In June 1835, Knox and Jefferson married, though they had not seen each other for two years from the time of Davis's transfer from Fort Crawford to St. Louis. The marriage, planned through the mails, took place in the home of Knox's aunt, in Louisville, Kentucky. Many of the Taylor family attended the wedding, though Zachary and his wife adamantly refused to sanction the marriage by their appearance. Davis, newly resigned from the army, took his young bride from Louisville to his brother's home, The Hurricane, for their honeymoon. The couple then moved on to his sister's home in Louisiana. From there Sarah exchanged letters with her reconciled parents, writing to her mother, "Do not make yourself uneasy about me, the country is quite healthy,"[64] and to her father she expressed her appreciation for the money he had sent to her.

Ironically, shortly after her protestations of the healthiness of her new home, both she and her husband contracted malaria. Davis recovered, Sarah did not. Barely three months after their marriage she died.

The first wife of Confederate President Jefferson Davis was laid to rest in the Davis family graveyard on the banks of the Mississippi.

OCTAVIA PANNEL AND MARGARET SMITH TAYLOR

Third and fourth children, third and fourth daughters of Zachary Taylor and Margaret Mackall Smith

Born: Octavia: August 16, 1816
      Margaret: July 27, 1819
Birthplace: Jefferson County, Kentucky
Died: Octavia: July 8, 1820
      Margaret: October 22, 1820
Age at Death: Octavia: 3 years, 8 months
        Margaret: 1 year, 3 months
Cause of Death: Probable yellow fever

DISEASE DEVASTATION

The short lives of two Taylor daughters should remind us of the ravages common to children before the medical discoveries of the twentieth century. Both Octavia Pannel and Margaret Smith Taylor were victims of a fever whose origin was unknown, but which especially attacked newcomers to the Mississippi delta. Once infected, the bodies of the children were helpless to evade the disease's onslaught, and the illness proceeded to death.

Zachary Taylor took his family, including the two little girls, to Bayou Sara, Louisiana, where he was engaged in the construction of a military road. Within months of their introduction to the region both girls became ill, and in July 1820, three-year-old Octavia died, to be followed by her younger sister in October of the same year.

A third daughter, Sarah, only slightly older than the two small children, was yet strong enough to survive the illness. But Sarah was to tempt fate twice by returning to the delta area following her marriage to Jefferson

Davis. Her mother's concern, expressed to Sarah upon her return to the delta was derived from experience with her two baby daughters' deaths. Thus, a third daughter, unmindful of her sisters' fates, would also die in the Mississippi delta.

MARY ELIZABETH TAYLOR BLISS DANDRIDGE

Fifth child, fifth daughter of Zachary Taylor and Margaret Mackall Smith

Born: April 20, 1824   *Birthplace:* Jefferson County, Kentucky
Died: July 26, 1909   *Age at Death:* 85 years, 3 months
Cause of Death: Unknown
Education: Unknown   *Profession:* Housewife, White House Hostess
Spouses: William Bliss, Philip Dandridge
Number of Children: None

THE CHARMER

Nicknamed "Betty," Mary Elizabeth Taylor, youngest of the Taylor daughters, was a beautiful and elegant woman. Possessing a natural poise and tact, she had large eyes, soft black hair, and a superb complexion, all of which combined to her family's benefit.

As Betty's mother opposed Zachary's acceptance of the nomination for president, when he was elected her mother refused to preside as White House hostess, true to the threat she had made prior to old "Rough and Ready's" election. Of necessity, "Miss Betty" took over the obligations of White House hostess in her mother's place. So well suited was she to the position, that a Washington, D.C., pundit observed she possessed "the art-lessness of a rustic and the grace of a duchess."[65] Such charm did not fail to attract many suitors, but it was her father's adjutant general, Major William Bliss, who captured her heart.

Sixteen months after he became president, Zachary Taylor died. The Bliss family moved from the White House and from Washington, D.C., never to return again.

In 1853 Bliss died, leaving Betty a childless widow. After several years, Betty met and married Philip Dandridge, of Winchester, Virginia. Living to a ripe old age, Betty retained the charm that had characterized her youth, and her home earned for itself the appellation Salon of the Valley of Shenandoah.

RICHARD TAYLOR

Sixth child, only son of Zachary Taylor and Margaret Mackall Smith

Born: January 27, 1826   *Birthplace:* Louisville, Kentucky

Died: April 12, 1879   *Age at Death:* 53 years, 3 months

Cause of Death: Malaria

Education: European schools, Harvard University, Yale University

Profession: Soldier, Plantation Manager, Politician, Author

Spouse: Louise Marie Bringier

Number of Children: 5

"ROUGH AND READY'S" ONLY SON

The only son of General "Rough and Ready" Taylor, Richard spent his childhood at army camps watching military maneuvers and acquiring for himself, from the enlisted men, a vocabulary that could only be described as crude, and which would remain with him throughout his life.

His mother, convinced that military posts were not the most suitable environments for the education of a gentleman, finally prevailed upon his father to send young Dick to Edinburgh, Scotland, to study Latin and literature. After two years of education in Scotland, Dick went to France to study for a year. When he returned to the United States he was privately tutored for a short time, to make up for certain deficiencies, and was admitted to Harvard in 1843 as a junior. But Harvard did not suit Dick, and he left to attend Yale, from which he graduated when he was twenty-three years old.

When Dick graduated, the dispute over the Texas boundary with Mexico, which had first begun as a dispute between the Texas Republic and Mexico, was about to flare into war with the United States. Dick joined his father, who was commanding the American troops in south Texas, and became his secretary and aide-de-camp until Dick was felled by fever. Leaving the army to recuperate, Dick traveled to Baton Rouge to the family's properties and worked on the sugar plantation. There he remained until his father was elected to the presidency, whereupon he again joined his father, to again serve as his secretary, but this time at the White House. Dick remained there until his father's death, sixteen months after the inauguration.

Marrying well, Dick was elected to the Louisiana State Senate, in which position he remained for four years. Elected to the state convention, established to decide the questions of secession from the United States of America, Dick opposed Louisiana's secession, but nevertheless went along with the majority in the end. Dick saw through all the "hoopla" and careless wishful thinking of his fellow delegates, and was later to reminisce that, "At that secession time and since, I marveled at the joyous and careless temper in which men, much my superior in sagacity and experience, consummated these acts."[66] When the war between the states commenced, Richard Taylor became Colonel Taylor of the Confederate Army, commanding an infantry regiment. Taylor and his men were on the march when the battle of Bull Run was fought, so that he and his troops missed that combat. But the enemy of soldiers everywhere, disease, ravaged the troops' ranks. Taylor devoted himself to nursing his men back to health from the dreaded killer, measles. Then, he himself was felled by fever, and his commanding officer ordered him to take leave to recover his health. Dick went to his sister's home, and she nursed him back to health. Fit for duty, he returned to the army and was promoted to the rank of brigadier general, though he protested the promotion as being undeserved and asked his brother-in-law, Jefferson Davis, president of the Confederate States of America, to revoke the promotion.

During the war, Taylor became involved in two important initiatives by the Confederate government, both of which came to nothing. President Davis, who trusted Taylor implicitly, gave him the mission of carrying communications from the Confederate government on a solution to the hostilities to the president of the United States, Abraham Lincoln. Taylor was also associated with General Robert E. Lee in an attempt to earn European support for the Confederacy. By 1864 General Taylor felt that the South could not win the war, but that he was honor-bound to continue fighting until the loss was unquestionable. Such was this commitment that the man who had opposed secession was the last general to surrender to Union forces. Jefferson Davis, desperately trying to continue the struggle after the surrender of Robert E. Lee, understood that when Taylor finally bowed to superior force the cause was lost.

At war's end, Dick returned to his plantation, from which he had been almost constantly absent for four years. In his last absence, his estate had been confiscated and sold. Out of pride he refused to ask for the restoration of his citizenship or restitution of his property. He accepted the difficult times after the war as punishment for a failure that he had long foreseen.

Dick, admired and respected by leaders on both sides of the Mason-Dixon line, represented Louisiana, suffering from military occupation and reconstruction, in attempts to secure relief from the government in Washington, D.C. There, even President Grant, who had served with Dick's father in antebellum days, accorded his former superior officer's son all the respect due to the scion of a comrade-in-arms and former president. Of course, after America's most bloody war, there were those on both sides who could never forgive nor look above the battle to respect the individual's merit. Thus, some northern newspapers in reporting the activities and movements of Dick Taylor always reminded their leaders of his diligence in the cause of rebellion.

In the last years of his life, Dick represented American business in Europe, as well as authoring his memoirs of the Civil War, titled *Destruction and Reconstruction*. Fighting malaria to the end, Dick lived long enough to finish his book and died in 1879, penniless though much honored and respected by former enemies and compatriots alike.

FOR FURTHER READING

Beard, Charles. *Presidents in American History*. New York, New York: Julian A. Messner, 1981.

Canfield, Cass. *The Iron Will of Jefferson Davis*. New York, New York: Harcourt, Brace Jovanovich, 1978.

Hamilton, Holman. *Three Kentucky Presidents: Lincoln, Taylor, Davis*. Lexington, Kentucky: University Press of Kentucky, 1978.

10 MILLARD FILLMORE'S CHILDREN

MILLARD POWERS FILLMORE

First child of Millard Fillmore and Abigail Powers

Born: April 25, 1828   *Birthplace:* Aurora, New York
Died: November 15, 1889   *Age at Death:* 61 years, 6 months
Cause of Death: Apoplexy
Education: Tutors, Cambridge Law School
Profession: Lawyer, Presidential Secretary
Spouse: None
Number of Children: None

DESTRUCTION OF PRESIDENTIAL DOCUMENTS

Was he trying to hide something? Or was it vengeance against his father that made Millard Powers Fillmore destroy his father's correspondence? What is certain is that his actions have left a historical void in our knowledge of the presidency of Millard Fillmore.

Called Powers throughout his life, Fillmore was educated in the law, including training under his father. Powers passed his New York bar examination and later became his father's White House secretary. Later he would, for a short time, open his own law office in Buffalo, New York. Records of his work, its quality and quantity, his associations, and cases, are lost forever in the same fire that consumed his personal correspondence with his father and family. From private practice Powers moved to a position in the federal court as a law clerk.

A clue to Powers's entire life may lie in his relationship to his mother. She was an invalid, and died shortly after her husband served his White House term. His father remarried. Powers, a bachelor his entire life, could not accept a replacement for his mother. Though his father requested in his will that Powers and the second wife try to get along, the battle of the inheritance was bitter. Fillmore left most of his belongings to his second wife in his will. Powers sued his stepmother and won. As soon as he could, Powers sold his winnings, the inheritance primarily of wine, silver, and a major book collection.

From the time of his lawsuit and his victory until his death, Powers lived as a guest at the Tifft House, a Buffalo, New York, hotel, spending his time talking with old cronies in the lobby of the hotel. Surviving his father by fifteen years, though in ill health for several years prior to his death, Powers died of apoplexy at the Tifft House. He left no known friends.

Powers's will, parts of which were printed in the *New York Times*, shocked society. In that will was a strange commandment—for the son of a president. "I particularly request and direct my executor at the earliest practicable moment to burn or otherwise effectively destroy all correspondence or letters to or from my father, mother, sister, or me, and under his immediate supervision. I hope to be able to do this myself before my death."[67] That provision was carried out.

Why should Powers want to destroy his family documents? The nation speculated then, and we can only speculate now. There is not a clue to understanding his reasons. Perhaps the letters would have made very interesting reading, and, perhaps, that is why they were destroyed.

Powers left bequests to some charitable institutions, the American Society for the Prevention of Cruelty to Animals, Young Women's Christian Association, and several churches and hospitals. He also left bequests to two aunts, as well as a sum of dollars to John Howcut, of Denver, whose relationship is not identified.

Powers was buried beside his father in Buffalo. But for the destruction of the papers it is possible to suggest that, perhaps, more could be said of the thirteenth president of the United States, other than "Millard who?"

MARY ABIGAIL FILLMORE

Second child, only daughter of Millard Fillmore and Abigail Powers

Born: March 27, 1832   *Birthplace:* Buffalo, New York
Died: July 26, 1854   *Age at Death:* 22 years, 3 months
Cause of Death: Cholera
Education: Sedgewick School, State Normal School, New York
Profession: White House Hostess, Teacher
Spouse: None   *Number of Children:* None

"AS IF SHE HAD BEEN BORN A PRINCESS"

Mary Abigail, called Abby by family and friends alike, spent her life "constantly thinking of some little surprise, some gift, some journey, some pleasure by which she could contribute to the happiness of others."[68] Described as an extrovert, and as gay, radiant, and charming, she was, however, never described as beautiful, yet her qualities attracted many people to her.

As a child her interest was music, although her formal education was far above that of her female contemporaries. In addition, Abby possessed her father's vitality and self-assuredness. Though she had prepared herself to become a teacher, it became necessary to fill her mother's shoes as White House hostess.

Fillmore's wife, Abigail, spent most of her life in semi-invalidism. Thus, in 1850 when Vice-President Fillmore became president on the death of Zachary Taylor, Abby, yet in her teens, took over the many responsibilities of mistress of the White House. In her new role, she was "as much at ease at the head of the presidential table as if she had been born a princess."[69]

Abby, like her older brother, never married. Shortly after her father's term ended in 1853, Abby's mother died, leaving Abby and her father to return to Buffalo where they buried Abigail, and Abby began her teaching career.

Only a year after her mother's death, Abby, continuing her characteristic helpfulness, traveled to East Aurora, New York, to visit her grandfather and help him settle in a new home. She went to help another, despite the illness she had suffered for days preceding. Within twelve hours after her arrival at her grandfather's new home, Abby was dead of cholera.

Like a fairy princess, she entered life, touched all that knew her with kindness, and was taken in the act of caring.

FOR FURTHER READING

Grayson, Benson Lee. *Unknown President: The Administration of Millard Fillmore*. New York, New York: University Press of America, 1981.

Kane, Nathan Joseph. *Facts about the Presidents*. New York, New York: The H. W. Wilson Company, 1981.

Snyder, Charles M. *The Lady and the President: The Letters of Dorothea Dix and Millard Fillmore*. Lexington, Kentucky: The University Press of Kentucky, 1975.

Taylor, Tim. *The Book of Presidents*. New York, New York: Arno Press, 1972.

11 FRANKLIN PIERCE'S CHILDREN

FRANKLIN AND FRANK ROBERT PIERCE

First and second children of Franklin Pierce and Jane Means Appleton

Born: Franklin: February 2, 1836
       Frank Robert: August 27, 1839
Birthplace: Franklin: Hillsborough, New Hampshire
            Frank Robert: Concord, New Hampshire
Died: Franklin: February 5, 1836
      Frank Robert: November 14, 1843
Age at Death: Franklin: 3 days
             Frank Robert: 4 years, 3 months
Causes of Death: Unknown

TWO SHORT LIVES

Almost nothing is known of the first two sons born to Franklin and Jane Pierce. It was the early deaths of these two boys that contributed to the mental instability that would eventually convince Jane that the Pierces must never again become involved in Washington, D.C., politics. But all of Jane's precautions were for naught as the last of these boys died, though Jane had convinced her husband to resign the Senate and return to New Hampshire and supposed safety. The boys died, leaving Jane with her only remaining child, son Benny.

When her last son died in a terrible railroad accident, Jane's last link with reality snapped. She was unable to comprehend the deaths of all of her children, and she spent her days as the nation's first lady communing with the dead children, for the most part confining herself to a White House sitting room, rather than involving herself in her husband's hated politics.

BENJAMIN PIERCE

Third child, third son of Franklin Pierce and Jane Means Appleton

Born: April 13, 1841   *Birthplace:* Concord, New Hampshire
Died: January 6, 1853   *Age at Death:* 11 years, 8 months
Cause of Death: Railroad accident

DEATH STALKS THE PIERCES

Benjamin, the thirdborn son of the Pierces, was the only one to survive beyond early childhood. The deaths of his brothers had instilled a horrible fear for Benny's life in his mother. Indeed, the family life of the Pierces came to revolve around concern for the life of their last son. Despite all precautions, fate would not spare the life of this child.

Shortly before the death of Benjamin's brother, Frank, the second son, Jane Pierce had convinced her senator husband to leave Washington, D.C., because "Washington is tainted by the evils of politics."[70] To placate his wife, Pierce resigned his Senate seat in 1842 and moved from Washington, D.C., back to Concord, New Hampshire, where he practiced law. While the sedate life of Concord suited Jane and her children, Pierce was never content away from the excitement and challenge of public life. But Jane's contentment was destroyed, when, in 1843, her second son died.

Pierce needed escape. The outbreak of the Mexican War in 1846 provided the perfect opportunity for leaving Concord. He joined the army and became a brigadier general, actively taking part in the war. Mother and remaining son stayed at home in New Hampshire. With her husband away she was free to lavish her full love and affection on her only remaining child. Pierce returned from the wars in 1848, and the family began, again, their quiet life.

But when Pierce was nominated as the Democratic-Republican presidential candidate in 1852, he leapt at the chance to reenter politics. Jane, on the other hand, prayed for his defeat. She detested politics and, even more, feared Washington, D.C. Unfortunately for Jane and Benny, Pierce won the election.

Defeated by her husband's victory, Jane made peace with Franklin and accepted the situation. To celebrate the election and Christmas 1852, the family set out for Boston by train. On the return journey the train wrecked. An axle broke, the train jumped the track, and it went over a fifteen-foot embankment.[71] Franklin and Jane were only slightly bruised. But when the cars settled, they saw their only son, crushed and lifeless, pinned beneath the railroad car. Jane Pierce was never to recover from the loss of her third son in such a tragic accident. She, who had fought so hard to keep her husband from returning to politics, was convinced "that Benny's fate was a divine punishment meted out for Pierce's political ambition."[72]

The shadow of Benny's death hung over the Pierce White House. The first lady came to the White House only to spend most of her time in the sitting room, scribbling notes to her dead Benny. Jane Pierce eventually retreated completely into a fantasy world, where she talked and played with her three dead sons.

FOR FURTHER READING

Bell, Carl Irving. *They Knew Franklin Pierce (and Others Thought They Did): A Sampling of Opinions about the 14th United States President Drawn from His Contemporaries.* Springfield, Vermont: April Hill, 1980.

Gerlinger, Irene. *Mistresses of the White House.* Freeport, New York: Books for Libraries Press, 1950.

Moses, John B., and Wilbur Cross. *Presidential Courage.* New York, New York: W. W. Norton, 1980.

12 ABRAHAM LINCOLN'S CHILDREN

ROBERT TODD LINCOLN

First child of Abraham Lincoln and Mary Todd

Born: August 1, 1843   *Birthplace:* Springfield, Illinois
Died: July 25, 1926   *Age at Death:* 82 years, 9 months
Cause of Death: Unknown
Education: Public schools, Phillips Exeter Academy, Harvard University
Profession: Lawyer, Business Executive, Politician
Spouse: Mary Harlan
Number of Children: 3

A CONTRAST IN THE CHARACTERS OF FATHER AND SON

Robert Todd Lincoln perhaps best personifies the character of an individual born into a family that would become American royalty, a recipient of opportunities offered to few in the age of his birth.

Born in Springfield, Illinois, he lived in the home Abraham purchased and enlarged during Bob's first sixteen years of life. He showed no exceptional ability in scholarship, and, in fact, his father observed early in his school years that, "He is quite smart enough. I sometimes fear that he is one of little 'rare-ripe' sort that are smarter at about five that ever after."[73] Certainly this observation was shown to be accurate when he attempted to enter Harvard College. He failed in sixteen of the seventeen subjects in which he was examined. Following this failure, he enrolled in Phillips Exeter Academy in Exeter, New Hampshire. Studying for a year, he finally obtained admission to Harvard. Years later Bob observed that upon his pronouncement that he would study law, his father gave him the only advice about his career that he was ever to receive. Abraham observed, "You should learn more than I ever did, but you will never have so good a time."[74] During Robert's attendance at Harvard, he took a short leave to attend his father's inauguration as president of the United States.

Almost immediately upon assumption of his term as president, Lincoln was faced with the inevitability of the Civil War. He called for 75,000 volunteers to protect properties of the Union, but a celebrated missing volunteer was his son, Robert. Though students and scholars left colleges, en masse, throughout the North, Robert steadfastly continued his studies. There is a great deal of opinion as to his reason for not enlisting, among them suggestions that he did not in deference to his mentally disturbed mother, or that Abraham did not want his son in the army, and still other opinions simply observe that Robert felt no obligation to enter the army merely because his father had declared the war.

However, upon Robert's 1864 graduation from Harvard, his father interceded and requested that General Grant find a position for his twenty-one-year-old son, saying, "having graduated from Harvard, [he] wishes to see something of the war before it ends. I do not wish to put him in the ranks, nor yet give him a commission, to which those who have already served are better entitled and better qualified to hold"[75] Grant responded by giving Robert the rank of captain, and his father immediately appointed Robert as assistant adjutant general of the army. Robert, therefore, "did manage to be at a camp around Petersburg, and at Appomattox to witness the surrender of Robert E. Lee."[76] Because Robert never actually served in a single battle of the Civil War, there is a certain irony when later northern newspapers were to carry the proclamation of "Robert Lincoln's distinguished service as an Army officer."[77]

On the fateful evening of Lincoln's assassination, Robert was in Washington in the White House. He would also be near both Garfield's and McKinley's assassinations. Following his father's funeral he immediately returned to his native state, Illinois, to enter a leading law firm, though he was not formally admitted to the Illinois bar until 1867. He rapidly developed a lucrative practice in Chicago and married Mary Harlan, the only daughter of Iowa's senator, in a small, rather stilted ceremony, due in large measure to his mother's erratic behavior.[78]

Continuing his law practice in Chicago, in 1876 Robert was elected to the only public office he was ever to hold through election, that of supervisor of the southern section of Chicago.[79] Between the years 1876 and 1881 Robert became closely allied with many Chicago-based major corporations, including the infamous Pullman Palace Car Company,[80] for which he acted as chief counsel.

In 1881 Robert Lincoln was appointed to Garfield's cabinet as secretary of war, a position he continued through Garfield's successor, Chester A. Arthur.[81] Robert then became an "almost ran" addition to presidential candidates. Three times he was mentioned for nomination as the Republican candidate for president. In 1880 his name was even submitted at the Republican party convention, where he received four votes. In 1884 he was mentioned, and in 1888 he was again named by Republicans hoping to entice support from his long-gone father's public image. However, as it was observed in 1884, that "no one claims that young Lincoln ever uttered a word or performed a solitary act showing superior ability, character or fitness to entitle him to the chief magistracy of the Republic,"[82] Lincoln continued to serve as secretary of war until the only Democratic president between Lincoln's administration and Woodrow Wilson, Grover Cleveland, was elected to the presidency.

Robert returned to law practice until Republican President Benjamin Harrison was elected. He was then appointed as minister to Great Britain, serving until Harrison's term ended in 1893.

Again back into law, which had, by this time, made him a very wealthy man, Robert became president of the Pullman Company, for which he had earlier acted as chief counsel. With this change in career from lawyer to business executive, Robert entered the arena for which he would acquire his own personal fame. Recognized as a major influence in industry, and responsible for a business that covered almost all railway lines in this time of tremendous railway development, with passengers numbering 9,618,438 a year, Robert Todd Lincoln was catered to, even by foreign dignitaries, as an "emperor of business."[83] He held this imperial position until his 1911 retirement.

The contrast in characters between father and son is evident. While his father suffered and achieved heroic stature through the sheer force of will and intellect, the son attained wealth and fame through his father's efforts. "Without risking the dangers of the battlefield, without service or exertion, he became Assistant Adjutant General of the Army. Without completing a law course he obtained membership in an outstanding law firm. Without any experience in military science he was appointed Secretary of War. Without any knowledge of diplomacy he became Minister to Great Britain."[84]

This, perhaps, is the most accurate epitaph for the son of one of this nation's most powerful and influential presidents, Abraham Lincoln.

EDWARD BAKER LINCOLN

Second child, second son of Abraham Lincoln and Mary Todd

Born: March 10, 1846   *Birthplace:* Springfield, Massachusetts
Died: February 1, 1850   *Age at Death:* 3 years, 11 months
Cause of Death: Unknown

A LINGERING DEATH

Born the second of four sons, Edward Baker, named after his father's close personal and political associate, Edward D. Baker of Illinois, did not survive childhood.

Edward was born when Abraham Lincoln was struggling to earn a living as a perambulating attorney in the Eighth Judicial Court District of Illinois. Riding "circuit" September to December each year, and then again from February to June, his father was absent from the family home in Springfield for most of Edward's few years of life. Describing his son to a friend, Lincoln wrote that Edward was not much like his elder brother, Bob, because Eddie was "rather of a longer order."[85]

When Edward died Lincoln wrote to his stepbrother, "We lost our little boy. It was not our first, but our second child. We miss him very much."[86] According to Lincoln, his son lay dying for fully two days. The love that Lincoln would shower on his other three sons can, perhaps, only be understood by the early loss of his second child, Eddie.

WILLIAM WALLACE LINCOLN

Third child, third son of Abraham Lincoln and Mary Todd

Born: December 21, 1850   *Birthplace:* Springfield, Illinois
Died: February 20, 1862   *Age at Death:* 11 years, 2 months
Cause of Death: Pneumonia

WHITE HOUSE GAMES

Willie Lincoln, believed to be his father's favorite child, was ten years old when his father was elected president of the United States. To Willie and his brother, Tad, the White House offered increased opportunity for the fun and games which characterized the two close brothers. Willie's boyish pranks kept the White House constantly in an uproar. For example, there was the occasion when he and his brother drove a goat through the drawing room, to the astonishment of the assembled visitors. Yet there was also a serious side to this Lincoln son, for he was particularly fond of drawing and writing poetry, some of which was published in newspapers.

Less than a year after the beginning of the Civil War, with newspapers screaming headlines of battles, there was also the announcement that "the president's son, William, aged ten or eleven years, died (this evening) of pneumonia."[87] Young Willie's untimely death was still another burden to the Lincolns, caught in the midst of the nation's tragedy. Lincoln and his wife were utterly distraught. Mary Todd Lincoln would never again enter the White House room where her son had died, nor even where his coffin had rested. So great was Lincoln's grief that it was a popular belief that Lincoln had Willie's body disinterred twice so that he might view it. Young Willie's remains were placed in a vault, in a Washington, D.C., cemetery, where they remained until his father's assassination.

Upon his father's assassination, Willie's body was removed from its resting place and put in the same funeral car with Lincoln's body, which then traveled across the country to the martyred president's interment in Springfield, Illinois. Of the over $7,000 expended for the funeral arrangements for the fallen president, $10 was spent so that Willie could accompany his father on their last trip, and the last public record of Lincoln's young son was that of the undertaker who noted the cost of his service as "removing remains of Willie $10."[88]

THOMAS LINCOLN

Fourth child, fourth son of Abraham Lincoln and Mary Todd

Born: April 4, 1853   *Birthplace:* Springfield, Illinois
Died: July 15, 1871   *Age at Death:* 18 years, 3 months
Cause of Death: Diphtheria
Education: Private schools

"COLONEL" LINCOLN

Eight years old when his father became the first Republican president of the United States, young Tad, as he was called, had spent earlier years in Springfield, Illinois. It was during his last summer spent in Springfield that Tad contracted scarlet fever, and though it is only an assumption by historians, it is probably the extremes of fever that caused the young man to have a great deal of difficulty in speaking, noted as "an unusual impediment in little Tad's speech [that] made it extremely difficult for him to pronounce certain words, and really impossible for him to ennunciate a name like Smith, for instance."[89] His impediment, whatever its cause, combined with the death of Lincoln's much loved Willie, endeared little Tad even more to his father.

Lincoln was not alone in his adoration of the small child; secretaries within the White House loved him, constantly deferring to him with affection. Described as merry, warm-blooded, and kindly, the little boy was, however, perfectly lawless. He ran freely throughout the White House, interrupting whatever struck his fancy. The president, catering to the little boy, would often let him play until he fell asleep, and then pick him up and carry him to bed.

On one occasion, young Tad, inspired by the war talk that filled the White House, was commissioned a second lieutenant in the army by Secretary of War Stanton. Tad believed the commission was real, not an unnatural assumption for a boy of his age and circumstances. The president did nothing to discourage the young boy's fantasy. Acting out the accepted fantasy, Lieutenant Tad overcame the night guards defending the White House in Civil War times, relieved them of their weapons, and mustered the gardeners and servants as his own guard, turning over the borrowed weapons to his troops. When Tad tired of being a lieutenant, his father promoted him to the rank of colonel. To enhance the credibility of the appointment, Lincoln ordered official stationery prepared with "Colonel Lincoln" upon it. Tad even sent telegrams signed Colonel Lincoln. In the course of carrying out his "colonel" duties, Tad found himself forced to sentence a doll to the death penalty, but the boy could not stomach the idea of actually carrying out the sentence. Appealing to his father to intervene to spare the life of the guilty doll, Tad called upon his father as president of the United States to exercise his constitutional power of pardon. With all solemnity, Lincoln heard the case and wrote, "The doll Jack is pardoned by order of the President. Signed, A. Lincoln."[90]

Upon Lincoln's assassination Tad came entirely under the care of his mother, Mary Todd Lincoln, who, throughout her life, suffered mental problems. His mother became obsessed that she and her little boy were abandoned in the world, poverty stricken. She took Tad with her to stay with her eldest son, Robert, but her erratic behavior soon disturbed the family. After a short stay with Robert, Mrs. Lincoln took Tad to Europe, where she alternately put him into private schools and then removed him, for no apparent reason. Throughout the European travels, she insisted on lodging in the cheapest accommodations available. With no apparent plan, mother and son returned to Chicago. Shortly after returning, Tad contracted diphtheria and died.

Mary Todd Lincoln, utterly devastated by the loss of her son, became even further removed from reality, and her only remaining child, Robert, was forced to commit her to a mental institution.

FOR FURTHER READING

Bruce, David K. *Sixteen American Presidents*. New York, New York: The Bobbs-Merrill Company, 1962.

Johannsen, Robert, ed. *The Letters of Stephen A. Douglas*. Urbana, Illinois: University of Illinois Press, 1961.

Oates, Stephan B. *With Malice Toward None: The Life of Abraham Lincoln*. New York, New York: Harper & Row, 1977.

Perling, Joseph J. *Presidents' Sons: The Prestige of Name in a Democracy*. Freeport, New York: Books for Libraries Press, 1971.

Sandburg, Carl. *Abraham Lincoln: The War Years III*. New York, New York: Harcourt, Brace and World, Inc., 1939.

Semones, Hattie. *Duel With Destiny*. Radford, Virginia: Commonwealth Press, 1976.

13 ANDREW JOHNSON'S CHILDREN

MARTHA JOHNSON PATTERSON

First child of Andrew Johnson and Eliza McCardle

Born: October 25, 1828   *Birthplace:* Greenville, Tennessee
Died: July 10, 1901   *Age at Death:* 72 years, 8 months
Cause of Death: Unknown   *Education:* Unknown
Profession: White House Hostess, Housewife, Mother
Spouse: David Trotter Patterson
Number of Children: 2

WHITE HOUSE ELEGANCE BEGAN WITH HER

She left her mark on the White House tradition when she filled the role of mistress of the White House, following the chaos of the Civil War years. Like several other daughters of presidents, Martha Johnson Patterson inherited the position of White House hostess because her mother was unable and unwilling to serve in that capacity. Unlike others that preceded her, Martha converted the jumbled White House of war years into the symbol of American elegance that it is today.

When Andrew Johnson took over the presidency following Lincoln's assassination in April 1865, the mansion showed the results of the war's impact and previous years of neglect and misuse. Civil War soldiers had wandered unchallenged throughout the entire White House, with the result that the furnishings were dirty and broken, soldiers had spat on the floors, they had slept throughout the mansion, and, quite literally, crowds had trampled the rugs to tatters.

Despite her father's difficulties with Congress, which eventually led to impeachment, Martha was able to convince influential congressmen that the White House deserved renovation. Congress appropriated $30,000 for interior redecoration. Despite the fact that this was a niggardly sum even in

1866, Martha accomplished such renovations that visitors were astounded. Everybody said that never before had the presidential home been so simply and yet so beautifully appointed. In addition to her pleasure in refurbishing the executive mansion, Martha felt great pride in the fine White House dairy, with prize cows grazing on what is today the White House lawn.

Possessing nervous energy very much like her father's, as well as the character of an extremely strong will, Martha accomplished much with very little. Raised by her mother in Tennessee, she once remarked, "We are just plain people from the mountains of Tennessee, placed in this position by a great tragedy. We have no desire to put on airs."[91]

When Lincoln was assassinated, Martha was a married woman with two lively children. Her husband, a senator from Tennessee, was a devoted husband and son-in-law, though a heavy drinker. The White House rang with parties for the children, and the entertainment gained for the Johnsons a reputation for graciousness and elegance. Assisted by her younger sister, Mary, they gave to the White House a character never before seen.

This simple girl from Tennessee, who described herself as "just plain people from the mountains,"[92] is, ironically, the individual most responsible for creating the image of the White House as the fashionable residence of the nation's first family.

CHARLES JOHNSON

Second child, first son of Andrew Johnson and Eliza McCardle

Born: February 19, 1830   *Birthplace:* Greenville, Tennessee
Died: April 4, 1863   *Age at Death:* 33 years, 2 months
Cause of Death: Suicide   *Education:* Unknown
Profession: Medical Doctor, Pharmacist, Soldier
Spouse: None   *Number of Children:* None

A SUICIDE

Charles Johnson, the eldest of three Johnson sons, was educated in pharmacy and medicine in accordance with the method of the day. He was a practicing physician as well as a partner in a drug store in Tennessee before the Civil War. As a political activist, opposed to Tennessee's secession from the Union, Charles put his medical skills at the service of the Union Army at the outbreak of the Civil War, when he joined the First Middle Tennessee Infantry as a surgeon.

In 1863, the son of Tennessee's governor and future president of the

United States died by his own hand. The much-loved son of Andrew, described as "his own worst enemy,"[93] unable to face the struggle between the states, completely exhausted, and addicted to stimulants, ended his own life. The funeral cortege was escorted by his own infantry regiment, as well as by the cavalry regiment commanded by his brother, Robert.

Charles, an easygoing, personable man until his Civil War involvement, was the first of three Johnson sons to come to an early end. His obituary was buried among headlines that spoke of the greater sorrow of the day—"General Grant Preparing to Bombard the City"[94] (Vicksburg, Mississippi). Thousands of other fathers would mourn their losses before the final act would be played in the greatest tragedy America has known.

MARY JOHNSON STOVER BROWN

Third child, second daughter of Andrew Johnson and Eliza McCardle

Born: May 8, 1832   *Birthplace:* Greenville, Tennessee
Died: April 19, 1883   *Age at Death:* 50 years, 11 months
Cause of Death: Unknown   *Education:* Unknown
Profession: Housewife, Mother
Spouses: Daniel Stover, William Brown
Number of Children: Johnson/Stover: 3
                                    Johnson/Brown: None

A SIMPLE WOMAN

Mary, the younger of the two Johnson girls, was a complete contrast to her sister Martha. While Martha was a dark-haired, grave child and woman, much like her father, Mary was fair, cheerful, and had a volatile temperament. The mother of three children before her father became president of the United States, she lived with her husband Daniel Stover, an east Tennessean with a spread of land in Watuga Valley, Tennessee. Her married life was thus spent in a home close to her birthplace.

During the Civil War the Stover home became the center for the entire Johnson clan. For part of the war, Mary's mother lived with the Stovers, and Mary spent much of her time catering to her mother's fears for her husband, Andrew. Mary's husband Daniel, like the Johnsons, a southerner by birth, fought in the Union's cause as a scout. Daniel would die from disease, the scourge of armies before twentieth-century medicine, leaving Mary a widow when her father entered the White House in 1865.

When Mary's father became president following the assassination of

Abraham Lincoln, Mary was called upon to serve, with her sister Martha, as White House hostess, as their mother was no longer capable of serving in this capacity. The White House reverberated with noises of Mary's and Martha's children during Johnson's administration.

At the conclusion of Johnson's presidency, he moved with his daughters back to their native Tennessee. Mary remarried in 1869. She moved into a home near her parents in order to be ever present to see to their needs. She and her new husband, William Brown, spent their summers at the Stover farm Mary had inherited from her first husband.

Mary, the constantly dutiful daughter, was, throughout her life, a pillar of strength and pleasure to her family. She shared with millions the tragedy of the Civil War, and further suffered the singular misfortune of the bitter presidency of Andrew Johnson.

ROBERT JOHNSON

Fourth child, second son of Andrew Johnson and Eliza McCardle

Born: February 22, 1834   *Birthplace:* Greenville, Tennessee
Died: April 22, 1869   *Age at Death:* 35 years, 2 months
Cause of Death: Alcoholism   *Education:* Unknown
Profession: Lawyer, Soldier, Presidential Secretary
Spouse: None   *Number of Children:* None

AN UNCOMPROMISING SOUTHERN UNIONIST

Robert Johnson, a southerner by birth and upbringing, fought for the northern cause in the Civil War. As a member of the Tennessee legislature while his father was military governor, Robert spoke against secession from the Union.

Going beyond words in his defense of the united Union, Robert organized an infantry regiment of Tennessee volunteers to fight to preserve the Union. Commissioned a colonel, Robert not only led his men but fought side by side with them. Because of his character, expressed through his very real concern for his troops, Robert Johnson earned a measure of respect and love accorded few commanding officers.

Following Lincoln's assassination, Robert's father became president of the United States. Robert immediately went to Washington, D.C., to become the president's private secretary. By all accounts Robert's work was exemplary.

But by early 1866, Robert's social drinking had definitely become serious drinking. Alcohol had become such an obvious problem for Robert that his father sought ways to remedy his illness by removing access to drink.

Devising a scheme in which Robert would take a long sea voyage, supposedly to investigate the slave trade on the African coast, the president planned that his son would abstain during the long trip. But national politics intervened and almost cost Andrew Johnson his office through impeachment. The trip was delayed over and over again because of the acute conflict between Robert's father and the Congress over reconstruction of the conquered South. When President Johnson had the time to turn his mind to his son's dilemma and finalize the projected sea voyage, his son refused to go.

Robert, a highly eligible bachelor, loose in Washington's society, nevertheless remained unmarried throughout his life. After his father's term as president, all of the Johnsons returned to Tennessee. The elder Johnson, far from removing himself from politics after his brush with impeachment, became a popular public speaker. It was during one of his speaking tours that Andrew Johnson was summoned back to Nashville, with news that his son Robert had died.

This respected, honorable man, who fought for his principles, became the object of passions that could not touch his father. Many of the obituaries for Robert were really arrows aimed at Lincoln's successor. Said one paper, "the devil came for the old man and not finding him took the son."[95]

ANDREW JOHNSON, JR.

Fifth child, third son of Andrew Johnson and Eliza McCardle

Born: August 6, 1852   *Birthplace:* Greenville, Tennessee
Died: March 12, 1879   *Age at Death:* 26 years, 7 months
Cause of Death: Unknown   *Education:* Unknown
Profession: Journalist   *Spouse:* Bessie May Kumbaugh
Number of Children: None

AN IMPRESSIONABLE BOY

Little is known of the youngest of the Johnson children, the namesake of his father. He was raised in the protected atmosphere of his Tennessee home, cared for by his mother, rarely seeing his politician father who only infrequently visited his home. Suddenly, the assassination of President

Lincoln hurled his father into the presidency, and changed the life of Andy, Jr. Thus, the only time that the impressionable boy had an opportunity to know his father was when he was the most powerful man in the nation.

After completing his schooling, following the end of his father's term as president, Andy entered a career in journalism. He organized a newspaper, the Greenville *Intelligencer*, when he was only twenty-one years old. In a short time he had acquired 800 subscribers, a sizeable number for the day, but the paper failed. Perhaps its failure was in part due to Andy's blatant and excessive concentration on his father's activities and accomplishments in the paper. Thus, the *Intelligencer* began well, but ended rapidly.

At the age of twenty-six Andy, Jr., died, surviving his father by only four years, and though he had married, young Andrew left no surviving children.

FOR FURTHER READING

Castel, Albert. *Presidency of Andrew Johnson*. Lawrence, Kansas: Regents Press of Kansas, 1979.

Miller, Hope Ridings. *Scandals in the Highest Office*. New York, New York: Random House, 1973.

Thomas, Lately. *The First President Johnson*. New York, New York: William Morrow & Company, 1968.

Williams, Frank B., Jr. *Tennessee's President*. Knoxville, Tennessee: University of Tennessee Press, 1981.

14 ULYSSES SIMPSON GRANT'S CHILDREN

FREDERICK DENT GRANT

First child of Ulysses Simpson Grant and Julia Boggs Dent

Born: May 30, 1850   *Birthplace:* St. Louis, Missouri
Died: April 11, 1912   *Age at Death:* 61 years, 11 months
Cause of Death: Cancer   *Education:* West Point
Profession: Soldier, Politician, Police Commissioner
Spouse: Ida Honore
Number of Children: 2

LIKE FATHER, LIKE SON

By the time he was thirteen years old, Frederick Dent Grant had already shown his preference for a military career. His experiences were not common to other thirteen-year-old boys, for Frederick's father was commander of the Union Army at the battle of Vicksburg, and the boy had accompanied his father on the campaign. When Grant took Jackson, Mississippi, it was his son who would, years later, lay claim to the honor. Running ahead of his father's troops young Frederick halted only at the sight of Confederate troops on the outskirts of the city. There he lay in wait for the Union soldiers. When his father's troops arrived, he proclaimed that he had been there first and upon him was the honor of laying siege to the city.

Entering West Point at fourteen, though with inadequate scholastic preparation, it took Frederick five years to complete the normal four-year course. Graduating as a second lieutenant, Frederick was assigned to the cavalry on patrol at the Mexican border. From this rather mundane assignment, nineteen-year-old Frederick was next transferred to Lieutenant General Philip Sheridan's command, as Sheridan's aide. The popular understanding was that he had received his new position because his father had recently become president of the United States. He served with Sheridan until his death and in 1889 he resigned from the army to accept President Benjamin Harrison's appointment to the post of minister to Austria.

In 1894 Frederick became New York City's police commissioner, a position he held for four years. But the call of the trumpet enticed him again to military service. Eighteen ninety-eight saw the beginning of the Spanish-American War, and Frederick, by virtue of his experience, quickly became Colonel Grant of the Fourteenth New York Infantry. From colonel, Frederick advanced to the rank of brigadier general, commanding the volunteers. At war's end he retained his rank, though in the regular army. Frederick was promoted to major general in 1906. His peacetime service included two tours of duty as commander of Governor's Island, New York, as well as the command of the Department of the Great Lakes.

Frederick's return to the military continued the path of his boyhood experiences. But during one brief period it seemed as if he would follow the pattern of his father, from the army to politics. In 1887 the Republican president nominated him for the cabinet position of secretary of state, but the Senate refused to confirm the nomination, agreeing with the *Boston Globe*'s observation that "the nomination of Colonel Grant would never have been though had he not been his father's son"[96] and Washington's *Sunday Herald* announcement that "everyone knows that it is only as the son of his father that he was given the place."[97] Thus, quickly began and ended the political aspirations of President Grant's son Frederick.

By 1912 Grant held the second highest military position in the United States, outranked only by Major General Leonard Wood, Washington, D.C., chief of staff. Returning to New York City from inspection of posts under his command at Portland, Maine, and as far as Galveston, Texas, Frederick took a leave of absence to spend some time with his wife, or so the press was informed.

Frederick underwent surgery for cancer, but the nature of his illness was kept secret. Ever since his father's terrible death from throat cancer, Frederick had lived in fear that he too would suffer the same death. His premonition was to prove accurate.

Seeking to evade possible publicity, Frederick and his wife registered under a false name in a New York hotel. On the evening of April 11, 1912, only hours after he had arrived at the hotel, the general began to choke. Doctors were called, but it was too late.

The press announced that Frederick had died of heart failure, complicated by diabetes and intestinal disorders, but the news of his real illness was not long kept secret. General Frederick Dent Grant was accorded a military funeral with all honors. Services were attended by thousands, including President Taft, the nation's vice-president, the mayor of New York City, and most of the highest ranking officers of the regular army and the National Guard.

A military caisson drawn by six horses escorted his coffin to its West Point burial ground. In the style of military funerals, his favorite horse, Pet, was led along the way of the procession, with the general's boots reversed in the saddle's stirrups. A final thirteen-gun salute ended the ceremonies of one of the nation's leading military men, the army's second General Grant.

ULYSSES SIMPSON GRANT II

Second child, second son of Ulysses Simpson Grant and Julia Boggs Dent

Born: July 22, 1852   *Birthplace:* Bethel, Ohio
Died: September 25, 1929   *Age at Death:* 77 years, 2 months
Cause of Death: Unknown
Education: Phillips Exeter Academy, University of Gottingen, Harvard University
Profession: Lawyer, Presidential Secretary, Businessman
Spouses: Josephine Chaffee, America Workman Wills
Number of Children: Grant/Chaffee: 5
                            Grant/Wills: None

U.S. MARRIES AMERICA

Born in Ohio and called "Buck" for most of his life because of his birthplace in the Buckeye State, Ulysses Grant II was but sixteen when his father went to the White House. But this "Buck" who was Ulysses Simpson Grant II was, in fact, the first Ulysses of the Grants. As Buck himself would later relate, his father's name was Hiram Grant until his West Point entrance, when a clerk mistakenly wrote a "U" initial rather than an "H," and thus rechristened Hiram S. Grant as U. S. Grant, the Ulysses being Grant's personal choice, given the limitation of the letter "U." However, the credibility of Buck's explanation is questioned by some authorities.

Buck graduated in 1874 from Harvard, having previously studied at Phillips Exeter Academy and the University of Gottingen, Germany. Admitted to the bar, Buck did not practice law, but rather served as his father's presidential secretary.

After Ulysses, Senior, left the White House, Buck became a junior partner in a large law firm, a remarkable achievement for so young and inexperienced a man. But despite the auspicious beginning, Buck's practice did not develop, and he rapidly became disenchanted with the law. Buck's interests shifted westward with his marriage to Josephine Chaffee, daughter of Colorado Senator Jerome B. Chaffee, as well as the attractions of the West's potential. He married Josephine, fathered five children and prospered in mining and land development—both western interests proved productive.

Following his wife's 1913 death, Grant, then sixty-one years old, married a widow in her early thirties by the name of Mrs. America Workman Wills. Children and friends opposed the marriage, but Grant, once a shy and retiring boy, flaunted his new wife, even going so far as to announce that the bulk of his estate would be hers upon his death. The Grants traveled the world, frolicking with nobility while U. S. II developed ideas of his own political destiny.

Returning to California, Buck commenced work to gain the Republican nomination for U.S. Senator from California. His goal was not entirely beyond reach, given his political heritage. But his political career was scuttled when it was proven that he had been involved in some bribery schemes.

At one time U. S. Grant II became the largest taxpayer in San Diego County. In the city of San Diego he built a unique "memorial" to his father—the U. S. Grant Hotel. Cynics proclaimed it to be the only dividend-paying "memorial" ever erected to a president's memory.

When Buck died, his big talk, the flamboyancy, and the facade of wealth crumbled. The great fortune upon which he had based all of his wild schemes was found to be no more than $10,000.

ELLEN WRENSHALL GRANT SARTORIS JONES

Third child, only daughter of Ulysses Simpson Grant and Julia Boggs Dent

Born: July 4, 1855   *Birthplace:* Wistonwisch, Missouri
Died: August 30, 1922   *Age at Death:* 67 years, 2 months
Cause of Death: Unknown   *Education:* Unknown
Profession: Housewife, Mother
Spouses: Algernon Charles Frederick Sartoris, Franklin Hatch Jones
Number of Children: Grant/Sartoris: 4
                    Grant/Jones: None

A BRITISH SUBJECT

Ellen Grant, called Nellie throughout her life, was General Grant's only daughter. At the age of thirteen, when her father entered the White House, Nellie moved into the elite circle of teenagers in Washington, D.C. It was in the atmosphere of international Washington that Nellie, at seventeen, met and married British diplomat Algernon Sartoris. The couple married in the White House, in a ceremony described by contemporaries as an extravaganza. The romantic story of a president's daughter and a distinguished diplomat and the splash of a White House wedding captured the public's imagination, and newspapers detailed her life from the wedding onward. When the couple moved to Britain, the English newspapers took up the story with the added twist that, from the British perspective, it was the president's daughter, "America's royalty," that intrigued the reader.

Four children were born to the couple, but shortly after the birth of the fourth, Sartoris died. Nellie was thus left as a British subject, which status she had attained by her marriage. Far from home and family, Nellie wanted to return to the country of her birth, and she petitioned the U.S. Congress for the return of her citizenship. An American citizen once again, Nellie returned to the United States, a widowed woman of means.

In 1912 she remarried. Her new husband, Franklin Hatch Jones, had been first assistant postmaster general in Grover Cleveland's administration, and would become head of the Illinois division of the Woodrow Wilson Foundation, an organization devoted to the support of scholarship. The couple were married in Nellie's summer home in Ontario, Canada. But only months after the marriage she became seriously ill from a disease that was never identified to the public. During the last seven years of her life she was paralyzed and was unable to partake of social life, so much a part of her former world. Ill health seemed the common misfortune of the Grants.

JESSE ROOT GRANT

Fourth child, third son of Ulysses Simpson Grant and Julia Boggs Dent

Born: February 6, 1858   *Birthplace:* St. Louis, Missouri
Died: June 8, 1934   *Age at Death:* 76 years, 4 months
Cause of Death: Unknown
Education: Cornell University, Columbia University
Profession: Engineer, Author
Spouses: Elizabeth Chapman, Lillian Burns Wilkins
Number of Children: Grant/Chapman: 2
                                    Grant/Wilkins: None

"SON-OF-A-GUN"

Jesse Root Grant, the youngest of the four Grant children, chose a life very different from that of his father. Selecting engineering as his career, Jesse studied at Cornell, though for a short period he was undecided and almost entered law when he studied at Columbia Law School for one year. Perhaps the trip Jesse took with his father around the world, following Grant's second presidential term, evoked a wanderlust in young Jesse. For after he had earned his engineering degree, Jesse became a world wanderer, traveling constantly as a free-lance mining engineer.

Though he married and fathered two children, the pattern of Jesse's life remained unbroken. He was not the type to settle down to a normal family relationship. Jesse continued to travel the world, spending little time at home. It must have been with more than a little humor when, in 1914, he filed divorce proceedings in Nevada, on grounds of desertion—by his wife. Mrs. Grant had the divorce set aside. Four years later Jesse tried again, and this time he was successful in obtaining his divorce on the grounds that his wife had deserted him. One week after the second divorce attempt became final, Jesse married a widow, nineteen years his junior. He was to outlive her by ten years.

In opposition to his father, Jesse was a Democrat. From his college days he took an active interest in politics, though never attempting to gain public office until 1908. Returning to New York City from a speaking tour in the South and West, Jesse astonishingly announced his candidacy for the Democratic nomination for the presidency of the United States. As it turned out it was William Jennings Bryan who was nominated and Bryan was soundly defeated by Republican William Howard Taft.

Jesse's final days were spent writing about his father. In his book, *In the Days of My Father: General Grant*, published in 1925, Jesse presents a picture of President Grant as "the kindest, most thoughtful and most abstemious man I ever knew."[98] The Grant that emerges from Jesse's memoir is not the man known to history. For most historians of Grant, he is known as a steel-hard man, a raucous ligh-liver, and a drunk. Surviving years beyond his brothers and sister, Jesse publicly defended his father, perhaps exceeding the truth.

FOR FURTHER READING

Faber, Doris. *Presidents' Mothers*. New York, New York: St. Martin's Press, 1978.

McFeely, William S. *Grant: A Biography*. New York, New York: W. W. Norton & Company, Inc., 1974.

Sadler, Christine. *Children in the White House*. New York, New York: G. P. Putnam's Sons, 1967.

15 RUTHERFORD BIRCHARD HAYES'S CHILDREN

BIRCHARD AUSTIN HAYES

First child of Rutherford Birchard Hayes and Lucy Ware Webb

Born: November 4, 1853   *Birthplace:* Cincinnati, Ohio
Died: January 24, 1926   *Age at Death:* 72 years, 2 months
Cause of Death: Unknown
Education: University of Michigan, Cornell University, Harvard University
Profession: Lawyer
Spouse: Mary Nancy Sherman
Number of Children: 5

TAX ATTORNEY

An army "brat" for the first ten years of his life, Birchard was sent to live with his uncle in Fremont, Ohio, so that he might prepare for entry into higher education. Undecided as to which college to attend, Birchard first went to school in Michigan and then, dissatisfied, he chose Cornell after lengthy consultations with his father.

Birchard's college education was uneventful. His father explained that his son's lack of academic distinction was because "his diffidence has kept him from improving his opportunity to learn to speak. He is an accurate, thorough student, not fond of books as I was, with an unusual fondness for statistics, especially for the preparation of tabular information."[99]

It was entirely fitting, therefore, that with this background and natural bent Birchard would enter Harvard Law School from which he graduated in 1877, shortly after his father had become president of the United States.

Though he began his law career in New York with a leading firm, within two years Birchard moved to Toledo, Ohio, and began a law practice specializing in taxation and real estate law; he continued for twenty-six years. In 1926 Birchard died.

JAMES WEBB COOK HAYES

Second child, second child of Rutherford Birchard Hayes and Lucy Ware Webb

Born: March 20, 1856   *Birthplace:* Cincinnati, Ohio
Died: July 26, 1934   *Age at Death:* 78 years, 4 months
Cause of Death: Unknown   *Education:* Cornell University
Profession: Presidential Secretary, Businessman, Soldier
Spouse: Mary Otis Miller
Number of Children: None

SOLDIER OF FORTUNE

Christened James Webb Hayes, he later changed his name to Webb Cook Hayes. Nobody seems to know why. Educated at Cornell, Webb was not a particularly good student, but his father did employ him as his confidential secretary during the Hayes presidency from 1877 until 1881.

After White House service, Webb moved from the political world to the business world and became an official in a small business enterprise. In time, under Webb's direction, the small firm reorganized, expanded, and absorbed numerous other businesses. The small enterprise was to become the giant multinational Union Carbide Corporation. Webb became rich, and even a bit more than rich, and he was able to indulge his other passion—war.

In 1898 Webb was commissioned a major in the U.S. Army, leading troops against the Spaniards in Cuba and Puerto Rico during the Spanish-American War. Wounded in action, he was awarded the Congressional Medal of Honor and promoted to the rank of lieutenant colonel. But the all too brief Spanish-American War only whetted Webb's appetite for military adventure.

In 1900 Webb was in China fighting in the Boxer Rebellion. In both 1911 and 1913 he was on the Mexican border, fighting bandits. At fifty-eight years of age Webb joined British and French brigades in Italy fighting in the first world war, before the United States was drawn into the carnage. When America did enter the war, Webb transferred to the U.S. Army. He was decorated for his service in both France and Africa.

Webb survived, and evidently enjoyed, three wars and numerous hazardous adventures before his 1934 death. Having achieved the dream of most men—real and substantial wealth—Webb repeatedly risked all for the heroic life, not unlike a more well-known man of his era, President Theodore Roosevelt.

RUTHERFORD PLATT HAYES

Third child, third son of Rutherford Birchard Hayes and Lucy Ware Webb

Born: June 24, 1858   *Birthplace:* Cincinnati, Ohio
Died: July 31, 1927   *Age at Death:* 69 years, 1 month
Cause of Death: Unknown
Education: University of Michigan, Cornell University, Boston Institute of Technology
Profession: Businessman, Librarian
Spouse: Lucy Hayes Platt
Number of Children: 3

RUTHERFORD "THE MILD"

Rutherford, characterized by his father as "the mild," was a tall, slender youth, who, at sixteen, was considered unfit for future hard work or hard study. However, proving to the contrary, Rutherford overcame early estimations and developed into a bright, jovial, and handsome man.

While his father was president of the United States, Rutherford studied at the University of Michigan and Cornell University, completing his undergraduate work in 1880. He continued graduate work at the Boston Institute of Technology until 1882. Returning to the family home in Fremont, Ohio, Rutherford became a cashier in a savings bank, a position of much higher status in those days than today. When the bank panic of 1892 hit, Rutherford is credited with guiding his bank through the difficult period.

As a rich uncle had founded the Birchard Library, Rutherford became a trustee for that library. In that fashion, quite by chance, Rutherford stumbled onto an avocation that was to become his passion—libraries. In 1895 he was a major founder of the American Library Association, today considered the major professional library association with thousands of members.

In creating what he called "mobile libraries" to bring books from libraries to the public, Hayes anticipated the "bookmobiles" of today's public library systems. It was also Rutherford who began the first reading room especially designed for children, an innovation which has become an American library standard.

In his own quiet way, the "mild" Rutherford made contributions to the American system of education and learning such as would only be exceeded, perhaps, by another man of Rutherford's time and passion, Andrew Carnegie, called "the father of the American library system."

JOSEPH THOMPSON HAYES

Fourth child, fourth son of Rutherford Birchard Hayes and Lucy Ware Webb

Born: December 21, 1861   *Birthplace:* Cincinnati, Ohio
Died: June 24, 1863   *Age at Death:* 1 year, 6 months
Cause of Death: Dysentery

HYDROENCEPHALITIS?

Joseph Hayes was born just before Christmas in the year the Civil War began. His father, stationed at Camp White, near Charleston, in the part of Virginia that stayed loyal to the Union, was not present at his birth and would not see his son until the boy was almost a year-and-one-half old, when the family arrived at the camp from their Cincinnati home.

Within a few short days of the family's arrival, the baby, already a sickly child, became further weakened by dysentery and died. The cottage that Rutherford Hayes had planned for a happy family reunion became, instead, a funeral parlor, when the little boy's body was placed on the table used as a makeshift bier.

Though his father had scarcely known the boy, he observed that "he was afflicted with some kind of mental disorder . . . that the boy's brain was excessively developed and that death had prevented further greater suffering."[100] From the description it appears likely that the child suffered from hydroencephalitis.

GEORGE CROOK HAYES

Fifth child, fifth son of Rutherford Birchard Hayes and Lucy Ware Webb

Born: September 29, 1864   *Birthplace:* Chillicothe, Ohio
Died: May 24, 1866   *Age at Death:* 1 year, 8 months
Cause of Death: Scarlet fever

CIVIL WAR NAMESAKE

Very little is recorded of the birth and death of the namesake of General Crook, who was so much admired by little George's father. The child was born only shortly after his father's hero was credited with winning a major Civil War battle, though later history would see Sheridan credited for the victory.

George, the second of the Hayeses' children to be born during war years, lived only slightly longer than the great war's end, when he succumbed to the dreaded disease, scarlet fever.

FANNY HAYES SMITH

Sixth child, only daughter of Rutherford Birchard Hayes and Lucy Ware Webb

Born: September 2, 1867   *Birthplace:* Cincinnati, Ohio
Died: March 18, 1950   *Age at Death:* 82 years, 6 months
Cause of Death: Unknown
Education: Tutors, finishing school   *Profession:* Housewife, Mother
Spouse: Harry Eaton Smith
Number of Children: 1

A SINGLE GIRL AMONG EIGHT

The only daughter among seven brothers, Fanny's earliest years were spent in Ohio where her father was the state's governor. Named after Hayes's much-loved sister, she was constantly pampered and catered to by all of the family, as well as her father's associates. On one occasion a massive doll house was presented to the little girl. When later carted to the White House all who saw it knew immediately that an important small child had taken up residence in the White House.

Only nine years old when her father became the nation's president, Fanny traveled frequently with her mother, her aunts, and her father throughout the nation. But Hayes, the consummate father, saw to it that his daughter took all lessons to make her a fine and proper lady, even including in her schedule dancing and swimming lessons. Fanny attended school during their days in Ohio with her close friend, another president-to-be's child, Molly Garfield. Later she completed her education in Connecticut at a finishing school.

Following the end of the Hayes presidency in 1881, Hayes returned to the Ohio family home to live a gentleman's life, involving himself and his family in interests in national affairs. Fanny was yet at home when her mother died in 1889, leaving Hayes distraught from the loss of his wife. The young daughter replaced her mother, filling the duties of hostess and travel companion, even accompanying her father to Bermuda in 1890.

Called "Fanny, the serious," while her brothers were identified as "Birchard, the bookish"; "Webb, the sportsman"; "Rutherford, the mild"; and "Scott, the adventurous"; Fanny's life changed following her father's death.[101] She married Harry Eaton Smith, bore one child, and after her husband's death she changed her name back to Hayes.

SCOTT RUSSELL HAYES

Seventh child, sixth son of Rutherford Birchard Hayes and Lucy Ware Webb

Born: February 8, 1871   *Birthplace:* Columbus, Ohio
Died: May 6, 1923   *Age at Death:* 52 years, 3 months
Cause of Death: Cancer   *Education:* Unknown
Profession: Businessman
Spouse: Maude Anderson
Number of Children: Unknown

"SCOTT, THE ADVENTUROUS?"

Only five years old when his father became president of the United States in 1877, he was described by his father as "our handsomest. Interesting, too honest to joke, or to comprehend a joke readily. He talks with some hesitation when excited and has many pretty ways. He says many queer things. He is fond of animals."[102] His father further described him as "an adventurer," which he would never become.

After Scott completed his education, he became an executive for a railroad spring and airbrake manufacturing company and eventually achieved financial success. Scott showed no interest in politics, but nevertheless was the closest to his father of the Hayes children. Indeed, it was to Scott that the former president wrote his last letter.

At the age of fifty-two Scott Hayes entered the hospital for an operation for a brain tumor, but he died before the operation could take place. Scott left a widow, but no direct descendants to follow him to his burial place in Fremont, Ohio.

MANNING FORCE HAYES

Eighth child, seventh son of Rutherford Birchard Hayes and Lucy Ware Webb

Born: August 1, 1873   *Birthplace:* Fremont, Ohio
Died: August 28, 1874   *Age at Death:* 1 year
Cause of Death: Unknown

A THIRD INFANT DEATH

The lastborn child and seventh son of Rutherford Hayes, Manning Force, survived only long enough to celebrate his first birthday, and then his life was suddenly cut short by a childhood disease.

Named after the son of Hayes's friend, Peter Force, with whom Hayes had attended Harvard, Manning was born only shortly after his mother's two brothers died. Manning brought some joy into an otherwise sorrowful family. But with his death he became one of three Hayes sons to die while yet babies.

FOR FURTHER READING

Davison, Kenneth E. *The Presidency of Rutherford B. Hayes.* Westport, Connecticut: Greenwood Press, 1972.
Eckenrode, H. J. *Rutherford B. Hayes.* New York, New York: Kennikat Press, 1963.
Whitney, David C. *American Presidents.* New York, New York: Doubleday, 1978.
Williams, T. Harry. *Hayes of the Twenty-Third: The Civil War Volunteer Officer.* New York, New York: Alfred A. Knopf, 1965.

16 JAMES ABRAM GARFIELD'S CHILDREN

ELIZA ARABELLA GARFIELD

First child of James Abram Garfield and Lucretia Rudolph

Born: July 3, 1860   *Birthplace:* Hiram, Ohio
Died: December 3, 1863   *Age at Death:* 3 years, 5 months
Cause of Death: Diphtheria

"LITTLE TROT"

Eliza, the first of seven Garfield children, became her father's pride and joy. Garfield, who had experienced some trepidation at the thought of fatherhood, came to adore his firstborn, whom he dubbed "Trot" after a literary character from a Dickens novel. Despite Garfield's undoubted affection for the girl, the press of his military and political duties allowed him little time to express that affection. Thus, Trot was usually under the care of her mother, living with her mother's parents.

Constantly in motion, demanding and giving affection freely, Trot completed, in Garfield's mind, the ideal family: his wife, his daughter, and himself. To house this ideal family, Garfield purchased the first family home for $825. Though the house badly needed repairs, it represented to Garfield the solid foundation of family life, which he had previously found difficult to imagine for himself. Soon after the move, a second child, Harry, was born.

But tragedy quickly intruded into the Garfield home. The joy of Garfield's election to Congress from Ohio was followed by the death of Trot from diphtheria. During her illness Garfield sat beside her. He later wrote, "We buried her . . . on the 3rd day of December, at the very hour she would have lived the fifth month of her fourth year. . . . It seems as if the fabric of my life were torn to atoms and scattered to the winds."[103] It was with his mind tormented by the death of his daughter that Garfield left for Washington, D.C., to enter upon his national political career.

HARRY AUGUSTUS GARFIELD

Second child, first son of James Abram Garfield and Lucretia Rudolph

Born: October 11, 1863   *Birthplace:* Hiram, Ohio

Died: December 12, 1942   *Age at Death:* 79 years, 2 months

Cause of Death: Unknown

Education: Williams College, Columbia University, Oxford University, England

Profession: Lawyer, Teacher, Politician, Businessman

Spouse: Belle Hartford Mason

Number of Children: 4

ENERGY CZAR

Born at the height of the Civil War, Harry, nicknamed Hal, entered Williams College about the time his father became president of the United States (1881), and graduated with a bachelor's degree in 1885. Hal went on to study law at both Columbia in New York, and Oxford, England. After completing his education, Harry opened a law office with his younger brother, James, in Cleveland, Ohio. Displaying a particularly strong aptitude for business, Hal became the vice-president of the Cleveland Trust Company, as well as developing other business interests, such as a coal syndicate to develop mines in Ohio.

Notwithstanding his involvement in business, it was the law that was Harry's career, and thus he became professor of contract law at Western Reserve College (later renamed Case Western Reserve University) near his Cleveland home. From Western Reserve, Hal moved to Princeton University, where, as a president's son, he taught politics. There he became friends with Princeton's president and future president of the United States, Woodrow Wilson. Then Williams College selected its former student as its president. Harry accepted and remained at Williams College as its president until America's entry into World War I.

War brought the need for organizing America's industrial power. President Woodrow Wilson called upon his old friend, Hal Garfield, to head the newly created Fuel Administration, which would control both the supply and distribution of the nation's energy resources. While Hal's innovations increased production of coal, his authoritarian attitude did bring national protests and earned for him the title of "dictator of the nation's fuel resources." Garfield was, however, awarded the Distinguished Service Medal at the war's conclusion.

After the war Hal returned to Williams College where he developed the Institute for Human Relations as a major resource for the study of international politics.

Hal's life ended in 1942 at the age of seventy-nine, and though he was primarily involved in academics for a major portion of his life, this president's son was a major contributor to the first regimentation and governmental control of American life, brought on by emergency needs created by the First World War.

JAMES RUDOLPH GARFIELD

Third child, second son of James Abram Garfield and Lucretia Rudolph

Born: October 17, 1865   *Birthplace:* Hiram, Ohio
Died: March 24, 1950   *Age at Death:* 84 years, 5 months
Cause of Death: Unknown
Education: Columbia University   *Profession:* Lawyer, Politician
Spouse: Helen Newell
Number of Children: 4

TEDDY'S SECRETARY OF THE INTERIOR

Fifteen-year-old James Garfield was with his father, traveling to meet his mother at the New Jersey seashore, when a man stepped from the crowd at the railroad station and shot the elder Garfield, the second assassination of an American president.

As Jimmy grew he developed an interest in sports. Lawn tennis and the newly invented game of baseball were his favorites, and perhaps because of his close association with his brother Hal, he also became fascinated by the law. Graduating from Columbia Law School in 1888, Jimmy married the daughter of a railroad president. The couple moved to a large Ohio farm where Jim raised cattle, but he continued his interest in the law and entered a partnership with his older brother, Hal.

Perhaps because of his name, James Garfield was elected to the Ohio state senate before his thirtieth birthday, thus beginning a career in politics. McKinley, whose fate it was also to be assassinated, appointed James to the United States Civil Service Commission, which oversees those federal jobs that have been removed from the partisanship of the spoils system. He was also appointed to a post in the Department of Commerce and Labor. Later, under Teddy Roosevelt, Jim headed investigations of monopolistic practices and price controls in industries such as meat, oil, and coal. Jim's abilities in these investigations prompted President Roosevelt to appoint him as U.S. secretary of interior, a position he held until the end of Roosevelt's administration in 1909.

Teddy and Jim had developed a mutual respect, and their friendship did not end when Roosevelt left the presidency. When Teddy decided to buck the Republican organization and form his own party, the Bull Moose party, it was Jim whom he called upon to help in his vigorous campaign. The defeat of the Bull Moose party ended not only Roosevelt's political activism, but Jim's as well.

In later years, Jim contributed his time and organizational abilities to the Red Cross effort in World War I. He also lent his support to Herbert Hoover in his second bid for the presidency, which, despite Jim's help, Hoover lost.

Dying in 1950, Jim's life had spanned the momentous changes in world history: from the end of the American Civil War to the Korean War, from the railway to the space program—and from Roosevelt to Roosevelt.

MARY GARFIELD STANLEY-BROWN

Fourth child, second daughter of James Abram Garfield and Lucretia Rudolph

Born: January 16, 1867   *Birthplace:* Washington, D.C.
Died: December 30, 1947   *Age at Death:* 80 years, 11 months
Cause of Death: Unknown
Education: Private schools   *Profession:* Housewife, Mother
Spouse: Joseph Stanley-Brown
Number of Children: 3

MOLLY, DEAR

Mary, the only Garfield daughter to survive beyond early childhood, was always called Molly. Born while her father was an Ohio congressman, Molly went to private schools in her native city, Washington, D.C. Educated far beyond women of her day, her scholastic abilities were a source of pride to her father.

Upon her father's election to the presidency, Garfield selected Joseph Stanley Brown to serve as private secretary (the name Stanley-Brown came later when he added the hyphen between his middle and last names, in the style of British aristocracy). Molly immediately developed a crush on her father's secretary. Fate seemed to conspire against the young girl, twice. On his way to join Molly and her mother at the New Jersey seashore, where Mrs. Garfield was recovering from malaria, a bullet struck her father, eventually resulting in his death. The same bullet appeared to also end Molly's romantic dreams, for when the Garfield administration ended, Molly and Joseph were separated. But the couple continued to correspond and develop their relationship.

In 1888 Joseph and Molly married and lived in New York City, where their three children were born. Molly, well suited to the role of wife and homemaker to a man of prestige, which her husband became following his graduation from Yale after their marriage, saw her husband become active in geological studies. Eventually he furthered his success in banking and railroads.

Joseph died in 1941 and she in 1947, having lived together long enough to celebrate their golden wedding anniversary.

IRVIN MCDOWELL GARFIELD

Fifth child, third son of James Abram Garfield and Lucretia Rudolph

Born: August 3, 1870   *Birthplace:* Hiram, Ohio
Died: July 18, 1951   *Age at Death:* 80 years, 11 months
Cause of Death: Unknown
Education: Williams College, Law School   *Profession:* Lawyer
Spouse: Susan Emmons
Number of Children: 3

ANOTHER WHITE HOUSE TERROR

The terror of the White House, Irvin McDowell Garfield, well deserved his reputation. "In bad weather he would ride high-wheeled bicycles indoors and careen down the staircase and through the corridors, gouging chunks from the historic wainscotting and scattering the lines of anxious office seekers waiting for an office with his father."[104] But his White House exuberance was short-lived, for his father was assassinated when Irvin was only eleven years old.

Irvin graduated from Williams College and continued on to law school, as did his older brothers. But, unlike both Jim and Hal who set up practice in Cleveland, Irvin went to Boston to begin his law practice. His clientele grew, and in time Irvin argued his cases before the Massachusetts Supreme Court, commanding astronomical fees for his services.

Surviving until the ripe old age of eighty, Irvin took part in charitable organizations as well as alumni activities of his old alma mater, Williams College, until only shortly before his death.

ABRAM GARFIELD

Sixth child, fourth son of James Abram Garfield and Lucretia Rudolph

Born: November 21, 1872   *Birthplace:* Washington, D.C.
Died: October 16, 1958   *Age at Death:* 85 years, 11 months
Cause of Death: Unknown
Education: Tutors, Williams College, Massachusetts Institute of Technology
Profession: Architect
Spouses: Sarah Granger, Helen Grannis Mathews
Number of Children: Garfield/Granger: 2
                        Garfield/Mathews: None

A LEADING ARCHITECT

Born in Washington, D.C., Abram was still a small boy when his father was assassinated, yet it was his father's strong beliefs concerning education that influenced the course of Abram's life. Garfield had come to the conclusion that the public schools were not adequate, stating that, "My faith in our public schools is steadily diminishing . . . the course of study is unnatural and the children miss a solid health growth."[105] In line with his father's beliefs, Abram was tutored by a young Englishman and eventually both Abram and his elder brothers received private tutoring from Dr. Hawkes, who was imported from the Montana Territory.

Whether private instruction proved better in the end, it certainly did not hinder the boy's academic advancement, for young Abram graduated from Williams College and took postgraduate studies at Massachusetts Institute of Technology, graduating in 1896. Upon graduating, Abram set out to make a grand tour of Europe with the object of studying, at first hand, the great architectural achievements of western civilization. With this tour he capped his academic education in architecture and prepared himself to his own satisfaction for a career as an architect.

Establishing his own architectural firm in Cleveland, Ohio, Abram's professional career coincided with the great age of American architecture. Abram's credits include Hiram and Kenyon Colleges, Cleveland's Babies and Children's Hospital and offices and homes of Cleveland's leading families. Abram was elected a fellow in the American Institute of Architects, as well as served two terms as the National Institute of Architects' director.

Achieving national recognition, Abram had been appointed by President Teddy Roosevelt to the National Council of Fine Arts in 1909. President Calvin Coolidge named him to the National Fine Arts Commission in 1925.

Abram once observed that "achievement and success will bring about this desirable personal publicity but personal publicity may hardly be depended upon to bring achievement and success."[106] At the age of seventy-five Abram remarried. Marrying a woman much his junior, he survived yet another ten years.

EDWARD GARFIELD

Seventh child, fifth son of James Abram Garfield and Lucretia Rudolph

Born: December 25, 1874   *Birthplace:* Hiram, Ohio
Died: October 25, 1876   *Age at Death:* 1 year, 10 months
Cause of Death: Whooping cough

"NOT AMISS"

The last of the Garfield children was destined to a short life. The family had been hoping for a girl. Instead, Edward, the third boy in a row appeared to the disappointment of all, and especially to young Molly Garfield, anticipating a little sister's birth. Garfield, straining at wit, punned, "We receive not when we ask amiss."[107]

It was during Garfield's campaigning in New Jersey that he was informed that his little son, "Neddie," as young Edward was called, was seriously ill. Garfield immediately rushed back to his Ohio home to be at the boy's bedside, but Neddie was unconscious from the ravages of whooping cough when his father returned home. For four days the parents waited and prayed for the recovery of their son. His brothers knew that Neddie had died when they returned home from school to find white crepe hanging on the door, symbolizing a death in the family.

Garfield, deeply pained at the death of his young son, tried to teach to his remaining children a philosophical view of death, never suspecting, of course, that they would have need for such consolation when he, himself, would be assassinated in a few short years.

Neddie was buried next to his sister, Trot, on Hiram Hill in Ohio.

FOR FURTHER READING

Doenecke, Justus D. *Presidencies of James A. Garfield and Chester A. Arthur*. Lawrence, Kansas: Regents Press of Kansas, 1981.
Leech, Margaret, and Harry Brown. *The Garfield Orbit*. New York, New York: Harper & Row, 1978.
Peskin, Allan. *Garfield*. Kent, Ohio: Kent State University Press, 1978.

17 CHESTER ALAN ARTHUR'S CHILDREN

WILLIAM LEWIS ARTHUR

First child of Chester Alan Arthur and Ellen Lewis Herndon

Born: December 10, 1860   *Birthplace:* New York, New York
Died: July 7, 1863   *Age at Death:* 2 years, 7 months
Cause of Death: Convulsions

A BRAIN AFFLICTION?

Born in late 1860 while his father was in the military, William Lewis Arthur was the first of three children to be born to Nell and Chester Arthur. The young couple and their child lived in "a plushly furnished two-story family hotel, near Twenty-second and Broadway," in New York City.[108] It would have been strange if the young couple, she from an aristocratic southern family and he a regular soldier in the U.S. Army, which would soon become the Union Army, had not felt the rising tensions from their different heritages, tensions that were just around the corner from Civil War.

When the boy died at the age of two-and-one-half, the couple were "prostrated with grief."[109] Chester wrote to his brother, and the child's namesake, of the boy's death saying, "We have sad, sad news to tell you. We have lost our darling boy. He died yesterday morning at Englewood, New Jersey, where we were staying for a few weeks—from convulsions, brought on by some affection of the brain. It came upon us so unexpectedly and suddenly. Nell is broken-hearted. I fear much for her health. You know how her heart was wrapped up in her dear boy."[110] His fears for his wife's health were justified, and though two other children were born to the couple, Chester Alan Arthur would enter the presidency as a widower with two young children.

The young parents, convinced that they had pushed their firstborn too hard and had demanded so much from him that his young brain was taxed, bore the blame for their first son's death. The result of William's early death, though childhood deaths were not uncommon at all in the day, would cause a great deal of pampering of the next child, also a boy, for fear that the same occasion of a young death would occur.

CHESTER ALAN ARTHUR II

Second child, second son of Chester Alan Arthur and Ellen Lewis Herndon

Born: July 25, 1864   *Birthplace:* New York, New York
Died: July 17, 1937   *Age at Death:* 73 years
Cause of Death: Unknown
Education: Princeton University, Columbia University
Profession: Playboy
Spouses: Myra Townsend Fithian Andrews, Rowena Dashwood Graves
Number of Children: Arthur/Andrews: 1
                      Arthur/Graves: None

PERPETUAL PLAYBOY

Born in New York City, just before the closing battles of the Civil War, Chester Alan Arthur II led a life that closely resembled that of European royalty. His father was on the staff of the governor of New York. His mother, who died shortly before her husband became president, was the daughter of a U.S. Navy officer, Captain William Lewis Herndon, discoverer of the source of the Amazon River headwaters, and came from a socialite background. Even as a young man, Chester Alan was accustomed to the life of a gentleman.

During his father's presidency, Alan, as the young man was called, was a student at Princeton. He disdained the simple life, reveling in luxuries available to him as the president's son. Thus, Alan often used both the president's yacht and his influence. The president, himself fond of titles and wealth, transmitted these characteristics to his children. In an era that often confused stilted formality with elegance, Alan conformed to the popular expectations of a "rake," earning for himself the nickname, "Prince of Washington."

In accordance with his father's wishes, Alan pursued law studies at Columbia University in order that he might eventually take over his father's New York City law firm. Attending his father during his father's final days,

Alan earned for himself an additional title of "presidential papers destroyer" when, following his father's instructions, he filled three garbage cans with his father's personal and official papers and burned them. Though he began the job of destroying all his father's papers, their complete destruction was stopped by the intercession of others.

Upon his father's death, Alan did not return to Columbia, but determined to take a six-month break in Europe. Arriving in Europe the six-foot four-inch, good-looking American rapidly became associated with the "Prince of Wales" set, the "jet set" of the time. Alan took to European high society as if he had been born to it. Not hesitating to trade on his father's office because he was a deceased U.S. president's son, Alan enjoyed all benefits normally reserved for royalty. The attractions of life in the capitals of Europe proved irresistible, and Alan never returned to Columbia to begin the career his father had envisioned. In a sense, Alan's European trip, begun as a six-month mourning period, was not to end until his death, for he would maintain residences both on the Continent and in the United States.

Twice married, the father of one child, Alan's career was the playboy life of polo, parties, and art. In later years, Alan made his home in Colorado, but even there, in the heart of America, he brought Europe with him, for Alan established the game of polo in the city of Cheyenne, Wyoming. Chester Alan Arthur II died in 1937 at the age of seventy-three, having thoroughly enjoyed his "romp" with wine, women, and song.

ELLEN HERNDON ARTHUR PINKERTON

Third child, only daughter of Chester Alan Arthur and Ellen Lewis Herndon

Born: November 21, 1871   *Birthplace:* New York, New York
Died: September 6, 1915   *Age at Death:* 43 years, 10 months
Cause of Death: Surgical complications
Education: Unknown   *Profession:* Housewife
Spouse: Charles Pinkerton
Number of Children: Unknown

A SECRET LIFE

Not yet ten years old when her father unexpectedly became president of the United States following Garfield's assassination, Ellen, called Nell, entered the White House under the care of her aunt, who served as both guardian of Nell and White House hostess to the widowed president.

Nell's life, prior to the White House days, was one of a young girl grow-ing up in a comfortable, upper-middle-class home during the depression-ridden 1870s. There was nothing of note in her pre-White House days, and her father insisted that his child's life remain private. Arthur, socially prom-inent, as well as extraordinarily handsome, was protective of his children, stating, on one occasion at least, "Madame, I may be the President of the United States, but my private life is nobody's damned business."[111] Nell, be-cause of this insistence on privacy, never became the object of massive press attention, and rarely was she even photographed.

Nell married Charles Pinkerton, and the couple, as best is known, lived their married life in upstate New York. Nell's death in 1915 was noted pri-marily for the highly unusual (for the day) medical treatment of blood transfusions employed to save her life, though the developing technology failed and did not save her life.

When Nell Arthur Pinkerton died, so ended the life of one of the most pri-vate of all presidential children.

FOR FURTHER READING

Doenecke, Justus D. *Presidencies of James A. Garfield and Chester A. Arthur*. Lawrence, Kansas: Regents Press of Kansas, 1981.

Kane, Joseph Nathan. *Facts about the Presidents*. New York, New York: The H. W. Wilson Company, 1981.

Reeves, Thomas C. *Gentleman Boss: The Life of Chester Alan Arthur*. New York, New York: Alfred A. Knopf, 1975.

18 GROVER CLEVELAND'S CHILDREN

RUTH CLEVELAND

First child of Grover Cleveland and Frances Folsom

Born: October 3, 1891   *Birthplace:* New York, New York
Died: January 7, 1904   *Age at Death:* 12 years, 3 months
Cause of Death: Diphtheria
Education: Miss Mary Fine's Private School

AMERICA'S SWEETHEART

Ruth Cleveland, the darling of the nation, bounced through the White House during her father's second term as president. Grover Cleveland had been reelected president after a break of four years. When the family entered the White House, Ruth was about one-and-one-half years old. When a third child was born to the Clevelands in the White House, Ruth became the eldest of Cleveland's three children to live in the White House.

Ruth's every move captured the attention of the nation. Her bouncing, blonde babyness was reported regularly in the press, earning for her the title of "Baby Ruth." When Cleveland's second term ended in 1897 and the family moved back to Princeton, New Jersey, where Ruth attended Miss Mary Fine's Private School, the nation continued to love the little girl.

In the very first days of January 1904, the "nation's sweetheart" developed "a mild attack of diphtheria." She was only ill for four days, and the illness was not diagnosed as serious. But "a sudden weakness of the heart, brought on by the diphtheria caused a rapid sinking spell."[112] Almost before her parents and the family doctor realized the critical nature of her illness, she was dead.

Ruth's obituary, carried in the *New York Times*, contained a list of her toys, including a pony and a tan go-cart and a bicycle. Further descriptions told of "rollicking good times" in the White House, as well as referring to the physical strength of her sister, who had fought a serious diphtheria attack the previous year.[113] Ruth's burial was simple and immediate, "owing to the contagious nature of the disease."[114] Miss Mary Fine's Private School closed for the balance of the week in honor of a much-loved student.

There are no photographs of "Baby Ruth" from the later years of her short life because the Clevelands feared the potential harm that might come to their children through public recognition. However, Ruth, "America's sweetheart," was not to be forgotten.

As the result of a 1921 Curtiss Candy Company employee contest, Ruth's nickname has now become known throughout the world as "Baby Ruth," the candy bar. The candy, originally named "Candy Cake," was renamed "Baby Ruth" for promotional purposes in sweet tribute to "America's sweetheart,"[115] Cleveland's eldest daughter, Baby Ruth Cleveland.

ESTHER CLEVELAND BOSANQUET

Second child, second daughter of Grover Cleveland and Frances Folsom

Born: September 9, 1893   *Birthplace:* New York, New York
Died: Unknown   *Age at Death:* Unknown
Cause of Death: Unknown
Education: Unknown   *Profession:* Housewife, Mother
Spouse: William Sydney Bence Bosanquet
Number of Children: 2

BRITISH SOCIETY

Esther, the second of Cleveland's daughters, was born shortly after her father entered the White House for his second term. Her father was a bachelor the first time he was elected to the presidency. In the four years intervening between his first term as president and his second term as president, Cleveland had married and sired a daughter and became the father of a second girl just after his second term began. The nation was delighted that Cleveland had fulfilled himself as a family man.

In 1918 Esther married England's Captain William Sydney Bence Bosanquet, the son of Sir Albert Bosanquet, whose family long represented prominence in British high society. Their wedding took place at no less a site than Westminster Abbey.

Esther and Bosanquet produced two children. No record of social or political prominence concerning this branch of the Bosanquet family is known, other than that Esther's husband died in 1967, leaving a very sizeable estate to the family.

MARION CLEVELAND DELL AMEN

Third child, third daughter of Grover Cleveland and Frances Folsom

Born: July 7, 1895   *Birthplace:* Buzzards Bay, Massachusetts
Died: June 18, 1977   *Age at Death:* 81 years, 11 months
Cause of Death: Unknown
Education: Westover School, Columbia University Teacher's College
Profession: Housewife, Mother, Social Leader
Spouses: William Stanley Dell, John Harlan Amen
Number of Children: Cleveland/Dell: 1
                          Cleveland/Amen: None

CRIME BUSTER'S WIFE

Eighty-one years old when she died in New York City, Marion Cleveland, youngest daughter of Grover Cleveland, had been involved in so many activities in the city that she acquired an admirable reputation as one of that city's social leaders and charity fund raisers.

Graduating from Westover School in 1916, Marion spent two years at Columbia University Teacher's College. Her first marriage was to William Stanley Dell, by whom she had one child, a daughter. In 1926 she married again, this time to the man that soon became one of New York City's more colorful personalities, John Harlan Amen. Though not flamboyant, even described as a bit absent-minded, Amen became the city's leading "racket buster" from 1928 to 1942, as special assistant to the U.S. attorney. It was Amen that began the application of antitrust laws to such diverse interests as corporations and gangsters. Marion's husband continued his public service when, after World War II, he served on the U.S. legal staff at the Nuremburg war crimes trials in Germany.

Marion died at eighty-one years, having outlived her second husband by almost an entire generation. Finally, after only being known as Amen's wife and the president's daughter, Marion managed to gain some measure of fame in her own name for her work and support of many charities.

RICHARD FOLSOM CLEVELAND

Fourth child, first son of Grover Cleveland and Frances Folsom

Born: October 28, 1897   *Birthplace:* Princeton, New Jersey
Died: January 10, 1974   *Age at Death:* 76 years, 3 months
Cause of Death: Unknown
Education: Phillips Exeter Academy, Princeton University, Harvard Law School
Profession: Lawyer
Spouses: Ellen Douglas Gailor, Jessie Maxwell Black
Number of Children: Cleveland/Gailor: 6
                      Cleveland/Black: None

"GROVER, JR."

Richard Folsom Cleveland, Grover's first son, was born after his father had left the White House, while Grover was a Princeton professor. The nation, which had been captivated by the little Cleveland girls during his term in office, expected the son would be named after his prestigious father. In the same expectation the press announced that Grover Cleveland, Jr., had been born. Fooling everybody, Cleveland chose his father's first name for his new son and his much-loved wife's maiden name for his son's middle name. Cleveland had always felt that the name "Grover" was a bother and refused to inflict the name on his newborn son. Despite Grover's best intentions the boy was often referred to in newspapers as "Grover, Jr."

Dick, as he was called by his friends and family, attended college preparatory school at Exeter, and later entered Princeton University. His mother, who remarried following her husband's death, chose a Princeton professor as Dick's stepfather.

At college Dick played football and participated in track events and was an extremely popular student. But Dick also had a serious side which emerged when he took part in the movement against the exclusive club system at Princeton, a battle which soon brought fame to Woodrow Wilson, then president of Princeton.

In June 1917, with the United States at war with the central powers, Dick left college to enlist in the Marine Corps, rising through the ranks to first lieutenant. After the war Dick returned to Princeton and graduated with a bachelor's degree in 1919. By 1921 he held his master's degree, also from Princeton.

The normal path of a well-to-do man provided the pattern for Dick when he took a vacation in Europe, met and married a socially acceptable bride, a graduate of both Vassar and Columbia, and, finally, studied law at Harvard and was admitted to the Maryland bar, becoming associated with a large Baltimore law firm.

Dick was often mentioned as a possible mayoral candidate, or for the position of the U.S. attorney, and even suggested for the vice-presidency, simply on the basis of his name. He refused all such suggestions, preferring to work for the Democratic party, though periodically accepting appointive Maryland state offices. Initially supporting Franklin Delano Roosevelt in 1932, by 1936 Dick had changed his mind and vigorously opposed the re-election of Roosevelt and the continuation of the New Deal. But by 1942 Dick and the party leaders were reconciled, and he received various appointments to government commissions dealing with the problems of young people, especially juvenile delinquency and education. Dick died in 1974 and is remembered today as a successful man, a good father, and a leader in his Baltimore community.

FRANCIS GROVER CLEVELAND

Fifth child, second son of Grover Cleveland and Frances Folsom

Born: July 18, 1903   *Birthplace:* Buzzards Bay, Massachusetts
Died: Unknown   *Age at Death:* Unknown
Cause of Death: Unknown
Education: Phillips Exeter Academy, Harvard University
Profession: Teacher, Actor
Spouse: Alice Erdman
Number of Children: 1

STAGESTRUCK

Born in Buzzards Bay, Massachusetts, the last of the five Cleveland children, his father had already reached the advanced age of sixty-six, and Francis was only five years old when his father died.

Francis grew up under the direction of his mother's second husband, Thomas J. Preston, Jr., a Princeton professor. As a young man Francis went to Exeter Academy and then on to Harvard with the class of 1925, though he did not graduate that year as he married instead. Francis studied drama, and though he taught at a private school, drama was his real love. This passion eventually led him to the stage, where he became a self-described actor, even appearing in a New York stage show.

At this juncture, entering what would seem the most public time of his life, Francis is lost to press coverage.

OSCAR CLEVELAND

Supposed illegitimate son of Grover Cleveland and Maria Crofts Halpin

Born: Unknown   *Birthplace:* Buffalo, New York
Died: Unknown   *Age at Death:* Unknown
Cause of Death: Unknown   *Education:* Unknown
Profession: Unknown   *Spouse:* Unknown
Number of Children: Unknown

DIRTY POLITICS

The legitimacy of Oscar Cleveland, his parentage, and the conditions of his birth became a major topic in the 1884 presidential election, when Democrat Grover Cleveland, a bachelor, was accused of fathering an illegitimate child.

The story began when Grover, a sheriff in New York state, met thirty-five-year-old widow Maria Crofts Halpin from New Jersey. He and his friends, the self-styled "rowdy reefers" (named in reference to fishing rather than "pot"), established a relationship with the newly arrived Maria in Buffalo. What the exact relationship was became a matter of discussion, for Maria claimed that Grover was the father of her baby boy, even giving the child the last name of Cleveland to indicate paternity. Maria demanded Grover marry her and legitimize her son. Grover considered the idea, but, according to his own later explanations, he was not sure the child was his, though he did not deny paternity and did periodically contribute to the support of both child and mother.

Within a year of the birth of her child, Maria became a heavy drinker and was committed to an asylum for a short time. Grover decided that, given the condition of Maria, the boy's future was questionable. What was needed was a normal family setting, and so Grover contributed $5 per week for the boy's care to an orphanage until such time as the boy was adopted. Sometime between 1875 and 1876 the boy was adopted by a prosperous Buffalo, New York, family who promised to educate the boy into a professional career.

Released from the asylum, Maria turned to Grover for money. She recognized that he had the potential for power and she felt he had a duty to compensate her. She requested that he set her up in business, which he did, loaning her $500, but the business failed. Maria then disappeared from Grover's life, only to reappear after Grover Cleveland had reached his first presidency.

During Cleveland's campaign for the presidency the first time, the illicit relationship of Grover and Maria emerged as a major issue. Cleveland was assailed by his opponent's (James Blaine) organizers as the father of an illegitimate child. Blaine's supporters invented the delightful ditty, "Ma Ma, where's my pa? Gone to the White House . . . ha ha ha!" as a campaign issue questioning Cleveland's morality.

Two years before the end of his first term, Cleveland was confronted by Maria, who demanded money, threatening that if it was not forthcoming, she would reveal more embarrassing facts to the public, thus ruining Cleveland's future in public life. Cleveland ignored the threat.

Oscar Cleveland's place in history is at the center of one of the most degrading presidential campaigns conducted by major political parties. The episode definitively illustrates the well-known political maxim that, if there is no valid issue, "sling mud." But in this case, the dirty work did not work. Cleveland was elected not only once, but would again return to the presidency after several years.

Though unsubstantiated, there have been periodicals of later days which stated that the supposed illegitimate son of Grover Cleveland by Maria Halpin died while in his late twenties of alcoholism, unable to face the origins of his birth.

FOR FURTHER READING

Leitch, Alexander. *Princeton Companion*. Princeton, New Jersey: Princeton University Press, 1978.

Miller, Hope Ridings. *Scandals in the Highest Office*. New York, New York: Random House, 1973.

Wallace, Irving. *Intimate Sex Lives of Famous People*. New York, New York: Delacorte Press, 1981.

19 BENJAMIN HARRISON'S CHILDREN

RUSSELL BENJAMIN HARRISON

First child of Benjamin Harrison and Caroline Lavinia Scott

Born: August 12, 1854   *Birthplace:* Oxford, Ohio
Died: December 13, 1936   *Age at Death:* 82 years, 4 months
Cause of Death: Unknown
Education: Military school, Lafayette College
Profession: Businessman, Engineer, Politician
Spouse: Mary Angeline Saunders
Number of Children: 2

VERSATILITY

Russell Benjamin Harrison, born in Oxford, Ohio, the son of an army officer, was six years old when the Civil War began, and observed later that "I was too young to know the causes which led to the war, and the great forces which were the factors in the intellectual struggle which preceded it, but I was in the Army [in later years] for a time, and I know what it all meant."[116] Russell's early schooling was at a military academy, and he completed his education at Lafayette College, in Easton, Pennsylvania, receiving an engineering degree at the age of twenty-three.

After graduation Russell traveled to his family's Indiana home and obtained a job as an engineer with the local gas and light company. After a brief time, Russell was appointed as assistant assayer of the U.S. Mint at New Orleans. He married influential Republican Senator Saunders's daughter, Mary (called Mamie), and then the newlyweds moved to Helena, Montana. Russell was appointed to the position of assistant U.S. treasurer, a position he held for eight years. Becoming involved in the cattle business in his adopted state, Montana, Russell was appointed as secretary of that state's Board of Stock Commissioners, and he acquired a financial interest in a cattle journal, eventually becoming its executive officer. But Russell's association with the journal brought more problems than credit when the publication was sued for libel over a number of articles. Criticism of his handling of the journal largely revolved around his inexpertise. Inexperience also characterized Russell's ventures into stock and feed, as well as his new publishing venture, the *Helena Daily Journal*, none of which were financial successes.

In 1889 Russell's father was inaugurated as president of the United States. During periodic visits to his father at the White House, Russell established a lasting friendship with a developing political figure, Teddy Roosevelt. The friendship was based on their mutual love of the West. It was a relationship that would stand Russell in good stead in future years. In 1890 Russell permanently moved to Washington, D.C., to become his father's official White House aide and then his secretary. Russell's wife, Mamie, took over the direction of White House social affairs as the president's wife was seriously ill. There was talk that his new financial success, coinciding with his Washington appointment, was not entirely due to economy and shrewd management, as his business ventures prior to the move had not shown a high level of business acumen. Nevertheless, in 1891, Russell became a major stockholder of a railroad, holding in excess of $500,000 worth of its stock. The *New York Times* suggested that some fraud was involved in the president's son's finances, but the accusations were dropped when no evidence was brought forward to prove that he had received stock in exchange for presidential favors. With new money, The Harrisons' life-style changed, and they sported a wardrobe that became the talk of the social set. "Where did the money come from?" questioned the press. Defenders said that it was natural for Russell to acquire information that allowed him to make judicious investments, and Russell even said that he was not aware that certain men of property were investing in his name; thus, he claimed, he received stocks without direct involvement in the financial affairs.

Russell's wife continued as the White House hostess during President Harrison's term, as Harrison's wife died of her lingering illness before his term was ended. During Harrison's unsuccessful election bid, the president, Russell, and his wife, as well as the president's wife's niece, all set out on a campaign swing. On the trip a certain fondness between niece and uncle-in-law blossomed and eventually led to marriage. Father and son became estranged over both the speed and the circumstances of the president's marriage.

From presidential secretary Russell became president of a street car company in Terre Haute, Indiana, where he stayed until the onset of the Spanish-American War in 1898. Commissioned as a major, Russell's most important command was that of the suburbs of Havana, Cuba, supervising evacuation of the Spanish troops after the war. Promoted to the rank of lieutenant colonel, Russell was made inspector general of the territory surrounding Santiago, Cuba, until his discharge in 1899 following a bout with yellow fever.

Russell, educated in engineering, drawn to journalism, and thrust into politics and business by his father's position, switched to the practice of law in Indiana after the end of his father's term. Among his clients was the Mexican government, and he became counsel for Mexico in Indiana, a position he held for twenty years, even while carrying on all of his other business interests and during his membership in the Indiana state legislature. Serving in both the House and the Senate of the Indiana legislature, his service also included chairmanship of the judiciary committees.

Extending a helpful hand to fellow veterans of the Spanish-American War, Russell was responsible for the appropriation of $1,000 for the organization of Spanish-American War veterans to stage an encampment. He later discovered that one-third of the $1,000 had been used to purchase jeweled medals for past commanders of the veterans' group. Outraged, Russell charged the veterans' organization with misappropriation of funds. For their part, the officials responded by calling him to appear before them to uphold his charges. Russell was able to defend himself from the charges and won his case. But in reality Russell lost the case, for he offended many of the state's leading citizens, and for the rest of his life he would suffer the social ostracism America reserves for those who offend upstanding members of society.

Russell's death at age eighty-two was barely noticed, as it coincided with the "hoopla" attached to the resignation of the British king, who left the throne for the love of a divorced American woman.

MARY SCOTT HARRISON MCKEE

Second child, only daughter of Benjamin Harrison and Caroline Lavinia Scott

Born: April 3, 1858   *Birthplace:* Indianapolis, Indiana
Died: October 28, 1930   *Age at Death:* 72 years, 6 months
Cause of Death: Unknown
Education: Private school, college   *Profession:* Housewife, Mother
Spouse: James Robert McKee
Number of Children: 2

A WHITE HOUSE BEAUTY

The beauty of Mary Scott Harrison McKee, eldest daughter of Benjamin Harrison, was said to rival that of other noted White House beauties, Dolley Madison, Lucy Hayes, and Frances Folsom Cleveland. Mary entered the White House when she was a widow with two children and became one of the celebrated hostesses during her mother's illness and following her mother's death. It was Mary, called Mamie, who introduced the custom of a White House Christmas tree. She wanted to introduce a home-like atmosphere into the mansion for her children's sake, and so she initiated the tradition which continues today.

Mamie began her life in Indianapolis. Her father, who was in his twenties when she was born, had to struggle to support not only his own two children, but also his four younger brothers and sisters. Under the financial strain of tending to all his burdens, Benjamin Harrison suffered a brief mental and physical collapse. However, her father's illness did not hinder Mary's education, for she remained in private school, regardless of cost, and even took private dancing lessons at home.

Entering college just as her father was coming into national prominence in the Republican party, Mamie's first introduction to the White House was as a guest of President Hayes, who invited the Harrison family to visit in gratitude for Benjamin's support. In 1881 Harrison became a Republican senator from Indiana, from which position he ascended to the White House. When the family moved to Washington, D.C., Mamie was her mother's nurse and constant companion during the illness from which her mother never recovered.

While in Washington, D.C., during her father's term as senator, Mamie maintained contact with her "boyfriend," James McKee, in Indianapolis, marrying him in 1884. Her father was elated when she gave birth to a boy, who was named Ben in honor of his grandfather.

By the time her father was elected to the presidency in 1888, Mamie was a widow. She moved to the White House with her two children to act as White House hostess. Victorian elegance and pretension were well mated to the explosive industrialization of this era in America. Mamie, her children, and the White House sparkled even in this most glittering, gaudy, and arrogant high society.

In his second campaign for the presidency, the widowed Harrison took his daughter with him on his campaign tour. The Harrison group also included her brother, and various other campaign associates, as well as Harrison's ward and Mamie's cousin, recently widowed Mary Scott Lord Dimmick, the woman that would take the place of Mamie's mother—much to Mamie's chagrin.

Mamie's disapproval of her father's second marriage in 1894 to his ward was never to abate, and years later her relationship with both stepmother and a stepsister were, at best, cursory. Mamie was survived eighteen years by her stepmother.

ELIZABETH HARRISON WALKER

Third child of Benjamin Harrison, only child of Benjamin Harrison and Mary Scott Lord Dimmick

Born: February 21, 1897   *Birthplace:* Indianapolis, Indiana
Died: December 26, 1955   *Age at Death:* 58 years, 10 months
Cause of Death: Unknown
Education: Westover School, New York University Law School
Profession: Lawyer, Writer, Businesswoman, TV and Radio Personality
Spouse: James Blaine Walker
Number of Children: Unknown

A TWENTIETH-CENTURY WOMAN

Born in Indianapolis following her father's presidency, the only child of Benjamin's second marriage, Elizabeth knew her father only a short time as he died before she was five. Her mother, Mary Scott Lord Dimmick, the former ward of Benjamin Harrison, was still a young woman and took her daughter on travels throughout Europe until her remarriage.

Elizabeth acquired an education that was exceptional even for males of the day. Graduating Westover School, she earned a bachelor's degree in both science and law, as well as earning a law degree from New York University Law School, eventually becoming a member of state bars in both New York and Indiana, all by 1919. In 1921 Elizabeth married the grand-nephew of her father's secretary of state, James Blaine Walker. The couple became prominent members of high society.

Elizabeth, a forerunner of today's liberated women, founded a monthly news service for women, "Cues on the News," which gave economic advice and investment tips to women. Eventually, Elizabeth's reputation grew and brought her an appointment to a national, all-male commission for economic development. Toward the end of her life Elizabeth was seen and heard frequently on television and radio, dispensing advice and commentary on economic issues, particularly those that affected women.

Only fifty-eight years old when she died in 1955, this president's daughter may well be ranked with such women as Eleanor Roosevelt, Helen Taft Manning, and Margaret Chase Smith, whose accumulated efforts were the foundation of the modern feminist movement.

FOR FURTHER READING

Beard, Charles. *Presidents in American History*. New York, New York: Julian A. Messner, 1981.

Kane, Joseph Nathan. *Facts about the Presidents*. New York, New York: The H. W. Wilson Company, 1981.

Van Steenwyk, Elizabeth. *Presidents at Home*. New York, New York: Julian A. Messner, 1980.

20 WILLIAM MCKINLEY'S CHILDREN

KATHERINE AND IDA MCKINLEY

Only two children of William McKinley and Ida Saxton

Born: Katherine: December 25, 1871
       Ida: April 1, 1873
Birthplace: Canton, Ohio
Died: Katherine: June 25, 1875
      Ida: August 22, 1873
Age at Death: Katherine: 3 years, 6 months
          Ida: 5 months
Cause of Death: Katherine: Typhoid fever
          Ida: Unknown

ENTWINED TRAGEDIES

The lives of the only two children of President William McKinley and his wife are so closely entwined that to speak of one is also to speak of the other.

The eldest of the daughters, Katherine, was born on Christmas Day when her father was a Canton, Ohio, lawyer. "Katie," as she was called, soon became the apple of her daddy's eye. In return Katie worshipped her father. But it was her mother, Ida, who smothered her with love until the birth of a second McKinley daughter.

The second McKinley, named Ida in honor of her mother, was born in the spring of 1873 following a difficult delivery. The difficulty of the birth left a physical imprint on her mother who suffered for the rest of her life with phlebitis and a nervous illness, as well as epilepsy. Little Ida died after only five months, and her mother was so disturbed by the death that she was never the same again.

After the infant Ida's death, the mother lavished on Katherine an all-consuming love reflected in her protectiveness and jealousy. Spending days in bed, in a state of depression, Ida wondered why God had placed such a punishment upon her. She demanded that both her husband and remaining daughter constantly shower her with displays of love and affection. Such was the extent of the mother's psychological needs that husband and child had to guard against displays of mutual affection, so the mother would not become jealous. Above all, Ida feared the loss of her firstborn. As in some melodrama of the day, the fear that haunted Ida came true. At three and one half, Katie died of typhoid fever.

Ida McKinley was shattered mentally and physically. Invalided for the rest of her life, she came to devote her entire being to her husband. In turn, McKinley lavished upon her the devotion, concern, and solicitude that might otherwise have been shared by his children. McKinley's public displays of affection for his wife, which so much endeared him to the American public, in large measure resulted from the death of Ida McKinley, his daughter who died so young.

Thus, it was the deaths of the McKinleys' only two children that brought the husband and wife closer together, and it was the public's perception of the loving couple that was the source of so much approval.

But the happy ending so often resolving the problems in a melodrama was not to be. Ida's husband William McKinley was assassinated, leaving the chronically ill woman to survive her husband by almost six years. Despite the heights to which William McKinley had risen, underlying all was the tragedy of childhood deaths and devastating illness.

FOR FURTHER READING

Gould, Lewis L. *Presidency of William McKinley*. Lawrence, Kansas: Regents Press of Kansas, 1980.

Morgan, H. Wayne. *McKinley and His America*. Syracuse, New York: Syracuse University Press, 1963.

Moses, John B., and Wilbur Cross. *Presidential Courage*. New York, New York: W. W. Norton, 1980.

Whitney, David C. *American Presidents*. New York, New York: Doubleday, 1978.

21 THEODORE ROOSEVELT'S CHILDREN

ALICE LEE ROOSEVELT LONGWORTH

Only child of Theodore Roosevelt and Alice Lee Hathaway

Born: February 12, 1884   *Birthplace:* New York, New York
Died: February 20, 1980   *Age at Death:* 96 years
Cause of Death: Unknown   *Education:* Private tutors
Profession: Housewife, Mother   *Spouse:* Nicholas Longworth
Number of Children: 1

IRASCIBLE ALICE

The woman who would become the "grande dame" of Washington, D.C., society was born in New York City to Teddy Roosevelt and his first wife, Alice Hathaway. As her mother died soon after Alice's birth, she was brought up by her father's second wife, Edith. Alice was seventeen years old when her father became president of the United States following the assassination of President McKinley in 1901.

Alice, a female version of the "man about town," was far in advance of her time. Independent, enthusiastic, and always in search of the new, Alice established herself in the public eye with such acts as her regular appearance in an open touring car, watching practice take-offs of the new "aeroplane" and dispensing alcoholic drinks to her companions and to whomever struck her fancy.

Unwilling to play second fiddle to her father, Alice, who married the thirty-six-year-old Ohio congressman, Nicholas Longworth, refused to have a traditional White House wedding. Dressed in her blue wedding gown, dramatically cutting the wedding cake with a sweep of a sword, Alice would not allow her father to upstage her at her own wedding, proclaiming, "My father always wants to be the corpse at every funeral, the bride at every wedding, and the baby at every christening."[117]

As the wife of a congressman, a man who became a powerful speaker of the House of Representatives, Alice became a leader of Washington society. Even after her husband's death in 1936 she continued her residence in Washington, D.C., and she continued to capture the imagination of America's public and press. Alice was more than a mere party giver, she was an acknowledged wit—a wit that became ever more sharp as she grew older. Her penetrating barbs were long remembered and often were so apt as to remain stuck to whomever was her target. Thus, Alice, who had met every president since the late 1880s president, Benjamin Harrison, described Harding as "a slob," Coolidge as "looking as if he had been weaned on a pickle," and presidential candidate Dewey as "looking as if he were a bridegroom atop a wedding cake . . . about to fall off." Fielding questions from the press on her eightieth birthday, Alice took full credit for calling them as she saw them. "I'm just a kindly amiable old thing. . . . If anyone takes that seriously, hah. . . . My specialty is detached malevolence."[118] One of her more famous remarks was, "If you haven't got anything nice to say about anybody, come, sit next to me."[119] Shortly before her health began to fade, well advanced in age, Alice was interviewed and said, "I don't think I'm insensitive or cruel. I laugh. I have a sense of humor. I like to tease. I must admit a sense of mischief does get hold of me from time to time. I'm a hedonist. I have an appetite for being entertained. Isn't it strange how that upsets people?"[120]

A widow of more than forty years, her only daughter dying at the age of thirty-one, Alice was survived by her granddaughter, her close and constant companion of later years. The ninety-six-year-old woman was a charmer to the end, and her barbs only hurt those whose skin was too thin and whose wit was too dull.

THEODORE ROOSEVELT, JR.

Second child of Theodore Roosevelt; first child of Theodore Roosevelt and Edith Carow

Born: September 13, 1887   *Birthplace:* Oyster Bay, New York
Died: July 12, 1944   *Age at Death:* 56 years, 10 months
Cause of Death: Heart attack
Education: Groton Preparatory School, Harvard University
Profession: Businessman, Politician, Soldier, Author
Spouse: Eleanor Butler Alexander
Number of Children: Unknown

A HERO OF BOTH WARS

As a father, Teddy Roosevelt was as equally demanding of his sons as he was of himself. Thus, it was that after sending his eldest son to Groton, the traditional Roosevelt preparatory school, and to Harvard University, Teddy sent Teddy, Jr., to learn business from the ground up. Like any other workman carrying his dinner pail, Teddy, Jr., worked in a carpet mill for a year until he was promoted to sales work.

What could be more natural for the sons of "Rough Rider" Teddy Roosevelt, hero of the Spanish-American War, than that they should be leaders of America's forces in the First World War? Thus, Teddy, Sr., who saw that America must be drawn into the European conflict, inspired all of his sons to enroll in military training for officers. The father's plans for his sons were realized when, following the predicted entry of America into the European conflict, Teddy, Jr., was promoted to lieutenant colonel and served in France at the battle of the Argonne Forest. Gassed in 1918, Ted was awarded the Distinguished Service Medal and the Distinguished Service Cross, as well as being decorated by several allied nations for gallantry.

Returning to the United States after the war, Ted ran for the New York Assembly in 1919. In response to the contention that he was running on his father's name, Ted replied, "My hat's in the ring too . . . and it isn't my father's."[121] From this beginning in politics, Ted's next step was an appointment by President Harding as assistant secretary of the navy, a position that was to involve young Ted in scandalous politics. The Teapot Dome scandals of the Harding administration concerned bribery and illegal payoffs, as well as the transfer of oil lands which had been set apart as the navy's strategic reserve in case of war, to avaricious high level government officials and, particularly, a petroleum magnate. Ted, himself, was never accused of any direct wrong doing. But the question arose as to how the assistant secretary of the navy did not detect the oil lease conspiracy in his department. Undaunted by his proximity to the scandal, Ted decided to run for the position of governor of New York against Democrat Al Smith. Naturally, Smith did not hesitate to recall to his audiences Ted's association with the Teapot Dome scandals, and Ted was soundly defeated in the election.

His father's son, the defeated Ted took his wife and went off to India and the Far East, later recounting his adventures in a book. There was a new president, Calvin Coolidge, when Ted returned to the United States. What could be more logical than Ted being appointed governor of Puerto Rico by Coolidge? Senate confirmation was rapid. From Puerto Rico, Ted's next appointment, by yet another Republican president, Herbert Hoover, was as governor general of the Philippine Islands. Upon the election of Democratic cousin, Franklin, the presidential appointments ceased, forcing Ted back into the comparative calm of the business world. Teddy heartily disliked his cousin and swore to keep the Republican Roosevelts separate from the liberal Roosevelts.

It was the second world war that again drew Ted from obscurity into a vortex of military action. With the rank of brigadier general, Ted was placed in command of the Twenty-sixth infantry which was his old unit from World War I. He served first in Africa and then in Italy. But it was in the Normandy landing, while the world waited, that Teddy entered the spotlight as commander of a division landing on the French coast.

Teddy, Jr., died during the Second World War. The public assumption, in line with the Roosevelt aura of "dying with their boots on," was that he died in combat. The truth is that, Teddy, exhausted from the rigors of battle, returned to London after the Normandy invasion. In July 1944 he died in his sleep. Posthumously, Teddy was awarded the Congressional Medal of Honor.

KERMIT ROOSEVELT

Third child of Theodore Roosevelt; second child, second son of Theodore Roosevelt and Edith Carow

Born: October 10, 1889   *Birthplace:* Oyster Bay, New York
Died: June 4, 1943   *Age at Death:* 53 years, 8 months
Cause of Death: Amoebic dysentery?
Education: Groton Preparatory School, Harvard University
Profession: Businessman, Executive, Soldier
Spouse: Belle Wyatt Willand
Number of Children: 4

FDR'S FISHING BUDDY

Beginning his life at Oyster Bay, on New York's Long Island, Kermit attended Groton Preparatory School and earned his bachelor's degree while his father was running for the presidency under the 1912 Bull Moose party banner.

Shortly after Kermit's father had left his almost two terms as president, Kermit traveled with the elder Roosevelt on big-game hunts in Africa for almost a year. On later trips, Teddy introduced Kermit to South America, and the two explored the area extensively, including forages into the wild and uncharted river country. Like his father, Kermit enjoyed the strenuous life, but very much unlike his father and his brothers, Kermit had little interest in politics. It was due to these travels that upon Kermit's completion of his schooling, he chose to go to South America to work in both engineering and banking.

Well before the United States became a party to the First World War, Kermit advocated America's involvement. But Kermit could not wait for the United States to enter the war, and when the British forces in Mesopotamia and Palestine offered Kermit a captain's rank, he jumped at the opportunity. For his service he was awarded the British Military Cross. When the United States entered the war, Kermit transferred to the U.S. field artillery, beginning a long experience with machine guns. Of all of the Roosevelt sons, Kermit was the only one to escape injury in World War I.

After the war, Kermit became an executive for a steamship line, and, in time, he formed his own Roosevelt Steamship Line, eventually merging with the International Mercantile Marine Company, of which he became vice-president, serving until his 1938 resignation.

Aware that war was imminent on the continent between Great Britain and Germany, Kermit went to Great Britain in September 1939 and joined the British army as a major, specializing in machine gun operations. Kermit was involved in the Norwegian campaign in 1940, then he was assigned to Egypt. Not bullets, but disease felled this old soldier and ended his service with the British army. In Egypt he contracted amoebic dysentery and was sent back to England, in time forced to resign from the British army and return to the United States to cure his illness. After treatment for almost two years, Kermit was pronounced cured and immediately joined the American army, receiving the rank of major. Assigned to intelligence, he was transferred to Alaska where he died from what the Army described as "natural causes."

Of the five Republican Roosevelt children, Kermit was the only one to establish cordial relations with his cousin, Democratic President Franklin Roosevelt, even spending time on fishing expeditions with the president. Kermit, like his father, was not a man of mean and narrow temperament.

ETHEL CAROW ROOSEVELT DERBY

Fourth child of Theodore Roosevelt; third child, only daughter of Theodore Roosevelt and Edith Carow

Born: August 13, 1891   *Birthplace:* Oyster Bay, New York
Died: December 10, 1977   *Age at Death:* 86 years, 4 months
Cause of Death: Unknown   *Education:* Private tutors
Profession: Housewife, Mother   *Spouse:* Richard Derby
Number of Children: 4

AMBULANCE ROUGH RIDER

Ethel Carow, the only daughter born to Teddy and his second wife, grew up in the Roosevelt compound at Oyster Bay, New York. When Ethel was ten years old her father became president upon the assassination of President McKinley. Described as a character, though tame in comparison to her half-sister Alice, Ethel was constantly in competition with her two older and two younger brothers. The liveliness of these children appealed to the American public and they took the Roosevelt children to heart with enthusiasm.

By the time she had become a teenager, Ethel was described as a perfect little lady, even a Sunday school teacher. In 1913 Ethel married a physician ten years her senior. While her father's repeated offers to lead Rough Riders in combat against the Germans in World War I were refused, Ethel and her husband took part in the war as working members of the American Ambulance Hospital in Paris.

Ethel and her husband had four children, several of whom became involved in politics in later years, and Ethel, ever the party stalwart, reappeared on the national political stage when, in 1960, she made the Republican party's seconding speech for Richard Milhous Nixon's nomination as that year's Republican presidential candidate.

ARCHIBALD BULLOCH ROOSEVELT

Fifth child of Theodore Roosevelt; fourth child, third son of Theodore Roosevelt and Edith Carow

Born: April 9, 1894   *Birthplace:* Washington, D.C.
Died: July 29, 1981   *Age at Death:* 87 years, 3 months
Cause of Death: Stroke
Education: Groton Preparatory School, Harvard University
Profession: Banker, Soldier
Spouse: Grace Stackpole Lockwood
Number of Children: 4

ANOTHER ROOSEVELT CONSERVATIONIST

Archie, the fourth of Teddy Roosevelt's children with his second wife, Edith Carow, fought in both world wars, and was an avid American patriot and Republican party supporter throughout his long life.

Graduating from Harvard in 1914, he attended an officer training school with his brothers just prior to America's entry into World War I. Rising to the rank of captain in the army, Archie was awarded the *Croix de Guerre* by the French and was severely wounded when saving the lives of three of his men under enemy fire. His father, Teddy, was not immediately told of the full extent of Archie's wounds, which were a knee and arm shattered by bullets. His father, with an enthusiasm not dampened by comprehension of the extent of his son's wounds, expressed undiminished enthusiasm for Archie's valor and for the righteousness of the war.

Undaunted by wounds that plagued him long after the war's end, Archie, well into his forties, convinced the army to take him on active service during World War II. Serving as a lieutenant colonel and batallion commander in New Guinea, Archie was again wounded and again distinguished himself, earning the Silver Star with Oak Leaf Cluster.

Archie's business career began after World War I, when he established a bond company, and ended with his move to Florida where he was a bank chairman of the board. Following his father's example in peace as well as war, Archie was an avid conservationist, becoming a member of the Boone and Crockett Club, which his father had founded in the late 1800s.

Later years saw Archie extremely concerned with the Communist threat to America. In testimony before the House un-American activities committee, he described the extensive infiltration (as he understood it) of the Communists into all levels of American life. At eighty-seven, the last surviving son of Teddy Roosevelt, Archie died in his Florida home from complications of a stroke.

QUENTIN ROOSEVELT

Sixth child of Theodore Roosevelt; fifth child, fourth son of Theodore Roosevelt and Edith Carow

Born: November 19, 1897   *Birthplace:* Washington, D.C.
Died: July 14, 1918   *Age at Death:* 20 years, 5 months
Cause of Death: War Casualty
Education: Groton Preparatory School   *Profession:* Pilot
Spouse: None
Number of Children: None

WORLD WAR I CASUALTY

Quentin Roosevelt was four years old when his father succeeded to the presidency following the assassination of President William McKinley in 1901. Quentin and his brother, Archie, earned a well-deserved reputation for White House pranks. Thus, on one occasion he and Archie somehow managed to transport a massive snowball onto the White House balcony, whereupon they ceremoniously dumped it onto their father as he exited with a guest. Typically, Teddy found the entire episode uproariously funny.

Quentin attended public schools in Washington, D.C., and Alexandria, Virginia, while his father was president. In 1917, when the United States entered the first world war, Quentin enlisted in the army. Fascinated by the new weapon, "aeroplanes," Quentin managed to become a superintendent of an airfield used to train flyers for combat. Taking lessons while managing the field, Quentin qualified as an aviator and went to France to fight the Germans.

In July 1918, Quentin was shot down. General Pershing, commander of the American Expeditionary Force in France, informed the former president that his youngest son had been killed in action. Teddy's war, the Spanish-American War, described by an American secretary of state as the "splendid little war," had brought glory, renown, and even the presidency. His son's war was the greatest horror the human race had thus far inflicted upon itself, and Quentin became one of the more than 8.5 million young men to be sacrificed.

FOR FURTHER READING

Blum, John Morton. *Progressive Presidents*. New York, New York: W. W. Norton, 1980.

Burnham, Sophy. *The Landed Gentry: Passions and Personalities Inside America's Propertied Class*. New York, New York: G. P. Putnam's Sons, 1978.

Churchill, Allen. *The Roosevelts: American Aristocrats*. New York, New York: Harper & Row, 1965.

Conrad, P. Roosevelt. *Great American Families*. New York, New York: W. W. Norton, 1977.

Egloff, Franklin R. *Theodore Roosevelt: An American Portrait*. New York, New York: Vantage Press, 1980.

Hess, Stephen. *America's Political Dynasties*. New York, New York: Doubleday & Company, Inc., 1966.

Miller, Nathan. *Roosevelt Chronicles*. New York, New York: Doubleday & Company, Inc., 1966.

Morris, Edmund. *Rise of Theodore Roosevelt*. New York, New York: Coward, McCann, 1979.

22 WILLIAM HOWARD TAFT'S CHILDREN

ROBERT ALPHONSO TAFT

First child of William Howard Taft and Helen Herron

Born: September 8, 1889   *Birthplace:* Cincinnati, Ohio
Died: July 31, 1953   *Age at Death:* 63 years, 10 months
Cause of Death: Cancer
Education: Harvard University, Yale University
Profession: Lawyer, Politician
Spouse: Martha Wheaton Bowers
Number of Children: 4

"MR. REPUBLICAN"

It was Robert's sister, Helen, who observed that Robert had wanted to become president of the United States since his attendance of his own father's inauguration in 1909. This son of William Howard Taft made three unsuccessful bids for the Republican presidential nomination.

Robert, the eldest of the Taft children, was educated at both Yale and Harvard, and graduated with the class's highest honors in 1913. He became a lawyer, but the practice of law did not satisfy this Taft. Robert set his sights on the presidency. Beginning his political career in 1920, Robert was elected to the Ohio House of Representatives, where he served three terms, the final term as speaker. From the Ohio House, Taft's political career advanced to the U.S. Senate. Robert Taft had foresight when he married Martha Bowers, a woman who possessed the social skills to complement Robert's political acumen. The political team of "Bob and Martha" was successful in electing Bob to the Senate in 1938 and thereafter until his death.

During his service in the Roosevelt Democratic Congress, Taft earned the identity of "Mr. Republican," because of his strong and vociferous opposition to the social programs of the New Deal. While in the Senate, Taft became the titular head of the Republican party. In 1947 he sponsored the Taft-Hartley bill, which replaced restrictions on organized labor. Despite this pro-business approach, he was considered by some a "middle-of-the-roader," for he also supported education and low-cost housing for the poor. "Mr. Republican" is also credited as one of the formative forces in the political education of the future Democratic president, Lyndon Baines Johnson.

Only two years after his election to the Senate, Bob Taft competed for the Republican nomination for the presidency. Out of that 1940 Republican convention came not the name of Robert Taft, but that of Wendell Willkie, a man who seemed even less likely than Taft to secure the nomination. A second bid for the presidential nomination came in 1948. Again, despite Taft's Senate experience and the name he had made for himself, he failed to capture the enthusiasm of the convention. The nomination was handed to New York's governor, Thomas E. Dewey. Taft's third and final attempt to fulfill his youthful dream of becoming president came in 1952. Unfortunately for Taft his competition was the war hero, Dwight Eisenhower. In contrast to Eisenhower's warmth and fatherly bearing, Taft appeared aloof and cold and more of a political machine than a flesh-and-blood leader of men.

Taft died of cancer in 1953, shortly after his wife, Martha, had suffered a stroke. He died at the very time when a Republican Congress was elected along with a Republican president, and when he was the acknowledged leader of the Republican Congress. Taft's untimely death was mourned by millions of Americans, both Republican and Democrat. Many have thought that his loss to the Republican party was a severe setback to cooperation between Congress and the president.

If there was anything that Taft stood for in the minds of many Americans, it was his idea of a balanced budget. Others mouthed the phrase; Taft, as in everything he did, meant it.

HELEN HERRON TAFT MANNING

Second child, only daughter of William Howard Taft and Helen Herron

Born: August 1, 1891   *Birthplace:* Cincinnati, Ohio
Education: Bryn Mawr, Yale University
Profession: Professor, Dean, College President
Spouse: Frederick Johnson Manning
Number of Children: 2

A LADY PROFESSOR

Regarded as frank and highly intelligent by all who knew her, and considered more liberal than her parents, Helen Herron Taft pursued a career uncommon to women of her day. Beginning her education in the Philippines where her father was governor general, she continued her education at the exclusive girl's school, Bryn Mawr, when the family returned from the Philippines. As an outspoken leader of the junior class, Helen set a pattern she would follow throughout her life, that of strongly but quietly speaking her mind to anyone that would listen.

In 1917, at the age of twenty-five, Helen was made acting dean of Bryn Mawr. In 1928 she was made acting president, and shortly thereafter she became that school's president. Considered a strong administrator as well as an excellent history professor, Helen had earned a Ph.D. for her study, "British Colonial Government after the American Revolution: 1782–1820."

Helen married Frederick J. Manning, a Yale professor of history. Two daughters were born to the Mannings, both of whom also married professors.

During her father's term as president (1909–1913) Helen left Bryn Mawr to act as her father's White House hostess when her mother was temporarily ill. As the daughter of a president, Helen stands in marked contrast to her contemporary, Alice Lee Roosevelt, the daughter of Teddy. While "Alice Blue" was flamboyant and conservative, Helen was quietly liberal. The press tried to inspire her popularity by writing of her activities and endowing her with the title "Helen Pink." Not surprisingly, the nation preferred "Alice Blue" Roosevelt to the academic "Helen Pink."

Yet of the two presidents' daughters, both born in the last of the Victorian age, it was, in fact, Helen Taft Manning who attained a position of responsibility and personal excellence uncommon to her generation's women. She was part of the transition generation of women who were born into an exclusive, male-dominated world, but she lived and earned prominence in a United States that, during her adulthood, made "full citizens" of its women.

CHARLES PHELPS TAFT

Third child, second son of William Howard Taft and Helen Herron

Born: September 20, 1897   *Birthplace:* Cincinnati, Ohio
Education: Yale University, University of Toledo
Profession: Lawyer, Politician
Spouse: Eleanor Chase
Number of Children: 7

"MR. REPUBLICAN'S" BROTHER

Charles Phelps Taft, the baby of the Taft family and eight years younger than his brother Robert, was a rambunctious, bright, mischievous child. The family favorite, Charlie, named after a wealthy uncle, was totally unlike his older brother as a child and as an adult, though comparisons would often be made.

When Charlie was only two years old his father became governor general of the Philippine islands. The family moved to Manila, where the Taft children received their early education. Charlie, as a youngster, was more interested in play than study. He was forever "cursed" with enthusiasm for his wide variety of interests, and his detractors would say that excessive enthusiasm was his major flaw.

Charlie, like his brother Robert, was educated at Yale and in the law. His education, unlike his brother's, was, however, interrupted when he decided to leave Yale and join the army as a private in the field artillery. While other men of his social and economic standings obtained commissions as officers, the son of a former president, characteristically, sought only to do his duty to his country. Serving on active duty in France during World War I, Charlie was promoted from private to sergeant major.

After the war, Charlie completed his education and entered into a law partnership with his brother. It did not work out. Indeed, the rift between the brothers was so deep that in 1927 Charlie refused to support his brother, Bob, on the Ohio Republican slate. Bob Taft, never a man to forget injury or insult, returned in kind when Charlie ran for mayor of Cincinnati. Robert Taft refused to support his brother, but Charlie won the mayoralty anyway.

Throughout his life Charles Phelps Taft involved himself enthusiastically in the public life of Cincinnati and the nation because of his love for people. He earned for himself the reputation of a warm human being devoted to the public's service.

FOR FURTHER READING

Anderson, Judith Icke. *William Howard Taft: An Intimate History*. New York, New York: W. W. Norton, 1981.

Patterson, James T. *Mr. Republican: A Biography of Robert A. Taft*. Boston, Massachusetts: Houghton Mifflin Company, 1972.

Pringle, Henry F. *The Life and Times of William Howard Taft*. Vol. 2. Hamden, Connecticut: Archon Books, 1939.

23 WOODROW WILSON'S CHILDREN

MARGARET WOODROW WILSON

First child of Woodrow Wilson and Ellen Louise Axson

Born: April 30, 1886   *Birthplace:* Gainesville, Georgia
Died: February 12, 1944   *Age at Death:* 57 years, 10 months
Cause of Death: Uremic poisoning
Education: Goucher College, Peabody Conservatory of Music, private music tutors
Profession: Pianist, Singer, Saleswoman, Advertising Writer
Spouse: None
Number of Children: None

"DISHTA," LEADING TO THE DISCOVERY OF THE DIVINE SELF

Margaret Woodrow Wilson, the first of three daughters of Woodrow Wilson's first wife, wandered through life, dreaming of a success that constantly eluded her pursuit.

When her father entered the White House and became president in 1913, Margaret was twenty-six and had already completed her formal education. Although her two younger sisters married during Wilson's first term, Margaret's interests did not lean toward marriage. Margaret sought a career in music.

Though Margaret took lessons for piano and voice for many years, the results of her study were not all that she wished. Although she sang once with the Chicago Symphony Orchestra during her father's term as president, the critics were not impressed. Her performances were damned with faint praise. Said one critic, "her voice had a sympathetic quality, which is its most commendable attribute."[122] Another critic observed that Margaret sang with "intelligence and feeling and without affectation."[123] Undaunted, she traveled to France to entertain the World War I Allied soldiers through song.

After the White House, Margaret worked as an advertising writer for two years. Her father died in 1924, leaving his considerable estate to his second wife, Edith. Margaret was to receive $2,500 per year, providing "that she did not marry."[124] Trained as a musician, with only $2,500 a year for financial security if she remained unmarried, Margaret had to make her own way in the world. From advertising she next became involved in oil stock speculation. Unfortunately, her oil stocks were found to be fraudulent. In the resulting lawsuit, Margaret was ordered to pay in excess of $10,000. Again, undaunted, in late 1927, Margaret moved from personal oil stocks to general sales of stocks and bonds to pay off her debts. It was not long until the 1929 stock market crash.

For the next decade, Margaret's press coverage is lost to the chaos of the Great Depression. We may speculate that she earned her living through music or, more likely, she took whatever jobs were available to survive. What is known is that sometime during the 1930s she became intrigued with the study of Indian cultures and religions during frequent visits to public libraries, as she later related.

In the early 1940s, Margaret surfaced. She was living in seclusion with Guru Siri Abobindo, in Pondicherry, India. She had taken the new name of "Dishta" which means "leading to the discovery of the divine self in every human being."[125] In an interview with a newspaper reporter, Margaret stated, "I am not homesick, in fact I never felt more at home anywhere, anytime in my life."[126]

Daughter of a two-term president, once at the center of public affairs of the world's most powerful nation, Margaret Woodrow Wilson died of uremic poisoning while living in India with a guru.

JESSIE WOODROW WILSON SAYRE

Second child, second daughter of Woodrow Wilson and Ellen Louise Axson

Born: August 28, 1887   *Birthplace:* Gainesville, Georgia
Died: January 15, 1933   *Age at Death:* 45 years, 4 months
Cause of Death: Surgical complications
Education: Goucher College, Princeton University
Profession: Housewife, Mother, Politician
Spouse: Francis Bowes Sayre
Number of Children: 3

A WOMAN IN POLITICS

As a child growing up in the college atmosphere of Princeton University, the daughter of Professor Woodrow Wilson would acquire a higher level of formal education than most women of her period. Jessie Woodrow Wilson attended Goucher College in Baltimore and Princeton University before beginning a three-year stint in social service work at a Philadelphia settlement house.

Jessie Wilson became Jessie Sayre in a White House wedding, the fifth daughter of a president to be married in the White House. Her husband, Francis Sayre, a professor of law at Harvard Law School, later served as both the Massachusetts state commissioner of corrections and as assistant secretary of state.

In support of her father's peace program following the first world war, Jessie became heavily involved in Democratic party politics and in working for the ratification of the Versailles Treaty and U.S. participation in the League of Nations. By 1928 she had achieved sufficient status within the party to be called upon to make the introductory speech for Alfred E. Smith's presidential nomination by the Democratic convention. She worked vigorously to elect the nation's first Catholic president. Smith lost, but Jessie had so impressed party leaders that she was asked to be a candidate for the Democratic nomination for the U.S. Senate from Massachusetts. She declined but continued to work for the party and a number of charitable causes.

Jessie died in January 1933. Just before her death, Franklin Delano Roosevelt began his many terms as president of the United States. As Jessie was, at the time of her death, secretary of the Massachusetts Democratic state committee, her death cut short a political career that would certainly have blossomed during the decades of the Democratic party's ascendancy.

ELEANOR RANDOLPH WILSON MCADOO

Third child, third daughter of Woodrow Wilson and Ellen Louise Axson

Born: October 16, 1889   *Birthplace:* Middletown, Connecticut
Died: April 5, 1967   *Age at Death:* 77 years, 5 months
Cause of Death: Unknown   *Education:* Princeton University
Profession: Housewife, Mother, Writer
Spouse: William Gibbs McAdoo
Number of Children: 2

HER FATHER'S DAUGHTER

She was considered the Wilson child that most resembled her father, both temperamentally and ideologically. Eleanor Randolph Wilson worked during her life as a writer, espousing her father's international viewpoints.

Her early years were spent on the Princeton University campus where her father was first a professor and then president of Princeton. In 1913 when Woodrow Wilson entered the White House with his wife and three daughters, the Wilson girls were thrust into the center of national attention. Eleanor later wrote, "when father first went to the White House, I thought I would die. . . . Suddenly we became goldfish in a bowl. . . . Utter strangers passed judgment on us, and we were plunged into a sea of etiquette and customs that we didn't understand a thing about. There were times when [I] wanted to dig a hole into the floor and disappear down it."[127]

She, like her elder sister, was married in a White House ceremony. At twenty-four years of age she married her father's secretary of the treasury, widowed, fifty-two-year-old William Gibbs McAdoo. Two children were born to the McAdoos, but the marriage failed. In 1934 Eleanor divorced McAdoo, pleading mental cruelty and receiving custody of the two girls. Following the divorce, Eleanor moved to California for the climate, which was more suited to her precarious health.

In California her life was active. She continued her writing and participated in numerous charitable organizations, including an organization dedicated to preserving her father's memory, the Woodrow Wilson Foundation. In 1959 Eleanor Wilson McAdoo made her last public appearance when she attended a "Life with Father" luncheon at the White House, honoring the sons and daughters of the former presidents. The last few years of her life were lived under the constant care of a nurse until she died at the age of seventy-seven.

FOR FURTHER READING

Garraty, John Arthur. *Woodrow Wilson: A Great Life in Brief*. Westport, Connecticut: Greenwood Press, 1977.

Mulder, John M. *Woodrow Wilson: The Years of Preparation*. Princeton, New Jersey: Princeton University Press, 1978.

Wilson, Woodrow. *President in Love: The Courtship Letters of Woodrow Wilson and Edith Bolling Galt*. Edited by Edwin Tribble. Boston, Massachusetts: Houghton Mifflin, 1981.

24 CALVIN COOLIDGE'S CHILDREN

JOHN COOLIDGE

First child of Calvin Coolidge and Grace Anna Goodhue

Born: September 7, 1906   *Birthplace:* Northampton, Massachusetts
Education: Mercersberg Academy, Amherst College
Profession: Businessman   *Spouse:* Florence Trumbull
Number of Children: 1

A "REGULAR FELLOW"

When President Warren G. Harding died in office, Vice-President Calvin Coolidge became president. The news reached John Coolidge, oldest of the Coolidge boys, while the seventeen-year-old was on military training exercises at Fort Devens, Massachusetts. When asked what it felt like to be the son of the president, John, in few words, observed, "It doesn't feel any different than when I was the son of the Massachusetts governor."[128]

John, described as a "regular fellow" although his father was in the White House, graduated from Mercersberg Academy in June 1924, and entered Amherst College. Earning the nickname "Butch," which stayed with him throughout his college days, John was active in the sport of boxing, as well as in college plays and Amherst's chorus. But what Calvin Coolidge demanded was excellence in scholastics. Even during the period of inauguration, John was not permitted to miss class for more than a single day. Coolidge's strict discipline and expectations for his son's deportment were high. Thus, while John was allowed to visit in the White House, Coolidge reminded John, "You are dining at the table of the President of the United States, and you will present yourself promptly and in proper attire."[129]

John's college life was not ordinary, for the Secret Service was in constant attendance upon him. Nevertheless, the young man achieved some popularity with his fellow students. In 1928 John graduated from Amherst, not the recipient of the highest academic honors, but with an excellent record of achievement. At that point in his life John did not really know what he wanted to do and what he wanted for his future. He was caught between the attractions of the study of law at Harvard and a business career, which he ultimately followed.

Despite the ever-present Secret Service during his Amherst days, John still managed to socialize and acquire a steady girl. Indeed, there was much press speculation that John would elope with Florence Trumbull, the popular daughter of the Connecticut governor. The couple did eventually marry, but they waited until 1929.

Making his home in Connecticut, John embarked on a business career by becoming a traveling passenger agent for the New York, New Haven, and Hartford Railroad, in which capacity he continued for ten years. Seldom was his name mentioned in print, but in 1938 John did take a small role in politics and served as delegate to the political convention, stressing his interest in helping the Republican party saying, "I'll be glad to do whatever I can locally to keep the Republican party alive."[130]

In 1940 John became ill and took a six-month leave of absence from his job. But the illness persisted, and within a year John resigned his railroad post. Recovering from his unnamed illness, John's next venture into the business world was not as an employee, but as an entrepreneur. Impressed with the need for increased accuracy for new business systems, John invested in a concern manufacturing printed business forms whose use would facilitate accurate record keeping and reporting. His father's example of precision in all things thus characterized John's life as it had his father's.

CALVIN COOLIDGE, JR.

Second child, second son of Calvin Coolidge and Grace Anna Goodhue

Born: April 13, 1908   *Birthplace:* Northampton, Massachusetts
Died: April 7, 1924   *Age at Death:* 16 years
Cause of Death: Blood poisoning
Education: Mercersberg Academy

DEATH FROM THE TENNIS COURT

The short lifetime of Calvin Coolidge, Jr., ended when the young man stubbed his toe while playing tennis on the White House grounds and the small injury caused blood poisoning, which ended his life.

Described as a rollicking boy, sixteen-year-old Cal was much like his mother, having a character full of fun and vigor with a ready ability to get along with his school classmates, very much unlike his father, who was called "silent Cal."

Within a short time of Coolidge's elevation to the office of the presidency, Cal, Jr., was gravely ill. Calvin Coolidge sat by the side of his son's bed while doctors tried to stop the spread of the infection that would cause the death of this much-loved son. Despite attempts at blood transfusions, by the time the seriousness of the illness was realized it was already too late. President Coolidge bemoaned the fact that, had he not been elected president, perhaps his son would not have died. The young man's death hit the family hard, and "silent Cal" was overcome by grief. Weeping unashamedly he told a close reporter friend, "I just can't believe it happened."[131]

Cal and Grace Coolidge arrived in the White House with two fine sons, to whom they had emphasized the values of honesty, thrift, truthfulness, and valor. The death of the younger boy aroused the sympathy of the nation and very nearly crushed the parents. Grace Coolidge would never get over the death of this child. She wrote a poem, later published, in which she described the intense emotions and feelings for her son.[132] Grace Coolidge never lost her feelings of despair over the tragic death of this special child.

FOR FURTHER READING

Kane, Joseph Nathan. *Facts about the Presidents.* New York, New York, 1981 ed.: The H. W. Wilson Company, 1981.

Lathem, Edward C., ed. *Meet Calvin Coolidge: The Man behind the Myth.* Brattleboro, Vermont: The Stephen Greene Press, 1960.

Lippmann, Walter. *Public Person.* New York, New York: Liveright Publishing, 1976.

Ross, Ishbel. *Grace Coolidge and Her Era: The Story of a President's Wife.* New York, New York: Dodd, Mead & Company, 1962.

25 HERBERT CLARK HOOVER'S CHILDREN

HERBERT CLARK HOOVER, JR.

First child of Herbert Clark Hoover and Lou Henry

Born: August 8, 1903   *Birthplace:* London, England
Died: April 9, 1969   *Age at Death:* 65 years, 8 months
Cause of Death: Cancer
Education: Stanford University, Harvard University
Profession: Engineer, Geologist, Inventor, Politician
Spouse: Margaret E. Watson
Number of Children: 3

ASSISTANT TO JOHN FOSTER DULLES

The son of the "great engineer" was himself to become a prominent engineer and geologist, highly respected for his contributions to geological exploration.

Born in London, England, where his father was working as an engineer, most of his childhood was spent accompanying his parents to far-flung points on the globe while his father practiced his profession. It was during his early childhood that Herbert Clark Hoover, Jr., began wearing a hearing aid because of partial deafness. But this handicap did not stop his mental development, and by 1925 he had earned his bachelor's degree from Stanford and shortly thereafter received his master's degree from Harvard, specializing in petroleum geology.

Among Herbert, Jr.'s, contributions to geology was the invention of a device which measured gasses that seeped to the surface from deep within the earth, identifying probable oil deposits. In later years Herbert, Jr., developed and assisted in the invention of mechanisms that would be used on American planes in World War II, receiving many patents for his work.

But it was not only in engineering that Herbert, Jr., made his reputation.

President Eisenhower appointed Herbert as under secretary of state, working with John Foster Dulles. Ike chose Herbert in recognition of his mediation of a dispute between Great Britain and Iran over the massive Iranian Abadan oil field. Herbert managed to satisfy all parties in the negotiations, a feat which earned Eisenhower's admiration and respect. Herbert, Sr., the former president, was still alive to see his son as the link between the "Grand Old Republican" party and Ike's modern Republicanism.

As secretary of state, Dulles was frequently ill, and Herbert, Jr., often acted in his stead. Despite Eisenhower's opinion, it was apparent that Herbert was not a born diplomat, though he did display excellent administrative ability in carrying out the policies established by others.

Herbert Clark Hoover, Jr., earned recognition for his own contributions, never relying on his name for unearned advantage. Characteristically, with a modesty that endeared him to friends, when he spoke about his father he never mentioned the fact that his father had been president of the United States. Once, while reflecting on his past, Herbert observed, "you know, my father was a mining engineer and we traveled a good deal."[133]

In 1969 Herbert died of cancer, leaving his widow and three children in California as the recipients of a large estate, earned by his own brilliance and ability. He was a self-made man, almost despite his father's position.

ALLAN HENRY HOOVER

Second child, second son of Herbert Clark Hoover and Lou Henry

Born: July 17, 1907   *Birthplace:* London, England
Education: Stanford University, Harvard Business School
Profession: Rancher, Miner, Banker, Businessman
Spouse: Margaret Coberly
Number of Children: 3

MASTER OF BUSINESS

Born in 1907, Allan, the second of the two Hoover children, was a student at Stanford University when his father became president. Journeying to the capital for his father's inauguration, he found neither the city nor his father's new home at the White House to his taste. So Allan went back to California, the family home, and completed his Stanford studies, earning a degree in economics.

Allan later returned to Washington, D.C., and the press found him an attractive subject, both in personality and appearance. Father and son took some trips together, but they were marred by Allan's illness, which the press, whether from sensationalism or not, suggested was serious. The press even tried to drum up a romance between the handsome, socially active young man and the Philippines' American governor general's daughter. The press proclaimed the two would marry momentarily, but such was not to happen.

Instead of marrying, Allan went to Harvard Business School in the fall of 1929, earning his master's degree in business administration.

Returning to California, Allan took over the management of his father's ranch, describing himself as a farmer, rancher, and even orchardist. Allan became wealthy but not by working for it. Instead, his father's successor to the presidency, Franklin Roosevelt, had instituted, with congressional approval, the farm-price support program as one of the New Deal measures to combat the depression. One of the provisions of the law was payment for not growing crops, to stop overproduction and keep prices high. Allan benefited from this program when he did not produce cotton on his land, and received payment for nonproduction.

By 1937 Allan's investments were secure, and he had expanded to banking and mining. When he married, his father, the only living ex-president of the day, attended the California wedding, and Allan's older brother served as best man.

FOR FURTHER READING

Best, Gary Dean. *Politics of American Individualism: Herbert Hoover in Transition: 1918–1921*. Westport, Connecticut: Greenwood Press, 1975.

Burner, David. *Herbert Hoover: A Public Life*. New York, New York: Alfred A. Knopf, 1979.

Lippmann, Walter. *Public Persons*. New York, New York: Liveright Publishing, 1976.

Rice, Arnold S., ed. *Herbert Hoover: 1874–1964*. Dobbs Ferry, New York: Oceana Publications, 1971.

26 FRANKLIN DELANO ROOSEVELT'S CHILDREN

ANNA ELEANOR ROOSEVELT DALL BOETTIGER HALSTED

First child of Franklin Delano Roosevelt and Anna Eleanor Roosevelt

Born: May 3, 1906   *Birthplace:* Hyde Park, New York
Died: December 1, 1975   *Age at Death:* 69 years, 7 months
Cause of Death: Cancer
Education: Private schools, Cornell University
Profession: Housewife, Mother, Newspaperwoman
Spouses: Curtis Bean Dall, John Boettiger, James Addison Halsted
Number of Children: Roosevelt/Dall: 2
                       Roosevelt/Boettiger: None
                       Roosevelt/Halsted: None

FDR'S LONE DAUGHTER

Anna Eleanor, the only daughter of Franklin and Eleanor Roosevelt, moved to Washington, D.C., when she was only seven years old. She had already begun her education at an exclusive girl's school and she continued in that same style in Washington. It has been suggested by Anna's mother that Anna was the recipient of too severe a discipline. Her mother protested, however, that the excessive discipline was given in complete innocence and ignorance of child training. Sometimes her mother's innocence of child-rearing led to ludicrous situations, such as when Eleanor put Anna into a wire contraption and hung the baby outside of the home so that she might have fresh air, which Eleanor believed was crucial to the good health and robust development of her baby. Neighbors, however, were outraged and threatened to call the Society for the Prevention of Cruelty to Children.

Completing school in 1925, the tall, blonde Anna Roosevelt was taken abroad by the family's domineering grandmother, Sara Roosevelt. Anna was not, at that time, interested in going to college, and this suited her grandmother who cautioned her granddaughter to avoid becoming a "grind" because men would be intimidated by her and she would end up an "old maid." Anna need not have worried of her ability to attract men, for she would eventually marry three times.

In spite of her grandmother's advice, Anna did decide to go to college, attending Cornell and studying agriculture because she loved the outdoors and animals. Her college days ended when she married Curtis Dall, a stockbroker about ten years her senior, when she was only twenty years old. Explaining her marriage to Dall, Anna pulled no punches saying, "I got married when I did because I wanted to get out."[134] What Anna referred to was the perpetual struggle between two strong-willed women, her mother and her father's mother, grandmother Sara. Anna's marriage did not last. Following the birth of two children in six years, the couple divorced. Shortly thereafter, Anna's father became president of the United States, and the family moved into the White House.

During Roosevelt's first campaign for the presidency in 1932, Anna met and fell in love with John Boettiger, a reporter for the *Chicago Tribune*. Though the paper was staunchly Republican, and, in particular, came to attack vehemently Roosevelt and his policies during the presidency, the newspaper's political attitude did not prevent Anna and Boettiger from marrying in 1935. Boettiger left the *Tribune* for public relations work, and then, courtesy of another Roosevelt enemy, William Randolph Hearst, he was made editor of the *Seattle Post Intelligencer*.

Leaving Seattle following public criticism of the Hearst and Roosevelt association, the couple purchased a shopping newspaper in Phoenix, Arizona, with the idea of turning it into a substantial daily newspaper. They poured every cent into the newspaper, as well as borrowed funds from mother Eleanor and brother Jimmy. The paper failed, and so did the marriage. Boettiger left Phoenix while Anna continued the struggle until the summer of 1948, justifying her persistence in the face of overwhelming opposition announcing, "I love a fight against a reactionary monopoly, and I hate to see the latter winning out in so many fields of endeavor in this country today."[135] In 1949 she and John divorced. Boettiger remarried, but on October 29, 1950, he committed suicide, jumping from the seventh floor of a New York hotel.

Anna, never defeated by life, began again. In 1952 she married Dr. James A. Halsted, a physician with a deep interest in psychosomatic medicine. She and her husband lived a quiet life in California, though periodically she and her Fulbright professor husband traveled to Iran and later to Washington, D.C., where he was with the Veterans Administration. In time the couple retired to upstate New York. Anna died in 1975 of throat cancer and was buried in her birthplace at Hyde Park. Anna's son by her first marriage changed his name from Dall to Roosevelt.

JAMES ROOSEVELT

Second child, first son of Franklin Delano Roosevelt and Anna Eleanor Roosevelt

Born: December 23, 1907   *Birthplace:* Hyde Park, New York
Education: Groton Preparatory School, Harvard University, Boston University Law School
Profession: Businessman, Politician, Teacher
Spouses: Betsy Cushing, Romelle Theresa Sneider, Gladys Irene Owens
Number of Children: Roosevelt/Cushing: 3
                                     Roosevelt/Sneider: None
                                     Roosevelt/Owens: None

HEADLINE MATERIAL

Described as having inherited "his father's charm, his father's boundless energy, and his father's speech and oratorial style,"[136] James, the eldest of Franklin and Eleanor Roosevelt's sons, was twenty-six years old when his father became president. James was educated at the exclusive boy's preparatory school, Groton, and continued at Harvard, finally completing his education at Boston University Law School. James then entered the insurance business.

Upon his father's election to the presidency, Jimmy, as he was called, believed it his right and duty to make suggestions for appointments in the new administration, as he had been his father's campaign manager for the important state of Massachusetts. Public reaction to the son advising the father was loud and negative. Jimmy escaped to Europe. Upon his return to the United States, there was talk that he was being considered for an appointment as the president's secretary. Public reaction to the projected appointment was so unfavorable that Franklin dropped the idea. Anyway, Jimmy had another career in mind.

In 1935, while he was not yet thirty years of age, Jimmy became president of the National Grain Yeast Corporation, involved in making industrial alcohol. Once more the public found fault with the president's son, for it was rumored that backers of the company had underworld connections, and that Jimmy's only credential for the presidency of the company was his connection to the chief executive of the United States. Under fire again, Jimmy resigned, giving as his reasons the conflict of time and pursuit of other, more important, interests.

Next, Jimmy joined his father when he traveled to the inter-American conference in South America, and served as his father's aide, with the rank of lieutenant colonel in the Marine Corps. Public criticism forced Jimmy's resignation from the Marine Corps, but he remained in his father's service.

In 1938 Jimmy was back at the insurance business, as a "super salesman" earning between $250,000 and $1 million per year in commissions. Again, the public raged. Jimmy defended both his integrity and his profits in a radio broadcast. From insurance, the young man went into the movie-production business and immediately became president of Goldwyn Studio Corporation, eventually establishing his own company, and actually producing two movies.

With World War II, Jimmy went into the marines as a captain and was sent as an observer to the Middle and Far East. In order to see front-line duty, Jimmy had to use the authority of his father's name to convince military superiors that his ulcers were not sufficient disability to hold him back from such duty. He was right. Jimmy not only participated in combat, but won the Silver Star for gallantry, serving at Guadalcanal, Tarawa, and Midway in the Pacific.

President Roosevelt died in 1945, the war ended, and Jimmy left active service and returned to settle in California, where he became a leading spokesman for the state's Democrats.

In time, Jimmy ran for the position of California's governor against Earl Warren. He was defeated. But Jimmy's political career was not ended. He served as a member of the House of Representatives for the Los Angeles congressional district, winning election repeatedly with a minimum of effort.

Following his political career, James Roosevelt returned to the business world, and today lives in California. Advanced in years, the much-publicized son of Franklin Delano Roosevelt has finally managed to escape headlines, though he regularly lectures at colleges throughout the nation.

FRANKLIN ROOSEVELT

Third child, second son of Franklin Delano Roosevelt and Anna Eleanor Roosevelt

Born: March 18, 1909   *Birthplace:* Hyde Park, New York
Died: November 8, 1909   *Age at Death:* 8 months
Cause of Death: Unknown

AN UNKNOWN FRANKLIN, JR.

The third child of Franklin and Eleanor, the first namesake of his father, died before he was nine months old. We can only speculate as to the emotional impact on the Roosevelt family caused by this loss. Not unnaturally, the death of a child at such an early age, within such a vibrant family, must have caused great pain. The man who would be the presidential giant of the twentieth century had not achieved fame in 1909 and chroniclers of the day paid no attention to merely another death, even though in a well-to-do, presidentially related family.

ELLIOTT ROOSEVELT

Fourth child, third son of Franklin Delano Roosevelt and Anna Eleanor Roosevelt

Born: September 23, 1910   *Birthplace:* Hyde Park, New York
Education: Groton Preparatory School
Profession: Businessman, Soldier, Writer
Spouses: Elizabeth Browning Donner, Ruth Josephine Googins, Faye Emerson, Minerva Bell Ross
Number of Children: Roosevelt/Donner: 1
                      Roosevelt/Googins: 3
                      Roosevelt/Emerson: None
                      Roosevelt/Ross: None

FLYING HIGH

Born only shortly before his father was elected to New York's state Senate, Elliott was the third child of four children to survive. He grew up in the family home at New York's Hyde Park. Elliott, like his other brothers, attended Groton. But then Elliott broke with family tradition when he went to work rather than continuing on to school. He entered the advertising business, and was relatively successful before his father became president.

Elliott developed a long and profitable interest in aviation, eventually becoming well known as an expert in the fledgling aviation industry. It was this interest that brought to Elliott a brief association with Anthony Fokker, and which would cause headlines and screams of favoritism by Roosevelt's enemies over Elliott's efforts on behalf of the German manufacturer of the Fokker airplane. Because of the notoriety, Elliott turned to the radio broadcast industry and settled at a ranch near Fort Worth, Texas, initially the home of his second wife, heiress Ruth Josephine Googins.

Just prior to the U.S. entry into World War II, Elliott received a commission as a captain in the U.S. Army Air Corps. His choice of military service again broke the Roosevelt family tradition of the navy, in which his father, his brothers, and even his uncle Theodore, had all been closely associated. During his wartime service, Elliott was awarded the U.S. Air Medal, the Legion of Merit, and the Distinguished Flying Cross with Oak Leaf Cluster, as well as being made Commander of the Order of the British Empire, receiving the French Legion of Honor, and the *Croix de Guerre* with Palm. Nevertheless, Elliott's promotion to the rank of brigadier general, which had to be made with congressional approval, caused South Dakota's Senator Bushfield to argue that "General Robert E. Lee had thirty-six years of service in the Army before he became a Brigadier General, General Eisenhower thirty years, General Pershing twenty-four years, and General MacArthur twenty-one years before reaching the rank of Brigadier General."[137] Despite Bushfield's objections, Elliott's four years of service were sufficient to earn him the promotion.

Bushfield's arguments had been exacerbated by recent headlines that reported that Elliott's dog had received more favorable treatment than the lowly soldier returning from the Continent, who did not have a presidential father. Elliott had, supposedly, "bumped" soldiers returning from European duty so that his dog could journey home. The press had a field day with the dog incident.

The end of the war and the death of his father should, therefore, have seen Elliott's activities relegated to newspapers' back pages. This was not to be the case.

It was revealed that Elliott had borrowed some $200,000 in 1939 only shortly before the war and he repaid only $4,000 of the debt. It was further claimed that the rest of the debt was written off—because he was the president's son. Defending himself, Elliott claimed the $200,000 had come from his wife. Following congressional inquiries nothing was proven or, for that matter, disproven.

Elliott quietly moved on to a new profession, writing a book about his father, *As He Saw It*, which was published in 1946. The book was reviewed, and for the most part it was agreed that the book was not a major contribution to FDR literature. One London critic even went so far as to observe that the book was so bad that it "proves nothing except that great men often have silly sons."[138]

Now living as a Texas resident, Elliott has, at last, moved back from the edge of notoriety to a quiet life on his ranch near Fort Worth.

FRANKLIN DELANO ROOSEVELT, JR.

Fifth child, fourth son of Franklin Delano Roosevelt and Anna Eleanor Roosevelt

Born: August 17, 1914
Birthplace: Campobello, New Brunswick, Georgia
Education: Groton Preparatory School, Harvard University, University of Virginia Law School
Profession: Lawyer, Politician
Spouses: Ethel Du Pont, Suzanne Perrin, Felicia Schiff Warburg Sarnoff, Patricia Oakes
Number of Children: Roosevelt/Du Pont: 2
                                    Roosevelt/Perrin: 2
                                    Roosevelt/Sarnoff: None
                                    Roosevelt/Oakes: None

THE CRUSADER

Franklin was almost nineteen years old in 1933 when his father became president. That same year he graduated from Groton Preparatory School. At school he had shown an aptitude for both scholarship and athletics. To continue his education, Franklin entered Harvard, but went traveling in France, England, and Spain before turning again to college life.

As the press constantly demanded news of the Roosevelt family, Franklin's college days were dogged by reporters in their desire to find interesting, amusing, and, perhaps, even scandalous stories for the public's consumption of Roosevelt news. Franklin resented this intrusion into his private life. Not by nature the quiet type, he, in one instance, seized a reporter's camera and smashed it to pieces, thereby making a newspaper story out of nothing.

In 1937, following a long courtship, Franklin married Ethel Du Pont, a member of a family that despised Franklin's father. Because of the "Romeo and Juliet" aspect of the marriage, the public's demand for intimate details of the relationship was insatiable. The newlywed Franklin completed his Harvard education and earned, as well, a law degree from the University of Virginia Law School. He began work as a clerk in a Wall Street law office for the munificent pay of $2,000 a year, a niggardly sum even in those days, but still a job in the midst of the depression.

Unlike some of his generation who became committed to social causes in the 1930s, but with the coming of personal prosperity tending to drop the cause, Franklin remained committed to his causes throughout his life. In 1965, he was appointed as chairman of the Equal Opportunity Commission by President Johnson. Franklin's social consciousness compelled him to enter public service and work against racial discrimination and in favor of expanded war veterans' benefits. President Truman appointed him to the U.S. Civil Rights Commission. But young Franklin could win elected office as well, and he served repeatedly as congressman from New York's twentieth district, though he failed to win when he sought the governorship of that state in 1966.

Franklin, Jr., also distinguished himself in World War II as a naval officer, earning the command of a destroyer escort and serving in both Atlantic and Pacific theaters of the war, and being awarded (among other awards) the Silver Star and the Purple Heart.

Married four times, and despite his patrimony, Franklin, Jr., was dropped from New York's *Social Register*, the "blue book" of social acceptability. In 1979, having lived in upstate New York on a 150-acre farm, Franklin put his estate up for sale, saying that he had grown tired of farming life and wanted to move to smaller quarters.

JOHN ASPINWALL ROOSEVELT

Sixth child, fifth son of Franklin Delano Roosevelt and Anna Eleanor Roosevelt

Born: March 13, 1916   *Birthplace:* Hyde Park, New York
Died: April 27, 1981   *Age at Death:* 65 years, 1 month
Cause of Death: Heart attack
Education: Groton Preparatory School, Harvard University
Profession: Businessman
Spouses: Anne Lindsay Clark, Irene Boyd McAlpin
Number of Children: Roosevelt/Clark: 3
                         Roosevelt/McAlpin: None

A REAGAN SUPPORTER

Seventeen years old when his father became president in 1933, John Roosevelt, along with the rest of the Roosevelt children, rapidly gained a reputation for playful and boisterous behavior. His mother called her youngest child "the most dignified of all my children," in defending her son against charges that during a 1937 European tour, John "squirted champagne in the face of the Mayor of Cannes, and roughed him with a bouquet of flowers."[139]

Shortly after John's return to the United States he married a Boston debutante, Anne Lindsay Clark, in a "small" Massachusetts wedding that included 30,000 onlookers along the wedding party's route. Following the wedding, John joined a Boston department store as a stock clerk, weekly earning $18.50. The press heartily approved of the young man and contrasted him with the sons of other wealthy men. Said one newspaper, "John Roosevelt, youngest son of the famous family, now happily married, is on his own, got himself a job, and is going to learn the art of merchandising. That's better than joining the colony of rich men's sons, idling away his times in a cocktail lounge and sponging on his parents as so many of them do."[140]

When the United States entered World War II, John quit his job and joined the navy, serving throughout the war. He was not in the United States at the time of his father's death near the conclusion of the war. Following the war, John settled in California and resumed his business career, becoming an executive in a clothing store chain, Filene's Sons, Inc. Living a private life uncharacteristic of the Roosevelts, his name suddenly appeared in print when a large photo of John crossing picket lines at his company was published in 1947 by *Life* magazine.

With the exception of the 1957 attempt to win the mayor's race following his return to New York City, John, unlike his political brothers, avoided political office, though he did act behind the scenes in supporting the candidacy of others. In New York, John became senior vice-president of Bache, Halsey, Stuart, Shields & Company, devoting his spare time to charitable fund-raising activities, including the polio foundation, which was so dear to his polio-crippled father.

Surprisingly, this son of FDR in his later years took a more active and open interest in politics and gave his support to the Republican party. He firmly supported Presidents Eisenhower, Nixon, and Reagan, as well as New York's Rockefeller and Javits, and Chase of neighboring New Jersey. Only shortly after Ronald Reagan's term as president began, John died of a heart attack in New York City.

FOR FURTHER READING

Boettiger, John R. *Love in Shadow*. New York, New York: W. W. Norton, 1978.

Burnham, Sophy. *The Landed Gentry: Passions and Personalities Inside America's Propertied Class*. New York, New York: G. P. Putnam's Sons, 1978.

Churchill, Allen. *The Roosevelts: American Aristocrats*. New York, New York: Harper & Row, 1965.

Perling, Joseph J. *Presidents' Sons: The Prestige of Name in a Democracy*. Freeport, New York: Books for Libraries Press, 1971.

Roosevelt, Elliott, and James Brough. *Mother: Eleanor Roosevelt's Untold Story*. New York, New York: G. P. Putnam's Sons, 1977.

Sadler, Christine. *Children in the White House*. New York, New York: G. P. Putnam's Sons, 1967.

Zilg, Gerald Colby. *Du Pont: Behind the Nylon Curtain*. New York, New York: Prentice-Hall, 1974.

27 HARRY S TRUMAN'S CHILD

MARGARET TRUMAN DANIELS

Only child of Harry S Truman and Elizabeth Virginia Wallace

Born: February 17, 1924   *Birthplace:* Independence, Missouri
Education: Gunston Hall, George Washington University
Profession: Housewife, Mother, Singer, Writer
Spouse: Clifton Daniels
Number of Children: 4

"ONE NICE GIRL"

Margaret, born during the years when her father was a hard-working haberdasher in Missouri, grew up as the center of her parents' attention. Called "my baby" or "Margie" or even "skinny," because of her perpetual dieting, Margaret was the only child the couple had, and she received the attention ofttimes reserved to only children, though she did not become the "spoiled brat" often associated with an only child. Truman righteously observed of his daughter, "She's one nice girl and I'm so glad she hasn't turned out like Alice Roosevelt and a couple of the Wilson daughters."[141] It was Harry's highest accolade. She was, and remains, a down-to-earth person, so much so that Harry later credited both her and her mother with keeping their feet firmly on the ground during the presidency as well as occasionally reminding Harry, when the power and prestige of the presidency elevated his own feelings of importance, that he, too, put on his pants one leg at a time.

Upon Truman's election to the Senate representing Missouri, in no small part resulting from his heroic opposition to a corrupt political machine, the family moved to Washington, D.C. Margaret and her mother not unnaturally felt some dread of the Washington, D.C., social world. The Washington establishment was unimpressed at the arrival of the new Missouri senator, and the family's penurious circumstances did nothing to change the impression until Truman became president of the United States. Money remained a perpetual family problem, even when Truman was the Democratic party's vice-presidential candidate.

Franklin Delano Roosevelt died shortly after his fourth election. Truman became president in a manner not unlike his distant relative, John Tyler, who had become the first vice-president to succeed to the office of president. The family life remained substantially the same. Margaret now had the opportunity to launch what she hoped would be a successful musical career, an aspiration not unlike Margaret Wilson's, the former president's daughter referred to by Truman in an earlier statement. In spite of Margaret's arduous devotion to her craft (and she would often practice voice to the accompaniment of her piano-playing father) her efforts were less than well received. In fact, it was a music critic's scornful analysis of her singing and her father's vitriolic response to the critic for which Margaret is most remembered by the public. On that occasion, a *Washington Post* critic, Paul Hume, described Margaret's performance, her voice quality, and her presentation in very unflattering terms. Harry, the presidential father, was enraged, and he publicly informed the nation of his opinion of the critic. Years later, in reminiscing about the incident, Harry, whose feelings the years had not mellowed, related the incident. "The next morning this Hume . . . wrote the dirtiest, meanest critique you ever saw. And I wrote him a letter. I wrote him a letter saying that if I could get my hands on him I'd bust him in the jaw and kick his nuts out [chuckle]."[142]

Harry's protectiveness of his daughter is understandable, given an assassination attempt on his life by Puerto Rican nationalists. Margaret's romantic opportunities, however, were strictly limited by security precautions. Margaret would periodically be humiliated when her father would send Secret Service men to find her when she was late in returning home. In this respect, the role of president's daughter had its negative impact, but there were positive sides for Margaret as well. Her father frequently sent her traveling in Europe as his personal representative. She made an excellent American ambassador, so much so that Harry laughingly remarked that the nation should fire its ambassadors and allow Margaret to fill their shoes.[143]

Shortly after her father left the White House, Margaret married. In 1956, having returned to the family home in Missouri, she married newspaperman Clifton Daniels and entered a quiet time of raising her family of four boys. In 1974 Margaret produced a book explaining her relationship with her father, as well as chronicling the Truman years in the White House. Thus, the daughter of Harry, "one nice girl," became a best-selling author.

FOR FURTHER READING

Hedley, John Hollister. *Harry S Truman: The Little Man from Missouri*. Woodburn, New York: Barron's Educational Series, 1979.

Ferrell, Robert H., ed. *Off the Record: The Private Papers of Harry S Truman*. New York, New York: Harper & Row, 1980.

Miller, Merle. *Plain Speaking: An Oral Biography of Harry S Truman*. New York, New York: Berkley Publishing Company, 1974.

Robbing, Jhan. *Bess and Harry: An American Love Story*. New York, New York: G. P. Putnam's Sons, 1980.

Robbins, Charles. *Last of His Kind. An Informal Portrait of Harry S Truman*. New York, New York: Morrow Publishing, 1979.

Truman, Harry S. *An Autobiography of Harry S Truman*. Edited by Robert H. Ferrell. Boulder, Colorado: Associated University Press, 1980.

_____. *Memoirs: Years of Trial and Hope*. New York, New York: Doubleday & Company, Inc., 1956.

Truman, Margaret. *Harry S Truman*. New York, New York: Pocket Books, 1974.

28 DWIGHT DAVID EISENHOWER'S CHILDREN

DWIGHT DOUD EISENHOWER

First child of Dwight David Eisenhower and Mary Geneva Doud

Born: September 24, 1917   *Birthplace:* Denver, Colorado
Died: January 2, 1921   *Age at Death:* 3 years, 4 months
Cause of Death: Scarlet fever

A FORGOTTEN CHILD

Most people are not aware that President Eisenhower was the father of two sons, for Dwight Doud Eisenhower survived only a short time. The family almost never spoke publicly of their firstborn, whose life ended from the effects of scarlet fever.

But, Ike, in his memoirs, later wrote that "this was the greatest disappointment and disaster in my life, the one I have never been able to forget completely."[144] After the construction of the Eisenhower Library, the remains of young Dwight were transferred to the building where a plaque marks the final resting place of Ike and Mamie's eldest son. At the dedication of the library, Eisenhower was seen to stare at the plaque with tears in his eyes.

JOHN SHELDON DOUD EISENHOWER

Second child, second son of Dwight David Eisenhower and Mary Geneva Doud

Born: August 3, 1923   *Birthplace:* Denver, Colorado
Education: West Point, Columbia University

Profession: Soldier, White House Aide, Teacher, Ambassador, Writer
Spouse: Barbara Jean Thompson
Number of Children: 4

A PHOTOGRAPHIC DUPLICATE

Born in Denver, Colorado, at the home of his maternal grandparents, John Sheldon Doud Eisenhower was named after his mother's father. By the age of two months, his mother, Mamie, overcame her dislike of the tropics and moved with her small son to join Ike in Panama. An account of John's school years reads like a travel guide through the nation's army bases until the family finally settled in Washington, D.C., long enough for John to graduate from the John Quincy Adams public school. Shortly after his graduation he and his mother moved to the Philippines with the general, where John attended the mission school on the islands for almost three years, though John graduated from Stadium High School at Tacoma, Washington.

John's memories of his father are based on a close feeling between father and son. They shared experiences such as hiking, flying lessons, and even cooking, comrades rather than superior versus inferior relationships which might characterize a career officer's association with his son.

Though his father never attempted to directly influence his son's choice of a career, the military camp made its mark, and John chose a career like his father's, though journalism and law were tempting to him. Competing furiously with thirty-five other candidates from Kansas, Eisenhower's state of official residence, John earned a much-desired West Point appointment.

With a natural aptitude for academics, young Ike, as he was often called, spent much of his time at West Point playing tennis, working on the yearbook, singing in the choir, and even acting as a tutor to lower classmen. He graduated from an accelerated three-year course in the 138th position in a class of 474. John's father was unable to attend his graduation, as Ike was directing his massive military operation on June 6, 1944—the Allied invasion of Europe.

John spent his graduation furlough with his father at the Normandy command post, and after further infantry training in the United States, he was assigned to staff duty in Europe, specifically working under General Omar Bradley. At war's end John returned to West Point, teaching, while he continued graduate studies in English and comparative literature, earning his graduate degree from Columbia University in 1950.

While serving as a front-line major in Korea, John was informed of his father's election to the presidency. Ike visited Korea, in partial fulfillment of campaign promises to end the war, and his son accompanied his president father on a tour of the battlefront. In 1953 John returned to the United States, where he spent the next five years stationed at various military posts, even doing a brief stint as a White House aide to his father until John Fitzgerald Kennedy's election.

Resigning his army commission in 1963, John determined to pursue a literary career, beginning a position with Doubleday Publishing, Inc., then taking a position with the Freedom Foundation, and finally turning his full attention to writing, specifically concentrating on his father's life.

Married, the father of four children, including a son who is the husband of former President Nixon's daughter, Julie, John is also today well recognized by the general public not only as the "general's son" but as the super salesman in television commercials promoting insurance for veterans.

FOR FURTHER READING

Cook, Blanche Wiesen. *Declassified Eisenhower: A Divided Legacy*. New York, New York: Doubleday, 1981.

Dulles, Eleanor Lansing. *Chances of a Lifetime: A Memoir*. New York, New York: Prentice-Hall, Inc., 1980.

Eisenhower, John S. D. *Strictly Personal: A Memoir*. New York, New York: Doubleday & Company, Inc., 1974.

Eisenhower, Milton S. *The President Calling*. New York, New York: Doubleday & Company, Inc., 1974.

Ferrell, Robert H., ed. *Eisenhower Diaries*. New York, New York: W. W. Norton, 1981.

Lee, R. Alton. *Dwight D. Eisenhower: Soldier and Statesman*. New York, New York: Nelson-Hall, 1981.

Neal, Steve. *Eisenhower's Reluctant Dynasty*. New York, New York: Doubleday & Company, Inc., 1978.

Richardson, Elmo. *Presidency of Dwight D. Eisenhower*. Lawrence, Kansas: Regents Press of Kansas, 1979.

29 JOHN FITZGERALD KENNEDY'S CHILDREN

CAROLINE BOUVIER KENNEDY

First child of John Fitzgerald Kennedy and Jacqueline Lee Bouvier

Born: November 27, 1957   *Birthplace:* New York, New York
Education: Radcliffe College   *Profession:* Researcher, Copy girl
Spouse: None
Number of Children: None

POOR LITTLE RICH GIRL

The phrase that is most descriptive of Caroline, the little blonde-haired, blue-eyed, dimpled daughter of the president was, to say the least, the "darling of the nation." The handsome parents, Jack and Jackie, and their equally photogenic child represented to the public the ideal family. The name Caroline took a rapid jump in popularity, with many parents naming their daughters after the Kennedy firstborn. She was part of the Kennedy style, and the nation came to anticipate Caroline's appearance ·in her father's oval office, during times of her choosing—not his. The antics of the child and the obvious loving warmth between father and daughter further endeared both to the nation. When Caroline's father was assassinated, the little girl's public image immediately changed from a laughing little face to a face that revealed pain and emotion far beyond her years.

Caroline's mother, Jacqueline Bouvier Kennedy, was not long a widow. The nation was shocked when she remarried and gave to her two young children a stepfather, Greek wheeler-dealer, billionaire Aristotle Onassis, a man much Jacqueline's senior. Caroline, naturally, could not escape the public's animosity to Jackie's new life. Both mother and daughter were chased throughout the world by photographers. Mother became a "jet-setter," and Caroline moved with her. The Kennedy image was tarnished, though the glamour remained. Neither the death of Onassis, nor Jackie's permanent return to the United States (and even conscious removal from the public eye) could reinstate mother and daughter to the "Camelot" image of former days.

Caroline, now the poor little rich girl, moved through her teen years to graduate from Radcliffe, the exclusive girls' college. Taking an apartment with roommates in Boston, she struck out on her own, though maintaining a close alliance with the Kennedy clan. At first Caroline moved some distance, both emotionally and geographically, from her mother, but recently Caroline Kennedy joined her mother at Jackie's new elaborate estate.

JOHN FITZGERALD KENNEDY, JR.

Second child, first son of John Fitzgerald Kennedy and Jacqueline Lee Bouvier

Born: November 25, 1960   *Birthplace:* Washington, D.C.
Education: Brown University   *Profession:* Student
Spouse: None
Number of Children: None

AN IMAGE OF SORROW

One of the indelible impressions of the Kennedy assassination must be the image of young John Kennedy, Jr., standing to attention before his father's grave and saluting the departed chief executive—his daddy. The agony of the nation was epitomized in the little boy's lost and bewildered appearance. The nation had lost its president and the boy had lost his father, and the double loss could be seen as the child stood by the grave. Only weeks before, the nation had been charmed and delighted by the overflowing love of Jack Kennedy and his son "John-John" when press photographs showed the young president tossing the little boy into the air and the obvious glee of the child captured the nation, as had the relationship of sister Caroline and her father.

In years that followed the assassination, John, like his sister, traveled throughout the world with his mother, who had married the Greek shipping magnate, Aristotle Onassis. Onassis, having children of his own, made no pretense of anything more than acceptance of his new wife's children. The male role model in the boy's life was not his stepfather, but rather his father's brothers, Robert (who was assassinated in 1968) and Ted Kennedy.

John's world travels ended when his mother was again widowed, and the little family returned to settle again in the United States.

Now a young man in his twenties and a student at Brown University, John has grown to remind many of the young John Fitzgerald Kennedy.

PATRICK BOUVIER KENNEDY

Third child, second son of John Fitzgerald Kennedy and Jacqueline Lee Bouvier

Born: August 7, 1963
Birthplace: Otis Air Force Base, Massachusetts
Died: August 9, 1963   *Age at Death:* 2 days
Cause of Death: Premature birth

FIRST PRESIDENTIAL NEWBORN SINCE CLEVELAND

Patrick Bouvier Kennedy, the second son of President Kennedy, was born five-and-one-half weeks prematurely, suffering from lungs that were not fully developed, not unlike the affliction also suffered by the elder son, John, at birth. Named for his grandfather and great-grandfather, Patrick Joseph, with his mother's maiden name for his middle name, the four-pound, ten-and-one-half ounce, seventeen-inch baby was beset with difficulties immediately upon his birth.

Delivered by caesarean section, Patrick had difficulty breathing immediately at birth. A day later, following attempts to stimulate his breathing, Patrick was transferred to the Children's Hospital Medical Center in Boston and placed in a high-pressure oxygen chamber. His mother remained in Falmouth, Massachusetts, at Otis Air Force Base hospital, where the child had been delivered. Patrick's father, President Kennedy, spent the night in the Boston hospital as the baby's condition grew worse.

The first child born to a president in office at the White House in 68 years, since the birth of Grover Cleveland's last daughter in 1895, the son's precarious health still did not cause the president of the United States to abandon his work load. While on the way to the Boston hospital during the limousine ride, the president signed into law four minor bills, which had recently passed in Congress. These bills became law with Kennedy's signature and mark the turmoil in this much-distressed family:

Public Law 88-90 Istle or Tampico Fiber–Duty-Free Importation

Public Law 88-91 Land Exchange–Wyoming

Public Law 88-92 Tanning Extracts–Duty-Free Import

Public Law 88-93 Heptanoic Acid–Duty-Free Import

All were signed August 8, 1963, during the urgency and concern of a presidential father for the life of his newborn son.

FOR FURTHER READING

Kennedy, Rose Fitzgerald. *Times to Remember*. New York, New York: Doubleday & Company, Inc., 1974.

Parmet, Herbert S. *Jack: The Struggles of John F. Kennedy*. New York, New York: Dial Press, 1980.

Toscano, Vincent. *Since Dallas: Images of John F. Kennedy in Popular and Scholarly Literature: 1963–1973*. Palo Alto, California: R & E Research Associates, 1978.

30 LYNDON BAINES JOHNSON'S CHILDREN

LYNDA BIRD JOHNSON ROBB

First child of Lyndon Baines Johnson and Claudia Alta Taylor

Born: March 19, 1944   *Birthplace:* Washington, D.C.
Education: University of Texas at Austin
Profession: Housewife, Mother, Politician
Spouse: Charles S. Robb
Number of Children: 3

"CINDERELLA"

"She's the smartest one and the one I worry about the most"[145] was her father's blunt appraisal about his eldest daughter, Lynda. Lyndon Baines Johnson, as a presidential father, approved of his daughter for displaying the qualities that he admired, intellect and strength of character, even going so far as to say that she was a woman who did not need to be taken care of by a man, as she was "so smart she'll be able to make a life for herself."[146] No idle flatterer, Johnson was so convinced of her abilities that he often consulted Lynda about his drafts of speeches. Lynda would reply by awarding the president on a grading system of "A," "B," or "C" (there is no record of "D" or "F" papers).

Lynda, however, was not always so comfortable with her father's political life. When Lyndon was still the House majority leader and Lynda yet a small girl, she was negatively affected by her parent's ambition and success. While her sister, Luci's, response to the situation was to resort to pranks, Lynda expressed her insecurity and resentment through compulsive eating, which had the expected results when she was described as a "butterball," a cause for further insecurity.

When her father entered the White House, Lynda was at the dating age and could not tolerate her "ugly duckling" self-image. Coincidentally with becoming the president's daughter, she also developed a relationship with Hollywood's perpetual "beach-boy bachelor," George Hamilton. Though the relationship was relatively short and its seriousness was strongly questioned by her father and the press (though apparently not by Lynda) she attempted to make herself over in the Hollywood image. To satisfy the demands of the publicity of her newly found glamour, Lynda even went to a Hollywood make-up artist to design and make over a new Lynda. Embarrassingly for Lynda, the nation's press detailed her make-over, including diagrams of her facial structure. The prince, however, did not slip on the glass slipper. Lynda was not to be a second Cinderella. While she was entranced by both her own image and Hollywood, Lyndon ribbed his daughter, however gently and cautiously. He waited until she graduated from the University of Texas to give her a two-month vacation to Europe, explaining his purpose, in the down-home style for which he was famous, as "Shucks, now she might even come back with that slick Hollywood boy out of her hair."[147] Lynda returned and Hamilton exited. Enter White House social aide, Marine Captain Charles S. Robb.

Robb, from an Ohio farm background, a recipient of a four-year Cornell scholarship and who would later be described as a mature "Ken doll," captured Lynda's attention. However, in years following Kennedy's assassination, presidential families have lived under the constant surveillance of the Secret Service. Despite Secret Service agents' guardianship, Robb and Lynda's relationship persevered until the Marine Corps officer and Lynda were married in a traditional military ceremony. The archway of crossed swords held by Robb's fellow officers added up to one of the most beautiful of White House wedding ceremonies.

From the Marine Corps, in which Robb served in Vietnam and was recognized for bravery, Lynda's husband went on to complete law school at the distinguished University of Virginia Law School. Only then did he enter politics. Elected as lieutenant governor of Virginia in his first attempt at public office, Robb furthered his political career when, in 1982, he was elected as Virginia's governor.

On her own account, Lynda has been active and has even served at President Carter's request as chairwoman of the National Advisory Council for Women. Thus, her father's judgment was accurate. Lynda has proven to be well able to take care of herself.

LUCY (LUCI) BAINES JOHNSON NUGENT

Second child, second daughter of Lyndon Baines Johnson and Claudia Alta Taylor

Born: July 2, 1947   *Birthplace:* Washington, D.C.
Education: National Cathedral School
Profession: Housewife, Mother, Businesswoman
Spouse: Patrick John Nugent
Number of Children: 4

BARE-FOOTED LUCI

Luci represented an image of femininity to the public, described by her father as so "appealing and feminine that there will always be some man around waiting to make a living for her."[148] But the president's attractive daughter, crowned by her father as queen of the Shenandoah Apple Blossom Festival in nearby Winchester, Virginia, was also tough-minded enough to carve a social life for herself, even during White House years. She asserted, "you have to be pushy to have any friends at the White House. No one will call you any more. You have to call them."[149] Behind her public facade was a strong-willed young girl.

Expected to personify all that was most wholesome in teenagers, Luci's independence caused her to rebel occasionally. And to her parents' dismay, she periodically tormented her mother by playing the piano too loudly while her mother was entertaining, or, in an even more shocking display, barging into a room full of her parents' invited guests in her bare feet. Such behavior in a president's child provoked comment, for the nation's people have come to apply a higher standard to children of the White House.

Because of Kennedy's assassination, which had elevated her father to president, the Secret Service intensified the protection of the new president's family. One result, as Luci entered the dating age, was to turn the dating game into an obstacle course. Heightened security, combined with the press's scramble for a story, led at least one boyfriend to sacrifice his romance with the president's daughter for the sake of his own health. One boyfriend escaped, claiming he was developing ulcers.

A convert to Catholicism during her father's term in office, Luci graduated from Washington's Episcopalian National Cathedral School. Periodically she and her father would attend the city's "Little Monk's" Church, and it was, perhaps, during one of these times that Luci asked the question in which her father took so much delight, whatever its authenticity: "Daddy, as an outsider, how do you feel about the human race?"[150]

Despite problems with maintaining friendships and dating, Luci eventually met and married Airman First Class Patrick Nugent, a Vietnam War veteran. The couple was married in Washington's National Catholic Shrine, which in itself caused an uproar, because the privilege of being married in the shrine had been denied to other couples. The date chosen for the wedding also created another uproar. The date selected was August 6, 1966, and it was the twenty-first anniversary of the day that the United States dropped the atom bomb on Hiroshima. Luci explained to the complaining organization, the Friends of Japan, that the date was a personal choice that had nothing to do with Hiroshima, Luci having been born after the bombing, and that the date would not be changed. The wedding, the first of a presidential daughter during the presidency since that of Alice Roosevelt Longworth early in the century, was on a grand scale. Luci, objecting to the size of the wedding which her parents developed, proclaimed, "This all happened because I wanted just my immediate family and friends. My parents invited only the immediate nation."[151]

The marriage lasted almost thirteen years, and four children were born to the couple before their 1979 divorce. Today Luci lives in Austin, Texas, not far from the Johnson family home, where her widowed mother still resides and where Luci spent so much of her time as a young girl.

FOR FURTHER READING

Bryant, Traphes, and Frances Spatz. *Dog Days at the White House: The Outrageous Memoirs of the Presidential Kennel Keeper*. New York, New York: Macmillan, 1975.

Cormier, Frank. *LBJ: The Way He Was*. Garden City, New York: Doubleday & Company, Inc., 1977.

Miller, Merle. *Lyndon: An Oral Biography*. New York, New York: G. P. Putnam's Sons, 1980.

Mooney, Booth. *LBJ: An Irreverent Chronicle*. New York, New York: Crowell, 1976.

Rulon, Philip Real. *Compassionate Samaritan: The Life of Lyndon Baines Johnson*. New York, New York: Nelson-Hall, 1981.

31 RICHARD MILHOUS NIXON'S CHILDREN

PATRICIA NIXON COX

First child of Richard Milhous Nixon and Thelma Catherine Ryan

Born: February 21, 1946   *Birthplace:* San Francisco, California
Education: Finch College   *Profession:* Housewife, Mother
Spouse: Edward Finch Cox
Number of Children: 1

A MODERN DAY CHARMER

Born only days after her father entered the race for California's twelfth district congressional seat in 1946, Tricia, as she came to be called, developed a personality quite different from that of her sister, Julie. Tricia is introverted, though "she is extremely effective whenever she has to do anything publicly, she doesn't like to do anything publicly."[152]

Twenty-two years old when her father became president in 1968, Tricia, a petite blonde weighing less than 100 pounds, worked as a tutor for third-grade school children in the Washington, D.C., ghetto while living in the White House. Tricia, unlike many White House residents, never felt constricted by her home. "I never feel alone in the White House," she said, "if I want privacy, I go to private parties and I don't tell people. I can't go out in crowds, people always recognize you, but I've found it possible to have a private life."[153] Displaying her ease in the role of president's child she periodically served as hostess for White House parties, and she charmed the nation when she conducted a televised tour of the White House as a one-hour CBS television presentation.

It was on Tricia that her parents pinned their hopes for a truly "royal" daughter, for she was not only linked in the press romantically with many of the nation's leading bachelors, but also with Britain's Crown Prince Charles. However, Prince Charles and Tricia had other ideas. The Nixons' first daughter held out for her own choice, "fast Eddy" Cox, whom she had met in college.

Edward Cox, whose family counted itself blue-blooded, tracing its ancestry back to Chancellor Robert Livingston who swore into office the first president of the United States, George Washington, became Tricia's fiancé in the spring of 1971. Neither of the families was excited about their children's choice of a mate. The Nixons had hoped for a more than "blue-blooded" liberal, as Cox was a member of "Nader's Raiders." From the Cox family point of view however, there were murmurs that the lowly Nixons were certainly far beneath the Coxes' lofty family heritage.

Despite the rumored objections on both sides, the couple was married on June 12, 1971 in the first outdoor wedding in the entire 171-year history of the White House. Both parents looked happy, though the wedding was delayed slightly by rain. The day after the wedding, political stormclouds gathered. On June 13, 1971, the *New York Times* lead story was the "Pentagon Papers," the papers initiating what would become a series of stories that led to the Watergate scandal.

As the Watergate scandal developed, Tricia and her husband stayed in the background. Tricia constantly proclaimed her father's innocence, saying it was "just jealous politicians who want his job," and predicting "that he would survive the ordeal and would not resign."[154] She was wrong. On the day of President Richard Milhous Nixon's resignation, August 9, 1974, Eddy and Tricia strolled in the White House rose garden, scene of their wedding, waiting for her father to make the announcement of his resignation as president of the United States.

In March 1979, Edward and Tricia Cox had their first child, giving the former president his first grandson when Tricia delivered, by caesarean section, Christopher Nixon Cox. In 1981 Tricia's thirty-four-year-old husband moved from his job with a prominent New York law firm to work for the Reagan administration in the newly created synthetic fuels energy system program, at a salary in excess of $52,000 per year.

JULIE NIXON EISENHOWER

Second child, second daughter of Richard Milhous Nixon and Thelma Catherine Ryan

Born: July 5, 1948   *Birthplace:* Washington, D.C.
Education: Smith College   *Profession:* Housewife, Mother, Writer
Spouse: David Dwight Eisenhower II
Number of Children: 2

A NIXON EXTROVERT

Julie—extroverted, gregarious, and constantly active—contrasts with the personality characteristics most commonly associated with the presidential Nixons. Born shortly after her father had become a member of Congress from California, Julie Nixon matured while her father acquired successively higher offices leading to the presidency.

When her father became president in 1968, Julie had already married her college sweetheart, David Dwight Eisenhower, grandson of former President Dwight David Eisenhower. The couple completed college, Julie at Smith College, and David at Amherst though at one time they both left their respective campuses to avoid possible difficulties from fellow college students during the U.S. bombing of Cambodia. During the early days of their marriage the couple rented, at an undisclosed rent, the $125,000 Bethesda, Maryland, home of her father's wealthy friend, Bebe Rebozo, causing some press notice. Shortly thereafter the couple moved to a more modest apartment.

When the Watergate affair developed, Julie vehemently defended her father. Throughout the affair Julie's faith in her father's innocence remained steadfast. Indeed, just before her father's resignation, the first in the history of the office, she insisted, "father will not resign" and "he is stronger now than he has ever been in his determination to see this through."[155]

In August 1978 Julie and David gave the former president his first grandchild, a girl, and in 1981 the couple had their second child, Alex Richard, named for a family friend and Julie's father.

It may be anticipated that in future years this couple, representing two presidential families, will be followed by the nation's press for, perhaps, no other reason than they represent two twentieth-century "royal" families.

FOR FURTHER READING

Atkins, Ollie. *White House Years: Triumph and Tragedy*. New York, New York: Playboy Press, 1977.

Brodie, Fawn. *Richard Nixon: The Shaping of His Character*. New York, New York: W. W. Norton, 1981.

Ehrlichman, John. *Witness to Power: The Nixon Years*. New York, New York: Simon and Schuster, 1982.

Klein, Herbert G. *Making It Perfectly Clear*. New York, New York: Doubleday, 1980.

Wills, Garry. *Nixon Agonistes: The Crisis of the Self-Made Man*. New York, New York: New American Library, 1979.

32 GERALD RUDOLPH FORD'S CHILDREN

MICHAEL GERALD FORD

First child of Gerald R. Ford and Elizabeth Anne Bloomer

Born: March 14, 1950   *Birthplace:* Washington, D.C.
Education: T. S. Williams High School, Wake Forest University,
Gordon-Conwell Theological Seminary
Profession: Businessman
Spouse: Gayle Brumbaugh
Number of Children: 2

A QUIET PRESENCE

The eldest of the Ford children, son Mike was born the year Gerald Ford entered his first congressional term in 1949. Educated in public schools near the family home in Alexandria, Virginia, during which time his father was constantly reelected to Congress from his home district in Grand Rapids, Michigan, Mike was, and is today, considered the most introspective of the Ford children. He did everything with intensity, a Ford characteristic, but most prominent in Mike—from skiing to studying and even to youthful games.

When Ford became president of the United States following a sequence of events that made him the only president to attain such an office without ever having been elected as president or vice-president, Mike was a twenty-three-year-old divinity student at a theological seminary near Boston, working on his master's degree. Fittingly, when his father was sworn into the presidency, it was Mike's Bible, especially purchased for the occasion, on which the president placed his hand to take the oath of office as prescribed in the Constitution of the United States. Ford's hand rested upon

"Psalm 20," which, appropriate to the situation of the United States on that day, begins "The Lord hear thee in the day of trouble."

Mike and his wife, Gayle, traveled from Boston to be with his father and mother, when, shortly after Ford became president, Betty Ford underwent a mastectomy. The Fords' eldest son and his wife were a major source of strength to the almost inconsolable president, often coming to sit with Michael's parents to pray.

JOHN GARDNER FORD

Second child, second son of Gerald R. Ford and Elizabeth Anne Bloomer

Born: March 16, 1952   *Birthplace:* Washington, D.C.
Education: T. C. Williams High School, Utah State University
Profession: Businessman
Spouse: None
Number of Children: None

A LATECOMER

The middle son of Gerald and Betty Ford, John, or Jack as he is called, is considered the brightest of the four children by those who know them, though his grades did not reflect his high I.Q. In fact, as a child Jack's school grades were so low that his teacher arranged for him to take special tests. As with some children of high intellectual ability, he did not achieve his potential early, nor in the schoolroom setting.

Growing up in Washington, D.C., where his father was a representative from the state of Michigan, Jack constantly encouraged his father to aspire to higher, more prestigious offices, telling him, when the speaker's position was open, to "Go for it, Dad." Naturally, his father's ascendancy to the vice-presidency following the resignation of Spiro Agnew thrilled the young man. Upon resignation of Richard Nixon, the first ever such resignation, Jack's father became president of the United States. For Jack it meant traveling with his parents to European capitals and even venturing into the Soviet Union, as well as periodically serving as his father's representative on speaking tours in the United States—"heady stuff" for a Utah State University graduate in forestry.

Perhaps something of the young man's character is reflected in his statement, following his father's 1976 loss of the presidential office to Jimmy Carter, when Jack observed, "You know, when you come so close, it's really hard to lose. But at the same time, if you can't lose graciously as you had planned to win, then you shouldn't have been in the race in the first place."[156]

STEVEN MEIGS FORD

Third child, third son of Gerald R. Ford and Elizabeth Anne Bloomer

Born: May 19, 1956   *Birthplace:* Washington, D.C.
Education: T. C. Williams High School, Utah State University, California Polytechnical Institute
Profession: Actor
Spouse: None
Number of Children: None

"THE YOUNG AND THE RESTLESS"

Only seventeen when his father became president, Steve Ford was a Washington "political brat," raised by the family nanny during his father's and mother's constant travels to fulfill the political duties of Ford's elective office. Completing his high school education, Steve was attracted by the life of ranching, and in pursuit of his interests he went west to work on a ranch. Though originally setting his goal on dentistry because "a dentist can be his own man, set his own hours. I could never shuffle papers eight hours a day," eventually he changed his mind.[157]

In 1981 Steve Ford, the former president's son, living in California near scenic San Luis Obispo, became involved in political activities to prevent the opening of the Diablo Canyon nuclear power plant on a major fault near the plant and ten miles from Steve's home. With the son, considered by some to be the most attractive, politically, as well as physically, observers suggest that at this time his career was not yet apparent.

Success came to this attractive young Ford with little effort. Taking a bit part in a popular daytime soap opera, "The Young and the Restless," young Steve met with popular approval by the viewing audience. His role was expanded until today he is well on his way to becoming a star of the series as well as a sex symbol to millions of avid viewers. With exposure such as young Steve is receiving, there is no telling where he might go.

SUSAN ELIZABETH FORD VANCE

Fourth child, only daughter of Gerald R. Ford and Elizabeth Anne Bloomer

Born: July 6, 1957   *Birthplace:* Washington, D.C.
Education: Holton-Arms School, Mt. Vernon College, University of Kansas
Profession: Photojournalist
Spouse: Charles Vance
Number of Children: 1

A SECRET SERVICE BLESSING

The only daughter and youngest of the four Ford children, Susan was born in the Washington, D.C., suburb of Alexandria, Virginia, when her father was a House of Representatives member from Michigan. As had her brothers, Susan studied at that city's public schools, until, when she was sixteen, her father became the nation's vice-president. Though she had worked in the White House during summer vacations selling books as souvenirs, as well as periodically working for her father in his capitol building office, when Gerald R. Ford became president, Susan was elevated to that rarified atmosphere of a president's daughter, living in the White House. Her teenage life changed.

Susan's father did not hesitate to make use of the Secret Service as a method of keeping tabs on his only daughter during both his vice-presidency and presidency. On occasion when Susan would arrive home later than scheduled her father would question, "What time did you get home last night?" Susan's general response of "oh, early" was immediately checked, when her father would refer to the agent's log for her arrival time. The use of the Secret Service with presidential children is well known, and privacy is little known. Father Ford, however, thought the Secret Service logs kept by the agents and designated to protect presidential families' children were a blessing for his parental role.

Susan, like the other Ford children, encouraged her father to run for the presidential office in 1976. When he was defeated, it was Susan, along with her mother and father, that made the final trip out of the United States before Carter's inauguration, when the family took a late November 1976 presidential trip to China.

In 1979, twenty-one-year-old Susan, a California resident, married Charles Vance. Ironically, he was a thirty-seven-year-old Secret Service agent, assigned to protect the former president's family. Perhaps Ford's assessment of the "blessing" of the Secret Service was prophetically accurate—at least for Susan. The couple married in California at a wedding held at the former president's home with 300 guests in attendance.

FOR FURTHER READING

Ford, Gerald R. *A Time to Heal*. New York, New York: Harper & Row, 1979.

Mollenhoff, Clark R. *The Man Who Pardoned Nixon*. New York, New York: St. Martin's Press, 1976.

Vesta, Bud. *Jerry Ford: Up Close*. New York, New York: Coward, McCann & Geoghegan, 1974.

33 JAMES EARL CARTER'S CHILDREN

JOHN WILLIAM CARTER

First child of James Earl Carter and Rosalynn Smith

Born: July 3, 1947   *Birthplace:* Portsmouth, Virginia
Education: Georgia Institute of Technology, University of Georgia Law School
Profession: Businessman, Lawyer
Spouse: Juliette Langford
Number of Children: 2

"POLITICS IS LIKE TAKING A BATH"

The eldest of the three Carter sons, John William, called Jack by family and media, is a successful businessman in his home state of Georgia. Though active in his political father's activities, he is first a businessman and then his father's campaigner. Claiming to have developed an early political sense with the story that, "Back when I was 13 my mother made me take a bath. I never liked it. Once I got in the bathtub, though, I liked it. The campaign is like that," Jack nevertheless has had limited time to devote to his father's profession.[158]

Perhaps because Jack is the eldest of Carter's children, he was able to speak with authority about his father's interests once his father's quest for a second term as president failed. Thirty-three-year-old Jack told reporters that though the loss of the office of the presidency was somewhat embarrassing, particularly referring to the sound defeat at the hands of the electorate, speaking for his parents he said, "but neither of my parents is taking it hard in the sense of being emotionally strung out about it."[159]

Living in Calhoun, Georgia, practicing law, as well as operating a grain storage business, this Carter son, too, may well enter the political scene in Georgia in the future. Though he has not acknowledged that he will run for a congressional seat from the state, Carter watchers do not discount the entry of this son into his father's arena.

JAMES EARL CARTER III

Second child, second son of James Earl Carter and Rosalynn Smith

Born: April 12, 1950   *Birthplace:* Honolulu, Hawaii
Education: Public schools   *Profession:* Businessman, Politician
Spouses: Caron Griffith, Ginger Hodges
Number of Children: Carter/Griffith: 1
                                         Carter/Hodges: None

POLITICAL STAND-IN

The middle of the three Carter sons and his father's namesake, James Earl, called "Chip" by his family and the press, is often viewed as most similar to his political father, both in appearance and ambition. However, the strong character of his mother is also to be seen in Chip, particularly in her "even-tempered, soft-spoken disposition."[160]

This son claims to have been an active political campaigner when he was ten years old, when he worked to gain support for John Fitzgerald Kennedy's election to the presidency in 1960. Campaigning actively for his father, seeking his first election to the Georgia state Senate, and eventually helping his father successfully reach the Georgia governorship, Chip and his mother proved to be the most politically active and effective of Carter's immediate family. The pair often substituted as stand-ins for father and husband, particularly during the period of the 1980 election when President Carter chose not to engage directly in domestic politics, claiming a higher priority, the Iranian hostage crisis.

Carter, discerning his best position for the campaign was at the communication and decision center of the White House, in the rose garden (which was the name tagged to his strategy) opted to have Chip and Rosalynn deliver needed political appearances and speeches during the early stages of the 1980 election.

Periodically introducing himself as "Amy's brother," referring, lightheartedly, to his younger sister's press coverage, Chip's political appearances were so traditional that "Chip kissed a few babies, cut one ribbon," and massaged local pride stating that "Virginia [or Michigan or Wisconsin] was one of the president's 'top targeted' states."[161]

Chip, the father of James Earl Carter IV, divorced from his first wife, but remarried in 1982. He feels today that his more than twenty years of political activism and involvement in the highest office of the land fit him for a political office. Despite his divorce, which today is less of a political disadvantage than in prior times, Chip plans to enter the Georgia legislative race, the same step that initiated his father on the road to the nation's presidency.

DONNELL JEFFREY CARTER

Third child, third son of James Earl Carter and Rosalynn Smith

Born: August 18, 1952   *Birthplace:* New London, Connecticut
Education: George Washington University
Profession: Businessman
Spouse: Annette Davis
Number of Children: None

THE UNKNOWN CARTER

In the heyday of mass media coverage and with a family which, by itself, attracted the most detailed attention perhaps ever experienced by a first family, Jeff Carter managed to remain a mystery to most of the public.

Graduating from George Washington University in Washington, D.C., specializing in computer cartography (a scientific technique used by demographers and city planners and even energy developers in planning space use) Jeff earned his bachelor's degree and immediately joined his instructor to found a computer consulting firm. It was a risk for both. At the beginning, the venture did not seem likely to succeed, as earnings fell well below a living wage for two.

But in 1980 Jeff's company's future dramatically brightened when the wife of Philippine President Marcos asked Jeff for assistance in her planned slum-clearance project. Jeff's presidential father, informed of the potential business deal by his son, gave his approval, though he insisted that the business be run as would any other business, without a presidential father. Perhaps Jimmy Carter had in mind press coverage of his brother Billy's business with the Libyan government. Nevertheless, Jeff and company received the Philippine government's contract, which would pay them in excess of $200,000, thus making sure that his out-of-work father would not have to support this Carter child.

AMY LYNN CARTER

Fourth child, first daughter of James Earl Carter and Rosalynn Smith

Born: October 19, 1967   *Birthplace:* Plains, Georgia
Education: Thaddeus Stevens School, Francis Junior High School,
Tri-County High School, (Ga.)
Profession: Student
Spouse: None
Number of Children: None

A PRESIDENTIAL ADVISER

Both public and press expected to enjoy the antics of the first young child to enter the White House since John Fitzgerald Kennedy's two small children in 1960. But Amy Carter did not prove to be charming press material, and, in fact, may have become the object of press barbs whose effect was directed at her father. This directly contrasted to the Kennedy children, John and Caroline, who could do no wrong and, in fact, enhanced Kennedy's image.

Trouble with the press began almost immediately for Amy Carter. Enrolled in a public school near the White House in a highly concentrated black area, Amy was to further her father's ambition to live as a man of the people, but Amy was forced to withdraw when any semblance of normal life was prevented by daily press attention to her, her teachers, and fellow students. The president's daughter could not be just one of the people, and sending her to a public school proved to be a mistake. It was a mistake as well, when, in some apparent attempt at normalcy, Amy was included in state dinners with visiting dignitaries in attendance. The girl read her books during what were clearly boring times for her, but the alternative of the young child's attempting to make polite conversation with heads of state was clearly impossible. The press even reported the titles of the books she read, making the entire attempted "down-home" atmosphere ludicrous.

The president's effort to reach the people through the "earthiness" and simplicity of a child went from the absurd to the politically disastrous. In the hotly contested race for the presidency during a crucial nationally televised debate with Carter's opponent Ronald Reagan, the president used his daughter as an authority for saying that the most important issue facing the nation was the control of nuclear proliferation. The nation roared with laughter. The image of the most powerful nation's head of state and leader of the free world seeking the advice of a thirteen-year-old girl on the fundamental issues facing the globe was too much for even the most ardent Carter supporters. Only days before the election one of the nation's sports heroes, Roger Staubach, himself the father of a girl named Amy, tweaked the president's nose on national television, when he said, "In fact, I talked to my daughter, Amy, this morning about it [when referring to the loss of a football game] and she said the number one problem was the bomb."[162]

In general, children have been political plusses to a politician, hence the constant "baby kissing" so typical of politicians. But in Carter's little Amy there exists strong repudiation of the time-worn maxim. From the contrived normalcy of the Carter White House, Amy has been thrust back to the family home in Plains, Georgia.

FOR FURTHER READING

Baker, James T. *Southern Baptist in the White House*. New York, New York: Westminster Press, 1977.

Blount, Roy, Jr. *Crackers: This Whole Many-Angled Thing of Jimmy, More Carters, Ominous Little Animals, Sad-Singing Women, My Daddy and Me.* New York, New York: Alfred Knopf, 1980.

Kucharsky, David. *Man from Plains: The Mind and Spirit of Jimmy Carter*. New York, New York: Harper, 1976.

Mazlish, Bruce, and Edwin Diamond. *Jimmy Carter: A Character Portrait*. New York, New York: Simon and Schuster, 1979.

Meyer, Peter. *James Earl Carter: The Man and the Myth*. Mission, Kansas: Andrews and McMeel, 1978.

Miller, William Lee. *Yankee from Georgia: The Emergence of Jimmy Carter*. Los Angeles, California: Time Books, 1978.

Mollenhoff, Clark R. *President Who Failed: Carter Out of Control*. New York, New York: Macmillan, 1980.

34 RONALD WILSON REAGAN'S CHILDREN

MAUREEN ELIZABETH REAGAN FILIPPONE SILLS REVELL

First natural-born child of Ronald Wilson Reagan and Jane Wyman

Born: January 4, 1941   *Birthplace:* Los Angeles, California
Education: Marymount College
Profession: Businesswoman, Politician, Television and Radio Personality
Spouse: John Filippone, David Sills, Dennis Revell
Number of Children: None

ANOTHER POLITICAL REAGAN?

A vocal, vivacious, and avid campaigner for her father in his quest for the presidency, Maureen Reagan, the eldest of the Reagan children, had joined the Republican party well before her father moved from the Democratic party into Republican ranks. With an enthusiasm not unlike that of an aging cheerleader, Maureen is, perhaps, the most memorable of the Reagan offspring, ofttimes to her father's chagrin. Maureen is an avid supporter of the Equal Rights Amendment, which Reagan has not supported, advocating women's full participation in society.

As the daughter of an actor and part-time politician, Maureen was educated in boarding schools, eventually attending Marymount College in Virginia, until she dropped out to become a struggling actress and singer, which business she quickly determined was not for her. Though she briefly hosted a talk show in California, Maureen found a more permanent use for her outgoing personality when she became an executive with a public relations firm for export promotion.

Three times married, most recently to a law student several years her junior, Maureen again came into the public eye when she sought the U.S. Senate seat from the state of California.

Given the intensity of Maureen Reagan, her strongly held opinions, and her fearlessness in front of the microphone, it is not likely that despite her loss in California's Republican primary election the American public has seen or heard the last of this Reagan child.

MICHAEL EDWARD REAGAN

First adopted child of Ronald Wilson Reagan and Jane Wyman

Born: 1945   *Birthplace:* Unknown
Education: Arizona State University   *Profession:* Businessman
Spouses: Pamela Putnam, Colleen Sterns
Number of Children: Reagan/Putnam: None
                            Reagan/Sterns: 1

AN ADOPTED SON

Ronald Reagan, during his first marriage to actress Jane Wyman, adopted a son, Michael. Michael attended various schools as a young man, receiving a football scholarship. But Michael turned down the offer and instead he married and devoted his time to motorboat racing. The interest in the sport continued while the marriage ended.

Working in various businesses, Michael eventually became an executive with a title company. It was in connection with another business that Michael achieved some notoriety. For, in seeking government business for the firm he represented, Michael, unfortunately, made use of his affiliation with his father, the president. He was severely criticized by the press for his use of presidential influence. Consequently, his father restated an earlier admonishment to exercise care not to seem to be using his father's position for personal gain. After first announcing that he would resign from the company, Michael then backed down and merely stated that under no conditions would he make use of his father's name for business gain.

Outside of his misstep, Michael appears to be the more staid of Reagan's four children. Living quietly in California with his second wife and child, he has provided Reagan with his only grandchild.

Intensely interested in his father's political career, Michael took only a modest part in the campaign, but gave freely of his advice. While Reagan had never appeared to the public to be weak or vacillating in his political positions, his son saw his father not living up to his potential for decisiveness and clarity. Thus it was Michael who informed the press that, "I'd tell him that he should come across strong more often."[163]

PATRICIA ANN REAGAN (DAVIS)

Third child of Ronald Wilson Reagan; first child of Ronald Wilson Reagan and Nancy Davis

Born: October 21, 1952   *Birthplace:* Los Angeles, California
Education: Northwestern University   *Profession:* Actress
Spouse: None   *Number of Children:* None

A FUTURE STAR

An entertainer like her father and her mother as well, Patty Davis took the stage name Davis from her mother's maiden name. Patty, however, does not share her family's political interests. Explaining why she did not actively campaign in her father's 1980 presidential race, she stated that she is "anti-political."[164]

Often called the family rebel, Patty dropped out of college to escape to the company of a rock musician, with whom she lived for some time. Expressing opposition to the Vietnam War and becoming part of the counterculture of the early 1970s, Patty and her family became alienated, only to be reunited when her father won election to the presidency. Patty, the former "San Francisco hippie," attended the inauguration in a Dior-designed gown.

Prior to the election, Patty appeared on television in some small dramatic roles. Immediately following the election, her career took a quick upturn. One of the country's leading agents accepted her as a client. The election, she candidly admitted, "has done wonders for my career."[165] But she did not entirely attribute her new-found success to her father's position, observing, "but it's not as if I slid into it. For years I've been going to auditions, getting a few parts, being turned down for others. I've worked as a waitress to pay the rent; I feel as if I've paid my dues."[166] Only time will tell whether the president's daughter has talent.

RONALD PRESCOTT REAGAN

Fourth child of Ronald Wilson Reagan; second child, first son of Ronald Wilson Reagan and Nancy Davis

Born: May 20, 1958   *Birthplace:* Los Angeles, California
Education: Yale University   *Profession:* Dancer
Spouse: Doria Palmieri   *Number of Children:* None

A DANCER'S FOOT-IN-MOUTH DISEASE

Ronald Reagan, son of his father's second marriage, was a fine student, but very early in life he became fascinated by the entertainment business to which he was constantly exposed in his California home. Of all the artistic forms of the theatre, dance was the artistic medium that most intrigued the young man. But it was not until his late teens that he began to study seriously. Earning a scholarship to New York City's Joffrey School of Dance and eventually becoming a regular member of the traveling dance troupe, Ronald embarked on a career which he still maintains. Critics have been kind to the president's son when he danced in the modest roles he has been given thus far, but they have not been kind about all of this son's actions.

Indeed, his own family was flabbergasted when Ronald dropped out of Yale University to become a ballet dancer while his father sought the presidency. Also of some concern to the family was his relationship with and marriage to an older woman. And, finally, the unwitting candor of this young man who refused to shake the hand of the ex-president, Jimmy Carter, at his father's inauguration, and his statement, reported in the national press, that President Jimmy Carter had the "morals of a snake," betrayed the young son's complete lack of the political sense that his father has so ably shown.

FOR FURTHER READING

Edwards, Lee. *Ronald Reagan: A Political Biography*. Belmont, Massachusetts: Nordland Publishing, 1980.

Smith, Hedrick, et al. *Reagan: The Man, the President*. New York: Macmillan, 1980.

Trimble, Vance H. *Reagan: The Man from Mainstreet U.S.A.* Oakville, Ontario, Canada: Mosaic Press, 1980.

APPENDIX: SHARED CHARACTERISTICS OF PRESIDENTS' CHILDREN

In the introduction to this book, we asked whether children of the presidents shared characteristics, and especially if it is an advantage in life to be born to a man who will be, or is, a president of the United States. Now we are able to answer these questions.

A review of their lives suggests that it is an advantage to have been born to a president. Opportunities for both male and female children far outstrip the national norm. Male children, in general, have achieved professional levels of high status; while females, particularly those of the eighteenth and nineteenth centuries, generally married men of wealth and influence. Following the general historical trend, women who reached maturity in the twentieth century have joined their male peers in professional achievements. In both males and females, however, there are exceptions to this observation.

The objection that may be advanced to the foregoing judgment is that these children would have achieved prominence despite their fathers' positions as presidents because they were part of "upper-class" America anyway. However, without a long, drawn-out argument, which may appear to be seeking the answer to "which came first, the chicken or the egg?" we can say that some of the presidents' families were not distinguished before taking office. Further, presidential fathers have not hesitated to use their own positions to advance the careers of their children—not unlike fathers in all walks of life.

As for other characteristics that presidents' children share, we have gathered some general information that may prove interesting, however it is interpreted.

The following tables display the common traits and vital statistics of the collected children.

MONTHS OF BIRTHS OF PRESIDENTIAL CHILDREN

Months of Birth	Numbers of Births in Descending Order of Months
January: 6	August: 18
February: 10	July: 17
March: 12	April: 16

Note: With the exception of Reagan's adopted son, adopted children and illegitimate children have not been included in the numbers.

April: 16

May: 10

June: 2

July: 17

August: 18

September: 15

October: 13

November: 8

December: 11

Unknown: 5

Total: 142

     1 Adopted

  143

September: 15

October: 13

March: 12

December: 11

February: 10

May: 10

November: 8

January: 6

June: 2

Most Common Month of Birth: August

Least Common Month of Birth: June

HOROSCOPE SIGNS OF PRESIDENTIAL CHILDREN

Aries: March 21–April 19   Males: 7   Females: 7

Jane Randolph Jefferson

George Washington Adams

Mary Tyler

Alice Tyler

John Alexander Tyler

Anne Margaret Mackall Tyler

Mary Abigail Fillmore

Benjamin Pierce

Thomas Lincoln

Mary Scott Harrison

Ida McKinley

Archibald Bulloch Roosevelt

Calvin Coolidge, Jr.

James Earl Carter III

Taurus: April 20–May 20   Males: 4   Females: 6

Lucy Elizabeth Jefferson II

John Tyler, Jr.

Letitia Tyler

Mary Elizabeth Taylor

Millard Powers Fillmore

Mary Johnson

Margaret Woodrow Wilson

Anna Eleanor Roosevelt

Steven Meigs Ford

Ronald Prescott Reagan

Gemini: May 21–June 21   Males: 3   Females: 1

Charles Adams

"Son" Jefferson

Pearl Tyler

Frederick Dent Grant

Cancer: June 22–July 22   Males: 8   Females: 8

Abigail Amelia Adams

John Quincy Adams

John Adams II

Elizabeth Tyler

David Gardiner Tyler

Ulysses S. Grant II

Ellen Grant

Rutherford Platt Hayes

Eliza Arabella Garfield

Marion Cleveland

Francis Grover Cleveland

Allan Henry Hoover

Lucy (Luci) Johnson

Julie Nixon

Susan Ford

John William Carter

Leo: July 23–August 22   Males: 12   Females: 5

Mary Jefferson

Charles Francis Adams

Octavia Taylor

Margaret Taylor

Robert Todd Lincoln

Andrew Johnson, Jr.

Manning Force Hayes

Irvin McDowell Garfield
Chester Alan Arthur II
Russell Benjamin Harrison
Ethel Carow Roosevelt
Helen Herron Taft
Herbert Clark Hoover, Jr.
Franklin Delano Roosevelt, Jr.
John Sheldon Doud Eisenhower
Patrick Bouvier Kennedy
Donnell Jeffrey Carter

Virgo: August 23–September 22   **Males: 8**   **Females: 3**
Thomas Boylston Adams
William Henry Harrison, Jr.
Robert Tyler
Frank Robert Pierce
Fanny Hayes
Esther Cleveland
Theodore Roosevelt, Jr.
Robert Alphonso Taft
Charles Phelps Taft
Jessie Woodrow Wilson
John Coolidge

Libra: September 23–October 23   **Males: 7**   **Females: 6**
Martha Washington Jefferson
Elizabeth Bassett Harrison
John Scott Harrison
George Crook Hayes
Harry Augustus Garfield
James Rudolph Garfield
Ruth Cleveland
Kermit Roosevelt
Eleanor Randolph Wilson
Elliott Roosevelt
Dwight Doud Eisenhower
Amy Carter
Patricia Reagan (Davis)

Scorpio: October 24–November 21   Males: 6   Females: 4

    Lucy Elizabeth Jefferson I

    John Cleves Symmes Harrison

    Carter Bassett Harrison

    Anna Tuthill Harrison

    Martha Johnson

    Birchard Austin Hayes

    Abram Garfield

    Ellen Herndon Arthur

    Richard Folsom Cleveland

    Quentin Roosevelt

Sagittarius: November 22–December 21   Males: 8   Females: 1

    Abraham Van Buren

    Martin Van Buren, Jr.

    Tazewell Tyler

    Lachlin Tyler

    William Wallace Lincoln

    Joseph Thompson Hayes

    William Lewis Arthur

    Caroline Kennedy

    John Fitzgerald Kennedy

Capricorn: December 22–January 19   Males: 3   Females: 5

    Susanna Adams

    Smith Thompson Van Buren

    Julia Tyler

    Mary Garfield

    Edward Garfield

    Katherine McKinley

    James Roosevelt

    Maureen Reagan

Aquarius: January 20–February 18   Males: 5   Females: 3

    John Van Buren

    Mary Symmes Harrison

    Richard Taylor

    Franklin Pierce

    Jesse Root Grant

Scott Russell Hayes

Alice Lee Roosevelt

Margaret Truman

Pisces: February 19–March 20   **Males:** 10   **Females:** 4

Thomas Boylston Adams

Robert Fitzwalter Tyler

Sarah Knox Taylor

Edward Baker Lincoln

Charles Johnson

Robert Johnson

James Webb Cook Hayes

Elizabeth Harrison

Franklin Roosevelt

John Aspinwall Roosevelt

Lynda Johnson

Patricia Nixon

Michael Gerald Ford

John Gardner Ford

Unknown Months and Days of Birth

Louisa Catherine Adams

Lucy Singleton Harrison

Benjamin Harrison

James Findlay Harrison

Anne Contesse Tyler

Lyon Gardiner Tyler

Michael Reagan (adopted)

STATES OF BIRTH OF PRESIDENTIAL CHILDREN

Ohio: 24

Virginia: 24

New York: 21

Massachusetts: 12

Washington, D.C.: 12

Indiana: 8

Kentucky: 5

Georgia: 4

Illinois: 4

Missouri: 5

New Hampshire: 3

Colorado: 2

Connecticut: 2

Hawaii: 1

Tennessee: 5

California: 4

New Jersey: 1

FOREIGN NATIONS AS PLACES OF BIRTH OF PRESIDENTIAL CHILDREN

London, England: 2

Berlin, Germany: 1

Paris, France: 1

St. Petersburg (Leningrad), Russia: 1

Unknown: 2

NUMBER OF CHILDREN PRODUCED BY PRESIDENTIAL CHILDREN, BY CENTURY

Eighteenth century: 23

Nineteenth century: 177

Twentieth century: 27

Presidential children who produced no children or whose number is unknown: 13

COMMON SCHOOLS OF PRESIDENTIAL CHILDREN

Harvard University: 20

Columbia University: 6

Cornell University: 6

Groton Preparatory School: 6

Yale University: 6

Princeton University: 4

West Point: 3

Phillips Academy: 2

Stanford University: 2

Williams College: 2

University of Virginia: 2

COMMON OCCUPATIONS OF PRESIDENTIAL CHILDREN

Politicians: Elected or Appointed

John Quincy Adams

Thomas Boylston Adams

Charles Francis Adams

John Van Buren

William Henry Harrison, Jr.

John Scott Harrison

Robert Tyler

John Tyler, Jr.

Harry Augustus Garfield

James Rudolph Garfield

Russell Benjamin Harrison

Theodore Roosevelt, Jr.

Robert Alphonso Taft

Charles Phelps Taft

Jessie Woodrow Wilson Sayre

Herbert Clark Hoover, Jr.

David Gardiner Tyler

John Alexander Tyler

Lyon Gardiner Tyler

Richard Taylor

Robert Todd Lincoln

Frederick Dent Grant

James Roosevelt

Franklin Delano Roosevelt, Jr.

Lynda Johnson Robb

James Earl Carter III

Maureen Reagan Filippone Sills Revell

Lawyers

Charles Adams

Thomas Boylston Adams

George Washington Adams

John Van Buren

William Henry Harrison, Jr.

Carter Bassett Harrison

Robert Tyler

John Tyler, Jr.

David Gardiner Tyler

Lyon Gardiner Tyler

Millard Powers Fillmore

Robert Todd Lincoln

Robert Johnson

Ulysses S. Grant II

Birchard Austin Hayes

Harry Augustus Garfield

James Rudolph Garfield

Irvin McDowell Garfield

Richard Folsom Cleveland

Elizabeth Harrison Walker

Robert Alphonso Taft

Charles Phelps Taft

Franklin Delano Roosevelt, Jr.

John William Carter

Writers/Editors

Thomas Boylston Adams

Charles Francis Adams

Smith Thompson Van Buren

Robert Tyler

Lyon Gardiner Tyler

Richard Taylor

Andrew Johnson, Jr.

Jesse Root Grant

Russell Benjamin Harrison

Elizabeth Harrison Walker

Theodore Roosevelt, Jr.

Eleanor Randolph Wilson McAdoo

Anna Eleanor Roosevelt Dall Boettiger Halsted

Elliott Roosevelt

Margaret Truman Daniels

John Sheldon Doud Eisenhower

Julie Nixon Eisenhower

Soldiers

Abraham Van Buren

Robert Tyler

Richard Taylor

Robert Todd Lincoln

James Webb Cook Hayes

Theodore Roosevelt, Jr.

Kermit Roosevelt

Archibald Bulloch Roosevelt

Charles Johnson   Quinton Roosevelt

Robert Johnson   Elliott Roosevelt

Frederick Dent Grant   John Sheldon Doud Eisenhower

Presidential Aides/Secretaries

John Quincy Adams   Robert Todd Lincoln

John Adams II   Robert Johnson

Abraham Van Buren   Ulysses S. Grant II

Martin Van Buren, Jr.   James Webb Cook Hayes

Smith Thompson Van Buren   Russell Benjamin Harrison

Robert Tyler   John Sheldon Doud Eisenhower

Millard Powers Fillmore

Teachers

John Quincy Adams   Francis Grover Cleveland

Letitia Tyler Semple   Helen Herron Taft Manning

Lyon Gardiner Tyler   James Roosevelt

Mary Abigail Fillmore   John Sheldon Doud Eisenhower

Harry Augustus Garfield

White House Hostesses

Martha Washington Jefferson Randolph

Eliza Kortright Monroe Hay

Mary Elizabeth Taylor Bliss Dandridge

Mary Abigail Fillmore

Martha Johnson Patterson

NUMBER OF CHILDREN BORN TO PRESIDENTS

Male: 85

Female: 58

Adopted: 2 (males)

Supposed illegitimate: 7 or 8

COMMON NAMES OF PRESIDENTIAL CHILDREN

John

Quincy Adams

Adams II

Van Buren

Cleves Symmes Harrison

Scott Harrison

Tyler, Jr.

Alexander Tyler

Coolidge

Aspinwall Roosevelt

Sheldon Doud Eisenhower

Fitzgerald Kennedy

Gardner Ford

William Carter

Mary, Maria

Jefferson Eppes

Hester Monroe Gouveneur

Symmes Harrison Thornton

Abigail Fillmore

Garfield Stanley-Brown

Scott Harrison McKee

James

Findlay Harrison

Webb Cook Hayes

Rudolph Garfield

Roosevelt

Earl Carter III

Charles

Adams

Francis Adams

Johnson

Phelps Taft

Robert

Fitzwalter Tyler

Todd Lincoln

Johnson

Alphonso Taft

Anna, Anne

Tuthill Harrison Taylor

Contesse Tyler

Margaret Mackall Taylor Wood

Eleanor Roosevelt Dall Boettiger Halsted

Lucy

Elizabeth Jefferson I

Elizabeth Jefferson II

Singleton Harrison Este

Margaret

Taylor

Woodrow Wilson

Truman Daniels

William

Henry Harrison, Jr.

Wallace Lincoln

Lewis Arthur

Abram, Abraham

Van Buren

Garfield

Edward

Baker Lincoln

Garfield

Martha

Washington Jefferson Randolph

Johnson Patterson

Richard

Taylor

Folsom Cleveland

Thomas

Boylston Adams

Lincoln

LONGEVITY OF PRESIDENTIAL CHILDREN

Survived Most Years

Alice Roosevelt Longworth: 96 years

Survived Shortest Period

Patrick Bouvier Kennedy

Died before Five Years Old

Susanna Adams: 1 year, 1 month

Jane Randolph Jefferson: 1 year, 6 months

"Son" Jefferson: 17 days

Lucy Elizabeth Jefferson I: 5 months

Lucy Elizabeth Jefferson II: 3 years, 6 months

J. S. Monroe: 2 years, 4 months

Louisa Catherine Adams: 1 year

James Finlay Harrison: 3 years

Anne Contesse Tyler: 3 months

Octavia Taylor: 3 years, 8 months

Margaret Taylor: 1 year, 3 months

Franklin Pierce: 3 days

Frank Robert Pierce: 4 years, 3 months

Edward Baker Lincoln: 3 years, 11 months

Joseph Thompson Hayes: 1 year, 6 months

George Crook Hayes: 1 year, 8 months

Manning Force Hayes: 1 year

Eliza Arabella Garfield: 3 years, 5 months

Edward Garfield: 1 year, 10 months

William Lewis Arthur: 2 years, 7 months

Katherine McKinley: 3 years, 6 months

Ida McKinley: 5 months

Franklin Roosevelt: 8 months

Dwight Doud Eisenhower: 3 years, 4 months

Patrick Bouvier Kennedy: 2 days

Died between Five Years and Twenty-One Years of Age

Benjamin Pierce: 11 years, 8 months

William Wallace Lincoln: 11 years, 2 months

Thomas Lincoln: 18 years, 3 months

Ruth Cleveland: 12 years, 3 months

Quentin Roosevelt: 20 years, 5 months

Calvin Coolidge, Jr.: 16 years

Survived beyond Seventy-Five Years of Age

> John Quincy Adams: 80 years, 7 months
> Charles Francis Adams: 79 years, 3 months
> John Tyler, Jr.: 76 years, 9 months
> Letitia Tyler Semple: 86 years, 7 months
> David Gardiner Tyler: 81 years, 2 months
> Lyon Gardiner Tyler: 81 years, 6 months
> Pearl Tyler Ellis: 87 years
> Mary Elizabeth Taylor Bliss Dandridge: 85 years, 3 months
> Robert Todd Lincoln: 82 years, 9 months
> Ulysses S. Grant II: 77 years, 2 months
> Jesse Root Grant: 76 years, 4 months
> James Webb Cook Hayes: 78 years, 4 months
> Fanny Hayes Smith: 82 years, 6 months
> Harry Augustus Garfield: 79 years, 2 months
> James Rudolph Garfield: 84 years, 5 months
> Mary Garfield Stanley-Brown: 80 years, 11 months
> Irvin McDowell Garfield: 80 years, 11 months
> Abram Garfield: 85 years, 11 months
> Marion Cleveland Dell Amen: 81 years, 11 months
> Richard Folsom Cleveland: 76 years, 3 months
> Russell Benjamin Harrison: 82 years, 4 months
> Alice Lee Roosevelt Longworth: 96 years
> Ethel Carow Roosevelt Derby: 86 years, 4 months
> Archibald Bulloch Roosevelt: 87 years, 3 months
> Eleanor Randolph Wilson McAdoo: 77 years, 5 months

Presidential Children Still Alive

> Helen Herron Taft Manning
> Charles Phelps Taft
> John Coolidge
> Allan Henry Hoover
> James Roosevelt
> Elliott Roosevelt
> Franklin Delano Roosevelt, Jr.
> Margaret Truman Daniels

John Sheldon Doud Eisenhower

Caroline Kennedy

John Fitzgerald Kennedy

Lynda Johnson Robb

Lucy (Luci) Johnson Nugent

Patricia Nixon Cox

Julie Nixon Eisenhower

Michael Gerald Ford

John Gardner Ford

Steven Meigs Ford

Susan Ford Vance

John William Carter

James Earl Carter III

Donnell Jeffrey Carter

Amy Carter

Maureen Reagan Filippone Sills Revell

Michael Reagan

Patricia Reagan (Davis)

Ronald Prescott Reagan

CAUSES OF DEATH OF PRESIDENTIAL CHILDREN

Disease

Diphtheria: Thomas Lincoln

   Eliza Arabella Garfield

   Ruth Cleveland

Whooping Cough: Lucy Elizabeth Jefferson II

   Edward Garfield

Malaria: Sarah Knox Taylor Davis

   Richard Taylor

Yellow Fever: Octavia Pannel Taylor

   Margaret Smith Taylor

Scarlet Fever: George Crook Hayes

   Dwight Doud Eisenhower

Amoebic Dysentery: Kermit Roosevelt

Cholera: Mary Abigail Fillmore

Convulsions: William Lewis Arthur

Dysentery: John Alexander Tyler

    Joseph Thompson Hayes

Pneumonia: William Wallace Lincoln

Typhoid Fever: Katherine McKinley

Cancer:

Abigail Amelia Adams Smith

Frederick Dent Grant

Scott Russell Hayes

Robert Alphonso Taft

Herbert Clark Hoover, Jr.

Anna Eleanor Roosevelt Dall Boettiger Halsted

Stroke/Cerebral Hemorrhage:

John Quincy Adams (cerebral hemorrhage)

Martha Washington Jefferson Randolph (apoplexy)

Charles Francis Adams (stroke)

Millard Powers Fillmore (apoplexy)

Archibald Bulloch Roosevelt (stroke)

Alcohol or Alcohol-Related Illness:

Charles Adams

John Adams II

William Henry Harrison, Jr.

Tazewell Tyler

Robert Johnson

Complications of Childbirth:

Mary Jefferson Eppes

Elizabeth Tyler Waller

Julia Tyler Spencer

Suicide:

George Washington Adams (drowning)

Charles Johnson (gunshot)

Death from Surgical Complications:

Ellen Herndon Arthur Pinkerton

Jessie Woodrow Wilson Sayre

War Death:

Quentin Roosevelt

Death from Accidents:

Benjamin Pierce (railroad accident)

Heart Attack:

Theodore Roosevelt, Jr.

John Aspinwall Roosevelt

Kidney Failure:

John Van Buren

Uremic Poisoning:

Margaret Woodrow Wilson

Blood Poisoning:

Calvin Coolidge, Jr.

Bilious Colic:

Alice Tyler Denison

Unknown*:

Susanna Adams

Thomas Boylston Adams

Jane Randolph Jefferson

"Son" Jefferson

Lucy Jefferson I

Eliza Kortright Monroe

J. S. Monroe

Maria Hester Monroe

Louisa Katherine Adams

Abraham Van Buren

Martin Van Buren

Smith Thompson Van Buren

Elizabeth Bassett Harrison Short

John Cleves Symmes Harrison

Lucy Singleton Harrison Este

John Scott Harrison

* Press records do not indicate exact cause of death.

Benjamin Harrison

Mary Symmes Harrison

Carter Bassett Harrison

Anna Tuthill Harrison

James Findlay Harrison

Mary Tyler

Robert Tyler

John Tyler, Jr.

David Gardiner Tyler

Lachlin Tyler

Lyon Gardiner Tyler

Robert Fitzwalter Tyler

Pearl Tyler

Anne Margaret Mackall Taylor Wood

Mary Elizabeth Taylor Dandridge

NOTES

1. Joseph J. Perling, *Presidents' Sons: The Prestige of Name in a Democracy* (1947; reprint ed., New York: Arno Press, 1970), p. 358.

2. Ibid., p. 370.

3. Lida Mayo, "Miss Adams in Love," *American Heritage* 16 (February 1965): 35–47. Cranch was Amelia's uncle on her mother's side. Letters to Royall were forwarded by Cranch.

4. Ibid., p. 87.

5. Ibid., p. 89.

6. Ibid.

7. Perling, *Presidents' Sons*, p. 9.

8. Ibid., p. 19.

9. Jack Shepherd, *The Adams' Chronicles* (Boston: Little, Brown, 1975), p. 210.

10. Ibid.

11. Perling, *Presidents' Sons*, p. 24.

12. Ibid., p. 28.

13. Fawn M. Brodie, *Thomas Jefferson: An Intimate History* (New York: W. W. Norton & Company, Inc., 1974), p. 109.

14. Christine Sadler, *Children in the White House* (New York: G. P. Putnam's Sons, 1967), p. 55.

15. There is some disagreement as to whether the child was born in France or whether he was born in the United States shortly after Sally's return to Monticello.

16. Brodie, *Thomas Jefferson*, pp. 23, 276–277, 392, 473.

17. Hope Ridings Miller, *Scandals in the Highest Office* (New York: Random House, 1973), p. 101.

18. Ibid.

19. William Penn Cresson, *James Monroe* (New York: Archon Books, 1971), p. 175.

20. Ibid.

21. Shepherd, *Adams' Chronicles*, p. 268.

22. Ibid., p. 310.

23. Ibid.

24. Ibid.

25. Ibid., p. 314.

26. Ibid., p. 271.

27. Ibid., p. 299.

28. Ibid., p. 322.

29. *New York Times*, 22 November 1886.

30. Shepherd, *Adams' Chronicles*, p. 41.

31. Ibid.

32. *New York Times*, 22 November 1886.

33. Shepherd, *Adams' Chronicles*, p. 244.

34. Sadler, *Children in the White House*, p. 103.

35. Perling, *Presidents' Sons*, p. 58.

36. Ibid., p. 59.

37. Ibid.

38. Ibid., p. 64.

39. Ibid., p. 66.

40. Ibid., p. 71.

41. Ibid., p. 72.

42. A practice not uncommon in the day, as "bounties" were paid to those who supplied bodies for medical students' research and studies of anatomy.

43. Perling, *Presidents' Sons*, p. 77.

44. Robert Seager, II. *And Tyler Too: A Biography of John and Julia Gardiner Tyler* (New York, New York: McGraw-Hill Book Company, 1963), p. 107.

45. Ibid., p. 108.

46. Perling, *Presidents' Sons*, p. 90.

47. Ibid., p. 92.

48. Ibid., p. 98.

49. Ibid., p. 99.

50. Seager, *And Tyler Too*, p. 102.

51. Ibid., p. 256.

52. Ibid., p. 349.

53. Ibid., p. 105.

54. Ibid., p. 521.

55. *New York Times*, 26 January 1874, p. 2.

56. Seager, *And Tyler Too*, p. 100.

57. Ibid., p. 339.

58. Ibid.

59. Ibid., p. 356.

60. Ibid., p. 546.

61. Ibid.

62. *New York Times*, 13 February 1935, p. 19.

63. Ibid.

64. Sadler, *Children in the White House*, p. 128.

65. Irene Gerlinger, *Mistresses of the White House* (Freeport, New York: Books for Libraries Press, 1950), p. 43.

66. Perling, *Presidents' Sons*, p. 118.

67. *New York Times*, 19 January 1889, p. 1.

68. Sadler, *Children in the White House*, p. 139.

69. Charles M. Snyder, *The Lady and the President: The Letters of Dorothea Dix and Millard Fillmore* (Lexington: The University Press of Kentucky, 1975), p. 51.

70. Edward T. James, et al., eds. *Notable American Women*, vol. 3 (Cambridge: Harvard University Press, 1980), p. 66.

71. Accidents of this type were common during the beginning of railroad expansion, resulting from faulty steel and poor construction.

72. James, *Notable American Women*, p. 67.

73. Perling, *Presidents' Sons*, p. 136.

74. Ibid., p. 137.

75. Ibid., p. 139.

76. Perling, *Presidents' Sons*, p. 140.

77. Ibid., p. 142.

78. Much information is available concerning Mary Todd Lincoln's illness, and Robert was later responsible for her commitment to a mental institution for a short duration.

79. Perling, *Presidents' Sons*, p. 143.

80. The Pullman Palace Car Company earned a place in history books when its model town near Chicago was hard hit by the 1893 depression. The company cut wages by one-third but did not reduce the rent of company houses. Workers, inspired by Socialist leader Eugene V. Debs, organized a strike, which was crushed by intervention from Washington, D.C.'s bayonet-supported forces under President Cleveland. The legal ground for the government's intervention was that the strike interfered with mail delivery.

81. Garfield was assassinated in 1881.

82. Perling, *Presidents' Sons*, p. 142.

83. Ibid., p. 147.

84. Ibid., pp. 148-49.

85. Carl Sandburg, *Abraham Lincoln: The War Years III* (New York: Harcourt, Brace and World, Inc., 1939), p. 381.

86. Ibid., p. 283.

87. *New York Times*, 21 February 1862.

88. Perling, *Presidents' Sons*, p. 132.

89. Ibid., p. 134.

90. Ibid., p. 135.

91. Gerlinger, *Mistresses of the White House*, p. 56.

92. Ibid.

93. Robert W. Winston, *Andrew Johnson: Plebian and Patriot* (New York: Henry Holt and Company, 1928), p. 494.

94. *New York Times*, 5 April 1863.

95. Perling, *Presidents' Sons*, p. 158.

96. *New York Times*, 12 April 1912.

97. Ibid.

98. *New York Times*, 9 June 1934, p. 15.

99. Perling, *Presidents' Sons*, p. 193.

100. Ibid., p. 151.

101. H. J. Eckenrode, *Rutherford B. Hayes* (New York: Kennikat Press, 1963), p. 47.

102. Perling, *Presidents' Sons*, p. 198.

103. Allan Peskin, *Garfield* (Kent, Ohio: The Kent State University Press, 1978), p. 156.

104. Ibid., p. 545.

105. Margaret Leech and Harry Brown, *The Garfield Orbit* (New York: Harper & Row, 1978), p. 189.

106. Perling, *Presidents' Sons*, p. 218.

107. Peskin, *Garfield*, p. 390.

108. Thomas C. Reeves, *Gentleman Boss: The Life of Chester Alan Arthur* (New York: Alfred A. Knopf, 1975), p. 32.

109. Ibid., p. 35.

110. Ibid.

111. Ibid., p. 275.

112. *New York Times*, 8 January 1904.

113. Ibid.

114. Ibid.

115. Curtiss Candy Company, Chicago, Illinois, was established in 1916 and incorporated into Standard Brands, Inc., in 1965.

116. Perling, *Presidents' Sons*, p. 238.

117. *Washington Post*, 21 February 1980.

118. Ibid.

119. Ibid.

120. Ibid.

121. Perling, *Presidents' Sons*, p. 256.

122. *New York Times*, 14 February 1944, p. 1.

123. Ibid.

124. Ibid.

125. Ibid.

126. Ibid.

127. *New York Times*, 7 April 1967, p. 37.

128. Perling, *Presidents' Sons*, p. 296.

129. Ishbel Ross, *Grace Coolidge and Her Era: The Story of a President's Wife* (New York: Dodd, Mead & Company, 1962), p. 216.

130. Perling, *Presidents' Sons*, p. 300.

131. John T. Lambert, "When the President Wept," in *Meet Calvin Coolidge: The Man behind the Myth*, ed. Edward C. Lathem (Brattleboro, Vermont: The Stephen Greene Press, 1960), p. 139.

132. Ross, *Grace Coolidge*, p. 128.

133. *New York Times*, 10 July 1969, p. 37.

134. Joseph P. Lash, *Eleanor and Franklin* (New York: W. W. Norton & Company, Inc., 1971), p. 301.

135. Ibid., p. 347.

136. Anna Rothe, ed., *Current Biography: Who's News and Why, 1950* (New York: The H. W. Wilson Company, 1950), p. 505.

137. Perling, *Presidents' Sons*, p. 330.

138. Ibid., p. 332.

139. Ibid.

140. Ibid.

141. Robert H. Ferrell, ed., *Off the Record: The Private Papers of Harry S Truman* (New York: Harper & Row, 1980), p. 109.

142. Merle Miller, *Plain Speaking: An Oral Biography of Harry S Truman* (New York: Berkley Publishing Company, 1974), p. 87.

143. Ibid., p. 33.

144. Dwight D. Eisenhower, *At Ease: Stories I Tell My Friends* (New York: Doubleday & Company, Inc., 1967), p. 181.

145. Frank Cormier, *LBJ: The Way He Was* (New York: Doubleday & Company, Inc., 1977), p. 112.

146. Ibid.

147. Ibid., p. 174.

148. Ibid., p. 85.

149. Ibid., p. 47.

150. Ibid., p. 151.

151. Ibid.

152. Helen Thomas, *Dateline: White House* (New York: Macmillan Publishing Co., Inc., 1975), p. 174.

153. Ibid., p. 176.

154. Ibid., p. 209.

155. Ibid., p. 207.

156. Gerald R. Ford, *A Time to Heal* (New York: Harper & Row, 1979), p. 436.

157. Bud Vesta, *Jerry Ford: Up Close* (New York: Coward, McCann & Geoghegan, 1974), p. 22.

158. *Houston Post*, 15 December 1980, p. 10.

159. Ibid.

160. Jacksonville *Times-Union*, 7 October 1980.

161. *Grand Rapids Press*, 25 September 1980.

162. *New York Times*, 4 November 1980.

163. "Four Reagans Used to Going Their Own Way," *Time*, 5 January 1981, p. 24.

164. Ibid.

165. Ibid.

166. "A Reagan by Any Other Name, Star-Elect Patti Davis Hopes for Her Own Landslide," *People*, 12 January 1981, p. 37.

BIBLIOGRAPHY

BOOKS

Basler, Roy P., ed. *The Collected Works of Abraham Lincoln*. Vols. 1–3. New Brunswick, New Jersey: Rutgers University Press, 1953.

Bonnell, John Sutherland. *Presidential Profiles: Religion in the Life of American Presidents*. Philadelphia, Pennsylvania: The Westminster Press, 1971.

Bradlee, Benjamin. *Conversations with Kennedy*. New York, New York: W. W. Norton & Company, Inc., 1975.

Brodie, Fawn M. *Thomas Jefferson: An Intimate History*. New York, New York: W. W. Norton & Company, Inc., 1974.

Bruce, David K. *Sixteen American Presidents*. New York, New York: The Bobbs-Merrill Company, 1962.

Bryant, Traphes, and Frances Spatz. *Dog Days at the White House: The Outrageous Memoirs of the Presidential Kennel Keeper*. New York, New York: Macmillan, 1975.

Burnam, Tom. *The Dictionary of Misinformation*. New York, New York: Thomas Y. Crowell Company, 1975.

Burner, David. *Herbert Hoover: A Public Life*. New York, New York: Alfred A. Knopf, 1979.

Burnham, Sophy. *The Landed Gentry: Passions and Personalities Inside America's Propertied Class*. New York, New York: G. P. Putnam's Sons, 1978.

Canfield, Cass. *The Iron Will of Jefferson Davis*. New York, New York: Harcourt, Brace Jovonovich, 1978.

Churchill, Allen. *The Roosevelts: American Aristocrats*. New York, New York: Harper & Row, 1965.

Cormier, Frank. *LBJ: The Way He Was*. Garden City, New York: Doubleday & Company, Inc., 1977.

Cresson, William Penn. *James Monroe*. New York, New York: Archon Books, 1971.

Davison, Kenneth E. *The Presidency of Rutherford B. Hayes*. Westport, Connecticut: Greenwood Press, Inc., 1972.

Dulles, Eleanor Lansing. *Chances of a Lifetime: A Memoir*. New York, New York: Prentice-Hall, Inc., 1980.

Eaton, Clement. *Jefferson Davis*. New York, New York: The Free Press, 1977.

Eckenrode, H. J. *Rutherford B. Hayes*. New York, New York: Kennikat Press, 1963.

Eisenhower, Dwight D. *At Ease: Stories I Tell My Friends*. New York, New York: Doubleday & Co., 1967.

Eisenhower, John. S. D. *Strictly Personal: A Memoir*. New York, New York: Doubleday & Company, Inc., 1974.

Eisenhower, Milton S. *The President Calling*. New York, New York: Doubleday & Company, Inc., 1974.

Ferrell, Robert H., ed. *Off the Record: The Private Papers of Harry S Truman*. New York, New York: Harper & Row, 1980.

Ford, Gerald R. *A Time to Heal*. New York: Harper & Row, 1979.

Gerlinger, Irene. *Mistresses of the White House*. Freeport, New York: Books for Libraries Press, 1950.

Hardy, Stella Pickett, and Tobias A. Wright. *Colonial Families of the Southern States of America*. New York, New York: Tobias A. Wright, 1911.

Hess, Stephen. *America's Political Dynasties*. New York, New York: Doubleday & Company, Inc., 1966.

Johannsen, Robert, ed. *The Letters of Stephen A. Douglas*. Urbana, Illinois: University of Illinois Press, 1961.

Kane, Joseph Nathan. *Facts about the Presidents*. New York, New York: The H. W. Wilson Company, 1981.

Kennedy, Rose Fitzgerald. *Times to Remember*. New York, New York: Doubleday & Company, Inc., 1974.

Lash, Joseph P. *Eleanor and Franklin*. New York, New York: W. W. Norton & Company, Inc., 1971.

Lathem, Edward C., ed. *Meet Calvin Coolidge: The Man behind the Myth*. Brattleboro, Vermont: The Stephen Greene Press, 1960.

Leech, Margaret, and Harry Brown. *The Garfield Orbit*. New York, New York: Harper & Row, 1978.

Miller, Hope Ridings. *Scandals in the Highest Office*. New York, New York: Random House, 1973.

Miller, Merle. *Plain Speaking: An Oral Biography of Harry S Truman*. New York, New York: Berkley Publishing Company, 1974.

Monroe, Haskell M. *The Papers of Jefferson Davis*. Vol. 1. (1808–1840). Edited by James T. McIntosh, et al. Baton Rouge, Louisiana: Louisiana State University Press, 1971.

Morgan, H. Wayne. *McKinley and His America*. Syracuse, New York: Syracuse University Press, 1963.

Patterson, James T. *Mr. Republican: A Biography of Robert A. Taft*. Boston, Massachusetts: Houghton Mifflin Company, 1972.

Perling, Joseph J. *Presidents' Sons: The Prestige of Name in a Democracy*. Freeport, New York: Books for Libraries Press, 1947. Reprint ed. New York, New York: Arno Press, 1970.

Peskin, Allan. *Garfield*. Kent, Ohio: Kent State University Press, 1978.

Pittman, Mrs. H. D., ed. *Americans of Gentle Birth*. Baltimore, Maryland: Genealogical Publishing, 1970.

Pringle, Henry F. *The Life and Times of William Howard Taft*. Vol. 2. Hamden, Connecticut: Archon Books, 1939.

Reeves, Thomas C. *Gentleman Boss: The Life of Chester Alan Arthur*. New York, New York: Alfred A. Knopf, 1975.

Rice, Arnold S., ed. *Herbert Hoover: 1874–1964*. Dobbs Ferry, New York: Oceana Publications, 1971.

Richardson, James D. *A Compilation of the Messages and Papers of the Presidents; 1789–1897*. Vol. 4. Washington, D.C.: n.p., 1897.

Roosevelt, Mrs. Theodore, Jr. *Day before Yesterday*. New York, New York: Doubleday & Company, Inc., 1959.

Ross, Ishbel. *Grace Coolidge and Her Era: The Story of a President's Wife*. New York, New York: Dodd, Mead & Company, 1962.

Sadler, Christine. *Children in the White House*. New York, New York: G. P. Putnam's Sons, 1967.

Sandburg, Carl. *Abraham Lincoln: The War Years III*. New York, New York: Harcourt, Brace and World, Inc., 1939.

Schachner, Nathan. *Thomas Jefferson: A Biography*. New York, New York: Appleton-Century-Crofts, Inc., 1961.

Seager, Robert II. *And Tyler Too: A Biography of John and Julia Gardiner Tyler*. New York, New York: McGraw-Hill Book Company, Inc., 1963.

Shepherd, Jack. *The Adams' Chronicles*. Boston, Massachusetts: Little, Brown, 1975.

Sievers, Harry J. *Hoosier Warrior: Through the Civil War Years 1833–1865*. New York, New York: University Publishers, Inc., 1960.

Snyder, Charles M. *The Lady and the President: The Letters of Dorothea Dix and Millard Fillmore*. Lexington, Kentucky: The University Press of Kentucky, 1975.

Taylor, Tim. *The Book of Presidents*. New York, New York: Arno Press, 1972.

Thomas, Lately. *The First President Johnson*. New York, New York: William Morrow & Company, 1968.

Truman, Harry S. *Memoirs: Years of Trial and Hope*. New York, New York: Doubleday & Company, Inc., 1956.

Truman, Margaret. *Harry S Truman*. New York, New York: Pocket Books, 1974.

Vesta, Bud. *Jerry Ford: Up Close*. New York, New York: Coward, McCann & Geoghegan, 1974.

Williams, T. Harry. *Hayes of the Twenty-third: The Civil War Volunteer Officer*. New York, New York: Alfred A. Knopf, 1965.

Winston, Robert W. *Andrew Johnson: Plebian and Patriot*. New York, New York: Henry Holt and Company, 1928.

Zilg, Gerald Colby. *Du Pont: Behind the Nylon Curtain*. New York, New York: Prentice-Hall, 1974.

REFERENCE BOOKS, NEWSPAPERS, AND OTHER SOURCES

Afro-American Encyclopedia. Vol. 5. "Thomas Jefferson and Sally Hemmings."

American Heritage. Vol. 16. Lida Mayo, "Miss Adams In Love," February 1965.

Biographical Directory of the United States Executive Branch: 1774–1977. Edited by Robert Sobel. Westport, Connecticut: Greenwood Press, 1977.

Curtiss Candy Company. Telephone interview. Chicago, Illinois, April 1981.

Colonial Families of the United States of America. Vol. 7. Edited by Nelson Osgood Rhoades. Bratenahl, Ohio: The Seaforth Press, 1960.

Colorado Springs Gazette.

Current Biography: Who's News and Why. Edited by Anna Rothe. New York, New York: The H. W. Wilson Company.

Cyclopedia of American Biography. Vol. 3. 1891. Reprint. Ann Arbor, Michigan: University Microfilms, 1967.

Florida Times-Union.

Grand Rapids Press.

Houston Post.

New York Times.

Notable American Women: 1607–1950. Edited by Edward T. James, et al. Cambridge, Massachusetts: Belknap Press of Harvard University Press, 1971.

Notable Men of Tennessee. Oliver Perry Temple, ed. New York: Cosmopolitan Press, 1912.

People.

San Francisco Archives, San Francisco Public Library, San Francisco, California.

Time.

Who's Who in America 1978–1979. Vol. 2. Chicago, Illinois: Marquis Who's Who, 1978.

Who's Who in the South and Southwest 1976–1977. 15th ed. Chicago, Illinois: Marquis Who's Who, 1976.

INDEX

Adams, Abigail (Mrs. John Adams), 7-13

Adams, Abigail Amelia (Nabby, Emmy) (daughter of John Adams), 5-8

Adams, Abigail Brown (Mrs. Charles Francis Adams), 31-32

Adams, Ann (Mrs. Thomas Boylston Adams), 13

Adams, Charles Francis (son of John Quincy Adams), 31-32; and brother's scandal, 29; in London, England, 12; as presidential candidate, 32; and Russia, 31; and slavery, 32; in Spain, 12; as vice-presidential candidate, 32

Adams, George Washington (son of John Quincy Adams), 27-29

Adams, John, 7-13; anecdote, xvii; minister to England, 8; grand-fatherly advice, 27

Adams, John, II (son of John Quincy Adams), 28-30

Adams, John Quincy (son of John Adams), 9-11, 27-33; anecdote, xvii; debts to Monroe, 24; and Russell Jarvis, 30; and Treaty of Ghent, 33; and William Henry Harrison, 47

Adams, Louisa Catherine (daughter of John Quincy Adams), 33

Adams, Louisa Catherine (Mrs. John Quincy Adams), 9-10, 27-33

Adams, Mary Catherine (Mrs. John Adams, II), 28-30

Adams, Thomas Boylston (son of John Adams), 13-14

Adams, Sarah (Mrs. Charles Adams), 12

Adams, Susanna (daughter of John Adams), 11

Agnew, Spiro, 183

Alexander, Eleanor Butler. See Roosevelt, Eleanor Butler

"Alice Blue Gown," 133

"Alice Blue" Roosevelt, 143

Amen, John Harlan (husband of Marion Cleveland), 120

Amen, Marion Cleveland Dell. See Cleveland, Marion

American Library Association (ALA), 101

"America's Sweetheart" (Ruth Cleveland), 119

Anderson, Maude. See Hayes, Maude

Andrews, Myra Townsend Fithian. See Arthur, Myra Townsend Fithian

Appleton, Jane Means. See Pierce, Jane Means

Arthur, Chester, 81, 114-116

Arthur, Chester Alan, II (son of Chester Alan Arthur), 115-116

Arthur, Myra Townsend Fithian (Mrs. Chester Alan Arthur, II), 115

Arthur, Ellen Herndon (Nell) (daughter of Chester Alan Arthur), 116-117

Arthur, Ellen Lewis (Mrs. Chester Alan Arthur), 114-116

Arthur, Rowena Dashwood (Mrs. Chester Alan Arthur, II), 115

ABOUT THE AUTHORS

Sandra L. Quinn and Sanford Kanter are in the Departments of History and Government at San Jacinto College, Houston, Texas. Dr. Quinn comes to her current position following a career in business, community affairs, research, and writing. She is the coauthor with Sanford Kanter of *How to Pass an Essay Examination* as well as the author of numerous specialized studies. Sanford Kanter has also written "Archbishop Fenelon's Political Activity" and "The Right of Property at the Beginning of the Third French Republic."